Meadows of Memory

*The Anne Burnett Tandy Lectures
in American Civilization
Number Eleven
Amon Carter Museum*

Meadows of Memory

Images of Time and Tradition in American Art and Culture

BY MICHAEL KAMMEN

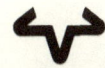

University of Texas Press, Austin

First paperback printing 2012

First Edition, 1992

Requests for permission to reproduce material from this work should be sent to
Permissions, University of Texas Press, Box 7819, Austin, Texas 78713-7819.

♾ The paper used in this publication meets the minimum requirements of American
National Standard for Information Sciences—Permanence of Paper for Printed Library
Materials, ANSI Z39.48-1984.

LIBRARY OF CONGRESS CATALOGING-IN-PUBLICATION DATA

Kammen, Michael G.
    Meadows of memory : images of time and tradition in American art and culture / by
Michael Kammen. — 1st ed.
      p.   cm. — (The Anne Burnett Tandy lectures in American civilization ; no. 11)
    Includes bibliographical references and index.
    ISBN: 978-0-292-74232-1
    1. Art, American.   2. United States in art.   3. Art and society—United States.
I. Title. II. Series.
N6505.K28 1992
758'.9973—dc20

          91-27637
          CIP

For Stanley N. Katz
and Douglas S. Greenberg

who do so much
to facilitate the scholarship
of so many others

Contents

Acknowledgments

I am deeply grateful to the staff of the Amon Carter Museum for their graciousness and courage in selecting someone untrained in the history of art to present the Tandy Lectures for 1989. I especially wish to thank Jan Keene Muhlert, the director; Irvin Lippman, assistant director; Rick Stewart, curator of Western painting and sculpture; Jane Myers, associate curator; Mary Lampe, technician extraordinaire; and Nancy Stevens, the publications coordinator, with whom it has been a privilege to work in preparing these essays to appear between covers.

Ruth Carter Stevenson, president of the museum's Board of Trustees, provided the most elegant hospitality imaginable; and William Howze, director of special programs at the museum, thoughtfully did so much to facilitate my visit and to ensure that every aspect of it would go smoothly.

The clear block of time required to prepare these lectures and revise them as essays was made possible by a generous grant from the Spencer Foundation. I very much appreciate the foundation's confidence and flexibility, particularly the cooperation of the late Lawrence A. Cremin and of Marion M. Faldet.

I am obliged to Dawn M. Drost and Jackie Hubble of Cornell University's History Department for converting my nineteenth-century penmanship into a twentieth-century typescript, and then cheerfully incorporating endless revisions at inconvenient intervals. I have also had the good fortune to work with three experienced and highly competent editors: sponsoring editor Shannon Davies, managing editor Barbara N. Spielman, and my meticulous copy editor, Alison Tartt. Once again, Anne Eberle made the index with critical care and dispatch.

There is an awkward problem that arises from the "poetic license" exercised by artists who paint trees. Sometimes trees that they believed to be elms actually may not have been. In other instances the artists simply did not care what the species really was. They preferred it to be an elm, so they called it an elm. Wayne A. Sinclair, professor of plant pathology in Cornell's College of Agriculture, has looked at the illustrations used in chapter 3 and informs me that a number of the trees may, in fact, not have been elms. In figure 3-20, for example, which Charles Burchfield titled *Old House and Elm Trees,* Professor Sinclair believes that we are really looking at three black locusts and an Eastern white pine! What ultimately matters, however, is the artist's allegorical or metaphorical intention. I am nonetheless grateful to Professor Sinclair for his iconoclastic expertise.

Finally, I owe a special debt to those who carefully read *in vitro* versions of these essays and gave me their candid suggestions for improvement: Alan Fern, John Higham, Carol Kammen, and Laura L. Meixner.

My very own meadows of memory recall "rootstock" that crossed rough oceans as well as metaphorical meadows. Because my grandparents originated in eastern Europe, I am fond of a passage written by Czeslaw Milosz, himself an immigrant to the United States, in his 1980 Nobel Lecture: "Those who are alive receive a mandate from those who are silent forever. They can fulfill their duties only by trying to reconstruct precisely things as they were and by wresting the past from fictions and legends."

Above Cayuga's Waters   M. K.

Sir Lewis B. Namier (1934)

When choosing the subject of these lectures, I was faced with the need to make a decision: was I to draw on work finished by me some time ago, or try to put before you that on which I now am engaged? In other words, should I offer you the fruit of my past research as a still-life, carefully arranged and with a decorative—dead—piece of salmon on top; or should I invite you into my workshop—with its unavoidable untidiness—and put before you the very incomplete results of my current efforts? I have chosen the second course because to me the sense of lectures such as these is in their subject still being alive in the lecturer's mind, not set, not yet in its final form, still subject to revision. I am told that before a mineral can express itself as a crystal, the substance must be absolutely dead because the slightest vestige of life would interfere with the process of crystallization. To my feeling, historical research should not—barring obvious exceptions—be put into print until it has crystallized. But once it has done so there it should remain, in the best shape its author was able to give it. And then its place is in the libraries, the universally accessible repositories of our past work and thoughts. In the lecture-room the unavoidable confusion of life seems to me preferable to the tidiness and decorum of the graveyard.

Introduction

There is no universal memory. All collective memory is supported by a group that is limited in space and time.
—MAURICE HALBWACHS (1950)

It may prove helpful if I indicate at the outset what I wish to accomplish in these Tandy Lectures, and also alert the reader to some basic assumptions and pervasive themes that characterize my approach.

First, I would like to broaden the customary connotations of such familiar phrases as "art history" and more particularly "historical art" because I believe that the complex role of the past in American painting has not yet achieved the attention that it warrants. Works of art that are manifestly historical in character have received substantial and insightful treatment.[1] I am nevertheless persuaded that other sorts of pictures—photographs as well as paintings—not ordinarily designated as "historical" were, in fact, meant to offer messages about trends and events, time and memory in the culture of the United States.

I firmly believe that it would be instructive to think about such pictures in terms of their implied narrative. Taken singly, they cannot tell a complete story. Each one, however, describes a carefully chosen moment and implies circumstances that must have preceded (and are likely to follow) the scene being viewed. Many of the pictures discussed in chapter 2, especially, are implied narratives of various sorts. The notion of implied narrative may conceivably enhance our sense of historical art as a complex genre.

Second, I hope to help illuminate the issue of American exceptionalism, which has been vigorously discussed and contested for more than a decade. At stake are such questions as these: How unique or distinctive has American civilization been? Have we become excessively parochial and chauvinistic by ignoring comparable qualities or tendencies that can be found in societies elsewhere?[2] In my view—which is not entirely original, but perhaps fresh in the particulars on which it is founded—some highly significant aspects of American iconography had Old World sources, to be sure, but those prototypes underwent important changes when they were transported to a new and different cultural context.[3] Just such a pattern will emerge with particular force in chapter 1.

Other noteworthy and representative pieces of American iconography pertaining to themes of time and tradition, however, are largely lacking in Old World antecedents; and those native emblems will be emphasized in chapter 3.[4] I shall suggest some manifestations of a rather melancholy tone in motifs derived from visions of unsettling circumstances and attempts at escape, from a sense of disconnectedness with the past, from anxious or naive moods of nostalgia, and so forth—motifs that have been minimized by the buoyant optimism ordinarily noticed in American romanticism, luminism, and "westering" art of the mid- and later nineteenth century.

Whereas chapter 1 takes emblems of time as its primary topic, and chapter 3 stresses exemplars of poignant change and persistence as symptomatic symbols, the middle lecture explores ways in which artists have used passages through space in order to make statements about history happening—by means of manifest and palpable events as well as latent and therefore less obvious ones. Overall, chapter 2 concerns varied illustrations of movement by a culture through time. I look at landscape art as a way of examining neglected dimensions of historical commentary in American visual culture. Spatial constraints have provided artists with some intriguing challenges to make observations on the passage of time as well as passages *through* time. I am disposed to emphasize diverse forms of *paysage* as multipurpose expressions of passage.

In the process I hope to show that symbolism in American art is less shallow than observers have been ready to perceive. Indeed, I would like to suggest that if American symbolism has not been a notably broad stream, it has steadily deepened during the past century and a half, thereby diverting currents from the Old World that may have obscured significant sections of seascape and landscape alike. Although I am obliged to recognize some familiar classics of the American canon along the way, I also intend to notice neglected works that are important and germane even though they may not be classified as masterpieces.[5]

While I appreciate Roger B. Stein's assertion that "we need to understand more deeply and more particularly that old truism about art: that form is the bearer of meaning, a way of giving shape to content," I have frequently found form determined by content.[6] Too often, moreover, the extant literature (exhibition catalogues, biographical studies, journal essays, etc.) seems preoccupied with form at the expense of content.

I must acknowledge, however—or at least convey as a caveat—recurrent patterns of caprice in the attribution of meaning to artists' use of allegorical symbols. One reads in a didactic label at the Detroit Institute of Arts, for instance, that the volcanic *Cotopaxi* (1862) by Frederic E. Church had immense impact upon the American public because it was perceived as a geological parable of the Civil War then in progress. To be candid, I am skeptical of such claims even when some speculative or tantalizing source can be invoked on their behalf.[7]

Painters themselves provide us with countless intimations that divining artistic meaning is an extremely slithery task. When Benjamin West did *Death on the Pale Horse* in 1796, for example, a large and foaming stallion at the right was ridden by a fierce mythological warrior. In West's monumental version of the very same theme painted in 1817, however, the stallion carried a figure of Christ the King.[8] Does anyone have a reliable explanation for that radical change? Not so far as I know. The lesson of such an alteration surely must be to proceed with caution. Let us keep in mind, then, a statement made by John La Farge in 1899: "It is not possible that a work of art should define like science and still move like poetry. . . . Because of the peculiarities of [the artist's] work . . . no person can explain that work perfectly in terms of words."[9]

I do not want to convey the impression, though, that randomness and enigma shroud the designs of American artists entirely. Quite the contrary, when we read what they wrote about their own work and about the work of those painters they most admired, we endlessly encounter the word-concept "truth." A representative example occurs in Marsden Hartley's 1921 homage to Winslow Homer: "In Winslow Homer we have yankeeism of the first order, turned to a creditable artistic account. With a fierce feeling for truth, a mania almost, for actualities."[10]

At the simplest or most basic level, "truth" has meant historical veracity. Emanuel Leutze, for instance, was obsessed by it. In preparing *Washington Crossing the Delaware* he had to have American rather than German models, even though he was then working in Düsseldorf. At another level, however, "truth" meant accuracy in the rendering of nature, in which case "fidelity" became a favored synonym for truth. At yet another level "truth" implied spiritual insight.[11]

The most common synonym for truth, however, and a key to comprehending its recurrent meaning in the artists' minds, is the word "authenticity." John Trumbull used the two words interchangeably. James Jackson Jarves used authenticity to criticize the "female statues" sculpted by Hiram Powers. Henry T. Tuckerman employed it to assess nineteenth-century writers as well as artists. He explained that his purpose in preparing *America and Her Commentators* (1864) was "to afford those desirous of authentic in-formation in regard to the United States a guide to the sources thereof."[12]

In the decades that followed the Civil War, expanded use of the camera facilitated greater degrees of authenticity in recording the American land-scape along with historical events related to alterations of the landscape. In Barbara Novak's view this phenomenon meant that authenticity would be-come a much less important criterion in American art—in fact, that tech-nology redefined the very meaning of "truth" in art.[13] Although I appreci-ate the validity and force of Novak's point, I feel that it applies primarily to the more accessible meanings customarily ascribed to truth and authen-ticity. At more sublime and subjective levels the painters' obsession per-sisted, as we have already seen with Marsden Hartley. We can also observe it in Edward Hopper's "Notes on Painting" (1933): "My aim in painting has always been the most exact transcription possible of my most intimate impressions of nature."[14] Although Hopper conceded the inevitability of subjectivism, he determined, nonetheless, to seek authenticity within the inescapable constraints of subjectivism.

I wish to stress an important lesson that research for these lectures has im-pressed upon me anew: namely, the elusiveness of attempts to impose a clear line of differentiation between elite and popular culture. A tendency remains, even among scholars, to assume that an investigation of painting from, let us say, 1790 until 1940 must necessarily involve an investigation primarily of high culture. The historical reality, however, is far more complicated.[15]

In 1789 John Trumbull wrote to Thomas Jefferson from London that he had placed his historical paintings of the battles of Bunker Hill and Quebec "in the hands of a print-seller and publisher" to be engraved. Just as soon as he returned to the United States, Trumbull explained, "I shall offer a subscription for prints to be published from such a series of pic-tures as I intend."[16] Within half a century the practice had become utterly commonplace. During the 1840s Fitz Hugh Lane produced lithographs at a rapid rate, especially his various views of Gloucester. For $1.50 a person could obtain a copy hand-colored by the artist.[17] Nor was this trend con-fined to famous works by celebrated artists. In 1851, the same year that Richard Caton Woodville painted *Waiting for the Stage Coach* (fig. 2-24), Goupil and Company produced a lithograph of the oil on canvas with an altered title better suited to the populace at large: *Cornered*. Prints of nine-teenth-century history paintings were routinely made and widely purchased, and various sorts of organizations facilitated the popular distribution of prints.

Art unions, moreover, sought to stimulate the aesthetic taste of Americans by creating a broadly based market for the sale of original works. By the later 1820s and 1830s the middle-brow public attended exhibits in significant numbers. By the 1840s and 1850s, shows remained open during evening hours so that working-class people could attend, and they did.[18] Historical themes with cosmopolitan appeal achieved the most astounding visibility. According to Henry T. Tuckerman in 1847, John Gadsby Chapman's *Landing of Columbus* was "originally sketched for a drop-curtain, and then furnished as a vignette for a newspaper for sixty-five dollars. In a few months it was reproduced in a London work, on bandboxes in the Bowery, in a tableau at the Olympic, and as a heading to the diplomas of the Madrid Historical Society."[19]

The democratization of responses to American art has proceeded fitfully ever since—for diverse reasons and with mixed reactions ranging from disdain by Henry James in 1875 to enthusiastic advocacy by Robert Henri in 1910 and a populistic rationale provided by Thomas Hart Benton one generation later. Henri spoke for numerous contemporaries (as well as for various artists soon to follow) in making his statement for "The New York Exhibition of Independent Artists":

> As I see it, there is only one reason for the development of art in America, and that is that the people of America learn the means of expressing themselves in their own time and in their own land. In this country we have no need of art as a culture; no need of art as a refined and elegant performance; no need of art for poetry's sake, or any of these things for their own sake. What we do need is art that expresses the spirit of the people of today.[20]

In the essays that follow, although constraints of time and space do not permit detailed discussions of the "popular" history of each work that is mentioned, readers are urged to regard many of these pictures as having been representative of the artists' "message" as well as the audience reached. When a picture remained obscure in either sense of the word—unknown or misunderstood—that will be duly noted.

Preparation of these lectures has led me to reconsider yet another misguided stereotype that perhaps I have shared with fellow students of American civilization who like to converse with contemporary artists: namely, that painters tend to be (at best) indifferent readers and (at worst) overtly anti-intellectual. What nonsense! We now know the actual contents of some of their personal libraries.[21] There is reason to believe that George

Caleb Bingham's intense interest in the fur-trader motif may have been partially inspired by Washington Irving's *Astoria* (1836), which described in detail the lives of French traders in the area of St. Louis, particularly those who had intermarried with Indians.

We know that one of Frederic Church's first landscapes, *View of Quebec* (1846), was based upon an engraving that he found in Benjamin Silliman, *Remarks Made on a Short Tour, Between Hartford and Quebec*, published in 1820.[22] A list of books in the library of Thomas P. Rossiter, who painted *Opening of the Wilderness* in about 1858 (fig. 2-22), indicates that he owned William Prescott Smith's *Book of the Great Railway Celebrations of 1857*. And we know that Jasper Cropsey, who painted *Starrucca Viaduct* in 1865, brought back to the United States a copy of Richard Beamish's 1862 biography of Sir Marc Isambard Brunel, who had been associated with construction of the Thames Tunnel. Equally relevant, Sir Marc was the father of the fabulously named Isambard Kingdom Brunel, who achieved fame as a railroad architect.[23]

Similarly Thomas Hart Benton, who between 1919 and 1926 undertook a massive series of murals known as the "American Historical Epic," became deeply engrossed in a four-volume history of the United States while stationed in Norfolk during World War I. In the years 1918–1920, Walt Kuhn completed twenty-nine paintings that he called his "Imaginary History of the West." Kuhn had avidly read books about the West since boyhood, and his personal library as an adult included fifty-nine titles representing most of the prominent writers on Western subjects.[24]

It hardly seems farfetched, therefore, to claim that Clio, the muse of history, has inspired a fair amount of the historical art produced in the United States from, let us say, Trumbull to Benton, a span approaching a century and a half. The circumstances under which the painters read, the highly eclectic nature of their literary explorations, and the uneven quality of what they consumed offer ample grounds for rethinking the persistent view that history books tend to be relatively inaccessible exemplars of high culture. Henry Ford's famous assertion that people learn history from objects rather than from books may be applicable to a great many modern tourists, yet much less so to painters of the American past. They learned from books as well as from experience. Their imagination, vision, and talent then took charge.

It is well known, of course, that quite a few American artists interacted with books for yet another reason: because they received commissions to illustrate them, particularly during the later nineteenth and early twentieth centuries. That aspect of art history has by now been richly documented.[25] My point is quite a discrete one: namely, that painters read history for pleasure, for research, and to fulfill urges that ranged from antiquarian curiosity to ardent patriotism.

No one should be astonished to find, by the way, that cerebration and aesthetic responsiveness got transmitted back and forth between artists and writers. In his *Talks About Art,* William Morris Hunt reminded students that "Hawthorne kept a notebook of hints which he obtained from Nature and from life; and to this he referred while writing his romances." In *The House of the Seven Gables* (which I shall turn to in chapter 3), Hawthorne makes reference to the "picturesque" and creates word-portraits comparable to painterly techniques that were popular at mid-century. Judge Pyncheon's face, for example, "was quite as striking, allowing for the difference of scale, as that betwixt a landscape under a broad sunshine and just before a thunderstorm." While writing *The House of the Seven Gables* Hawthorne mused to his publisher that "many passages of this book ought to be finished with the minuteness of a Dutch picture, in order to give them their proper effect."[26] Perhaps he had Vermeer in mind.

Although the visual arts provide the principal subject of these essays, I shall also attempt to draw interlineations with American literature— fiction as well as nonfiction—because each enhances our appreciation of the other.[27] Both are products of the same cultural context. As Henry T. Tuckerman noted in 1864, our writers painted with words instead of pigments. Native authors conveyed "the truth of history, nature, and character as regards this country. They are, to the mass of American Travels, what the finished picture is to the desultory series of offhand sketches from nature."[28] Asher B. Durand's great romantic icon, *Kindred Spirits* (1849), in which William Cullen Bryant and the shade of Thomas Cole commune, is no idiosyncratic lucubration. It simply says on canvas, quite compellingly, what many others were then essaying in print.

We should also acknowledge that for native authors and artists alike, coming to terms with history as a subject or force may have seemed more problematic than coming to terms with the past per se. Having been scornful of written history in "Nature" (1836), Ralph Waldo Emerson contrived a rationale for redeeming it just five years later when he gave "History" the lead in a new collection of essays. "Let it suffice," he wrote, "that in the light of these two facts, namely, that the mind is One, and that nature is its correlative, history is to be read and written. . . . History no longer shall be a dull book."[29]

We know all too well that American artists affirmed the notion that "nature is its correlative." Much less apparent to us, however, is the ongoing effort to define the proper character and purpose of history painting in Nature's Nation. As early as 1812, George Murray lamented "what appears yet wanting, a *national gallery* of the works of American artists consisting of subjects from our own history." Such complaints swiftly became a leitmotif of young republican culture.[30]

Anyone who has read the manifestos and correspondence of nineteenth-century American artists knows that most of them sought a suitably indigenous mode of expression. Considering how many of them were attracted to Italy, Germany, and other parts of Europe—often for prolonged periods—the motives that prompted their patriotic quest went well beyond jingoistic chauvinism. They reasonably believed that a new environment ought to elicit new visions, new subjects, and new modes of rendering both. Joshua Taylor summarized the situation succinctly some two decades ago: "The emphatic protestation [by artists] of being purely American is the proclamation of a social attitude, not a description of style. That the artist wished to feel himself different from his European colleagues is of sociological importance."[31]

The manifold ways in which they succeeded in doing so require, in my view, greater attention to historical content in American art and to attitudes generally than we find in the circumscribed and problematic commentary concerning the genre that is customarily identified as "historical painting." In 1929 an interviewer asked Charles Demuth, "What do you look forward to?" His response, "The Past," was intended to be only partially ironic.[32] His reply made explicit a profoundly intriguing ambivalence that had characterized American art for generations: present-mindedness regarding technique blended with a belief that, for better and for worse, the palpable past had determined the present and consequently could not be ignored.

As a point of reference for the distinctiveness of the story that follows in these essays, it may be helpful to invoke Jerome H. Buckley's summary view of the anxieties faced by British Victorians in coming to terms with the nexus of time and art:

> If it could restore even briefly a sense of integration, unity, and design, art
> could reduce to harmless illusion the terror of time, the separation of then and

when, before and after. Modern man might then return to the facts of change and history, progress and decadence, private past and public present, with an unproven yet sustaining conviction of continuity.[33]

Buckley contends persuasively that the "great polar ideas" of Victorian Britain were the idea of progress and the idea of decadence, "the twin aspects of an all-encompassing history."[34]

The dynamics of social thought and culture were connected yet curiously different in the United States when compared with Europe. Chapter 1 looks at patterns of iconological change in viewing the process by which the past is recorded and remembered. Time, truth, and history eventually became conflated here into a catch-all designation: Memory. Chapter 2 re-examines selected aspects of American landscape art and finds a more encompassing historical vision than what is usually ascribed to it. Chapter 3 describes and explores what I believe have been the dominant icons of collective memory and tradition in American culture. Although the argument there is closely aligned in approach with that of chapter 1, I have settled upon this overall sequence in order to achieve some sense of movement through time. The chronological locus of chapter 1 is primarily early modern and makes its way to the United States fitfully and incompletely. The locus of chapter 2 is predominantly nineteenth-century and American. The concluding chapter charges forward into the twentieth century and carries the discussion more closely to our own time and experience.

I would not claim that all of the pictures discussed in these lectures rank among the finest examples of American art. But aesthetic inferiority does not connote or correlate with cultural inconsequence. Nor do I believe that each of these works was fully understood when it first went on exhibition. I do insist, however, that a high proportion of the art discussed here mattered intensely to the artists themselves. These were labors of love, statements of various sorts that their creators felt compelled to make. Daniel Chester French had no commission to carve *Memory* (fig. 1-29). Nor did Thomas Hart Benton have a commission for his unfinished murals known as the "American Historical Epic," nor Walt Kuhn for his "Imaginary History of the West."

I firmly believe that these works were especially close to the hearts of their creators and were intended as statements about the determinative significance of a meaningful or problematic past. Subsequently, with the passage of time, their importance and their quintessential Americanness has begun to be appreciated. (As Emanuel Leutze wrote from Düsseldorf to a friend in 1854: "We will paint 'American pictures'.") Some of them are now regarded as truly national icons. It is my hope that these essays may enhance the slow yet incremental process of perceiving and ultimately possessing them by making them our very own.

Notes

1. See William H. Gerdts and Mark Thistlethwaite, *Grand Illusions: History Painting in America* (Fort Worth, 1988); Donelson F. Hoopes, *American Narrative Painting* (Los Angeles, 1974); Hermann Warner Williams, Jr., *Mirror to the American Past: A Survey of American Genre Painting: 1750–1900* (New York, 1973).

2. See, e.g., Laurence Veysey, "The Autonomy of American History Reconsidered," *American Quarterly* 31 (Fall 1979): 455–477; Carl N. Degler, "In Pursuit of an American History," *American Historical Review* 92 (Feb. 1987): 1–12; Michael Kammen, *Sovereignty and Liberty: Constitutional Discourse in American Culture* (Madison, Wis., 1988), pp. 5, 102, and chap. 4; Alex Inkeles, "Continuity and Change in the American National Character," in *The Third Century: America as a Post-Industrial Society,* ed. Seymour Martin Lipset (Stanford, 1979), pp. 390–416; and Harold M. Hyman, *American Singularity: The 1787 Northwest Ordinance, the 1862 Homestead and Morrill Acts, and the 1944 G.I. Bill* (Athens, Ga., 1986).

3. For a fine examination of precise and complex traditions in the iconology of early modern Europe as retained in simplified and often ambiguous or vague ways in America, see Roland E. Fleischer, "Emblems and Colonial American Painting," *American Art Journal* 20, no. 3 (1988): 3–35, esp. 30, 33; Richard H. Saunders and Ellen G. Miles, *American Colonial Portraits, 1700–1776* (Washington, D.C., 1987).

4. I find Panofsky's distinction between iconography and iconology useful, and I especially like Leo Marx's application of that distinction to the American scene. For the most part I too will apply it. See Erwin Panofsky, "Iconography and Iconology: An Introduction to the Study of Renaissance Art," in *Meaning in the Visual Arts: Papers in and on Art History* (New York, 1957), pp. 26–54; Leo Marx, "The Railroad-in-the-Landscape: An Iconological Reading of a Theme in American Art," *Prospects: An Annual of American Cultural Studies* 10 (1985): 77–117, esp. pp. 105, 110.

5. An important move in that direction can be found in Albert Boime, *Art in an Age of Revolution, 1750–1800,* vol. 1 of *A Social History of Modern Art* (Chicago, 1987); and in Roy Porter, "Review Article: Seeing the Past," *Past & Present,* no. 118 (Feb. 1988): 186–205. In writing about political prints, Porter asks: "What (if anything) do printed pictures say which was not already being said verbally elsewhere?" (p. 190).

6. Roger B. Stein, "Structure as Meaning: Towards a Cultural Interpretation of American Painting," *American Art Review* 3 (Mar. 1976): 67. It has been noted that

nineteenth-century Americans who wrote about art valued content above form, "the idea" above "rules," "historical and poetical associations" above technique. See Lillian B. Miller, "Paintings, Sculpture, and the National Character, 1815–1860," *Journal of American History* 53 (Mar. 1967): 700–701. But for a twentieth-century perspective, see Ben Shahn, *The Shape of Content* (Cambridge, Mass., 1957), p. 53: "Form is the very shape of content."

7. The label follows a suggestive text by Katherine Manthorne, *Creation and Renewal: Views of Cotopaxi by Frederic Edwin Church* (Washington, D.C., 1985), 49–51; but a more judicious and plausible interpretation will be found in David C. Huntington, *The Landscapes of Frederic Edwin Church: Vision of an American Era* (New York, 1966), 11–20.

8. See Helmut von Erffa and Allen Staley, *The Paintings of Benjamin West* (New Haven, 1986), pp. 146–149.

9. John La Farge, "Concerning Painters Who Would Express Themselves in Words," *Scribner's Magazine* 26 (Aug. 1899): 256. See also Francis Haskell, "Visual Sources and *The Embarrassment of Riches*," *Past & Present*, no. 120 (Aug. 1988): 216–226, who calls attention to "unresolved contentions" in pictures and the possibility that the artist "meant us to be unsure."

10. Marsden Hartley, *Adventures in the Arts: Informal Chapters on Painters, Vaudeville and Poets* (New York, 1921), p. 42.

11. See John W. McCoubrey, ed., *American Art, 1700–1960: Sources and Documents* (Englewood Cliffs, N.J., 1965), pp. 116, 157, 178; Alfred Frankenstein, *William Sidney Mount* (New York, 1975), p. 143 (Mount's diary entry for August 19, 1846). For an obsession with historical authenticity equal to (if not greater than) Leutze's, see Thomas Hart Benton, *An Artist in America*, 4th ed. (Columbia, Mo., 1983), pp. 255, 344–345, 352–353, 358–359.

12. Henry T. Tuckerman, *America and Her Commentators. With a Critical Sketch of Travel in the United States* (New York, 1864), pp. iii, 424, 430, 434; McCoubrey, ed., *American Art, 1700–1960*, p. 41; James Jackson Jarves, *The Art-Idea*, ed. Benjamin Rowland, Jr. (Cambridge, Mass., 1960), p. 212. For Robert W. Weir's explicit concern for authenticity in American historical art, see Henry T. Tuckerman, *Artist-Life: Or Sketches of American Painters* (New York, 1847), p. 138.

13. Barbara Novak, *Nature and Culture: American Landscape and Painting, 1825–1875* (New York, 1980), p. 177. See also Weston J. Naef et al., *Era of Exploration: The Rise of Landscape Photography in the American West, 1860–1885* (Boston, 1975).

14. Robert Goldwater and Marco Treves, comps., *Artists on Art, from the Fourteenth to the Twentieth Century* (New York, 1945), p. 471.

15. For new work that breaks with such assumptions, see Lawrence W. Levine, *Highbrow/Lowbrow: The Emergence of Cultural Hierarchy in America* (Cambridge, Mass., 1988); Karal Ann Marling, *Wall-to-Wall America: A Cultural History of Post-Office Murals in the Great Depression* (Minneapolis, 1982).

16. McCoubrey, ed., *American Art, 1700–1960*, pp. 41–42.

17. John Wilmerding, *Fitz Hugh Lane* (New York, 1971), pp. 28–29; Richard J. Boyle et al., *In This Academy: The Pennsylvania Academy of the Fine Arts, 1805–1976. A Special Bicentennial Exhibition* (Philadelphia, 1976), p. 110.

18. Patricia Hills, *The Painters' America: Rural and Urban Life, 1810–1910* (New York, 1974), p. 25; McCoubrey, ed., *American Art, 1700–1960*, pp. 117, 126, 147; E. Maurice Bloch, *The Paintings of George Caleb Bingham: A Catalogue Raisonné* (Columbia, Mo., 1986), pp. 12–13.

19. Tuckerman, *Artist-Life,* p. 156. See also Mark Thistlethwaite, "Patronage Gone Awry: The 1883 Temple Competition of Historical Paintings," *Pennsylvania Magazine of History and Biography* 112 (Oct. 1988): 574; Erika L. Doss, "Borrowing Regionalism: Advertising's Use of American Art in the 1930s and '40s," *Journal of American Culture* 5 (Winter 1982): 10–19.

20. McCoubrey, ed., *American Art, 1700–1960,* p. 174; see also pp. 163–164, 175, 201, 205.

21. See Elizabeth Johns, "Washington Allston's Library," *American Art Journal* 7 (Nov. 1975): 32–41; David Tatham, "Winslow Homer's Library," *American Art Journal* 9 (May 1977): 92–98. For a representative example of the stereotypical twentieth-century American artist as anti-intellectual, see Laurie Lisle, *Portrait of an Artist: A Biography of Georgia O'Keeffe* (New York, 1980), pp. 357–358, 382, 416.

22. *View of Quebec* is in the Wadsworth Atheneum, Hartford, Connecticut. There is some doubt whether Church ever visited the city of Quebec.

23. See Mark Thistlethwaite, "The Artist as Interpreter of American History," in Boyle et al., *In This Academy,* pp. 99–120; Susan Danly Walther, *The Railroad in the American Landscape: 1850–1950* (Wellesley, Mass., 1981), pp. 85, 88; William Sidney Mount to John M. Gardner, May 28, 1863, in Frankenstein, *William Sidney Mount,* p. 375.

24. Henry Adams, *Thomas Hart Benton: An American Original* (New York, 1989), pp. 86–88; Matthew Baigell, *Thomas Hart Benton* (New York, 1973), pp. 62–79; Fred S. Bartlett, *Walt Kuhn: An Imaginary History of the West* (Colorado Springs, 1964), esp. pp. 8–9.

25. See Kathleen A. Foster, *Edwin Austin Abbey (1852–1911): An Exhibition Organized by the Yale University Art Gallery* (New Haven, 1973). Howard Pyle and N. C. Wyeth provide other obvious examples.

26. William Morris Hunt, *Talks About Art* (London, 1878), p. 2; Nathaniel Hawthorne, *The House of the Seven Gables: A Romance* (1851: Boston, 1900), pp. 34, 170, and xiii. For Hawthorne's relationship with Leutze, see Barbara S. Groseclose, *Emanuel Leutze, 1816–1868: Freedom Is the Only King* (Washington, D.C., 1975), pp. 58–59, 118; and see Kent Ljungquist, *The Grand and the Fair: Poe's Landscape Aesthetics and Pictorial Techniques* (Potomac, Md., 1984).

27. See Mario Praz, *Mnemosyne: The Parallel Between Literature and the Visual Arts* (Princeton, 1970). Although Praz titles chapter 2 "Time Unveils Truth" and chapter 7 "Spatial and Temporal Interpenetration," his concerns in those chapters bear little relationship to my emphases in chapters 1 and 2 below.

28. Tuckerman, *America and Her Commentators*, p. 430. See also James T. Flexner, "Tuckerman's *Book of the Artists*," *American Art Journal* 1 (Fall 1969): 53–57; and Barbara Haskell, *Charles Demuth* (New York, 1987), p. 129.

29. *The Complete Works of Ralph Waldo Emerson* (Boston, 1903), 2:38–40.

30. Boyle et al., *In This Academy*, pp. 101, 110; Bloch, *Paintings of George Caleb Bingham*, pp. 19–23; Thistlethwaite, "Patronage Gone Awry," p. 572. For comparable statements made by Daniel Webster between 1809 and 1852, especially his address titled "The Dignity and Importance of History," see Paul D. Erickson, *The Poetry of Events: Daniel Webster's Rhetoric of the Constitution and the Union* (New York, 1986), pp. 54–56.

31. Joshua Taylor, "The Historical Problem of American Art," *American Art Review* 1 (Sept. 1973): 29–30; William H. Gerdts, "The American 'Discourses': A Survey of Lectures and Writings on American Art, 1770–1858," *American Art Journal* 15 (Summer 1983): 61–79; Bloch, *Paintings of George Caleb Bingham*, pp. 16–17, 21.

32. Charles Demuth, "Confessions," *Little Review* 12 (May 1929): 30. On January 5, 1928, N. C. Wyeth wrote to James Boyd, the American historical novelist whose works Wyeth illustrated for Scribner's: "How I do yearn for the technical ability to put down in color and pattern the things that are almost tearing my insides out." Boyd Papers, box 3, Southern Historical Collection, University of North Carolina, Chapel Hill.

33. Jerome Hamilton Buckley, *The Triumph of Time: A Study of the Victorian Concepts of Time, History, Progress, and Decadence* (Cambridge, Mass., 1966), p. 153. Some comparable themes (and some striking contrasts) are traced by T. J. Jackson Lears in *No Place of Grace: Antimodernism and the Transformation of American Culture, 1880–1920* (New York, 1981). Lears' period coincides with only the final phase of Buckley's, and I have reservations about the representativeness of Lears' dramatis personae.

34. Buckley, *Triumph of Time*, p. 13. See also Henry Kozicki, *Tennyson and Clio: History in the Major Poems* (Baltimore, 1979); and Peter Paret, *Art as History: Episodes in the Culture and Politics of Nineteenth-Century Germany* (Princeton, 1988).

35. Leutze to Montgomery C. Meigs, Feb. 10, 1854, in Justin G. Turner, "Emmanuel Leutze's *Westward the Course of Empire Takes Its Way*," *Manuscripts* 18 (Spring 1966): 6.

Meadows of Memory

1.
Truth, Time, and History

. . . that clock time which spaces us apart so inhibitingly, divides young and old, keeps our living through the same experiences at separate distances.

—EUDORA WELTY (1984)

The title of this first essay is taken from a work of the same name painted by Goya late in the 1790s (fig. 1-17). The picture is profoundly apropos because it brings together, more engagingly than any other, three familiar figures of considerable importance in Western art. Two of them, Father Time and Clio (the muse of history), have distinctive and discrete allegorical derivations, and I shall look sequentially at the separate lineage of each. Goya's rendering of their convergence, however, calls to our attention the principal themes of this chapter: anxiety induced by the inevitable passage of time (and by its irreversibility); humankind's desire to remember historical events reliably; and the need to differentiate between truths that are "merely" revealed and history that has been faithfully recorded.

We will return to *Truth, Time, and History* for a closer look after we have established the nature and significance of its several components. In order to do so we must take a brief look at Father Time, first in Europe and then in America; at the changing depictions of Clio in European art; and then at visible signs of connectedness between Time and History, because each one becomes more interesting when they interact. The reader should be aware at the outset, however, that the historical evolution and periodization of Truth, Time, and History are not tidily synchronized and consequently do not present us with perfectly coherent patterns. Although they converge (and even interact) in certain artistic statements, each allegorical concept had its own origins, its own development, and its own discrete attractiveness to particular painters at particular times. The concepts maintain a rather stubborn historical autonomy—even when they become connected.

The essay then examines the American inheritance, casual use, and transformation of these materials through the iconology pertaining to history being recorded; the presentation of clocks and watches emblematic of "time's pulse"; the gradual conflation of Truth, Time, and History into the intriguing but sometimes elusive notion of Memory; and finally, as a logical transition to chapter 2, the motif of burial in American landscape painting—a theme in which traditional notions of Father Time persist, yet one in which Clio, the maiden, manages to transcend and even transport mortality. The artist (Clio's surrogate?) has figuratively rendered the ephemeral nature of life, and in so doing has transmitted it as a visually enduring icon of spiritual transfiguration. Testimonial evidence gives way to testamentary Truth, if not consolation.

Father Time and His Symbols in Transition

Scholars have not neglected the complex and long-evolving quadripartite mythology of Saturn-Cronus, Father Time, the notion of a Watchmaker God, and Father Christmas. Samuel L. Macey, moreover, has called our attention to the ambiguities inherent in such symbols:

> Saturn-Cronus simultaneously represents the past Saturnalian Age of Gold and the present awesome Time the Destroyer; Father Time develops from the saturnine Time the Destroyer into the present sentimental patriarch who attempts to hold back Death; and the Watchmaker God uses a model that, during the second century of its existence, can be viewed either as a benevolent clockwork universe or a malevolent clockwork diabolism.[1]

Relevant to our concerns in this context is the matter of mythological genealogy: in antiquity Cronus, later combined with Chronos (Time), was the father of the gods; Memory was the mother of the muses (including Clio); and Truth was (perhaps even remains) the daughter of Time.[2]

Equally pertinent are permutations that have occurred in the artistic representations of Time, especially during the fourteenth century (note Petrarch's richly illustrated *Triumph of Time*) and the fifteenth century (note Pieter Brueghel's *Triumph of Time*). Time's sickle was then replaced by a scythe; and during the Renaissance Father Time's persona came to be separated from that of Death, and the hourglass emerged as an iconic accompaniment to Father Time.[3]

In the sixteenth century a Paduan follower of Andrea Mantegna produced a triptych titled *Triumph of Time* in the center and flanked on the left by *Triumph of Fame* and on the right by *Triumph of Divinity*. Time is depicted as a very old man holding a cross and standing on a rather fantastic cart drawn by two stags.[4]

Between the later fifteenth and the mid-seventeenth centuries, Father Time actually became the antagonist of Death. The former assumed many of the iconological "duties of Death" while gradually being depicted less harshly or fearfully than the dreaded skeletal specter, as in *Men and Animals Struggling Against Death and Father Time* (c. 1620), by David Vinckboons or a member of his circle, and Philips Wouwerman's *Knight Vanquishing Time, Death, and Monstrous Demons* (1662).[5] By the mid-eighteenth century Father Time was rarely portrayed without his full panoply of equipment—the hourglass, scythe, and extended wings—yet commonly appeared as a benevolent rather than a malevolent figure, and was often no longer shadowed by Death.[6] This development may very well have accompanied the emerging idea of progress, which implied humankind's collective capacity to triumph over time and the mortality of individuals.

These transitions and transformations, allowing due consideration for cultural lag, are reflected in the history of American iconography as well as literature through the beginning of this century, when Father Time steadily faded as an imaginative figure.

During the seventeenth century he joined Death on New England gravestones. On Timothy Lindall's tomb in Salem, Massachusetts, Death and Father Time appear to glower across the stone as adversaries (fig. 1-1). In a superb example of the stonecutter's art, Joseph Tapping's headstone at the King's Chapel Burial Ground in Boston (c. 1678), Father Time seems to be staying the hand of Death, who is attempting to snuff out the candle of life (fig. 1-2).[7] Similarly, on the footstone of John Foster, who died in 1681 at Charleston, Massachusetts, Father Time tries to restrain a skeletal grim reaper (fig. 1-3). Taken together, in tension and in concert, these figures of Time and Death determine just how long the flame of Christian life will burn.[8] Foster, by the way, was an astronomer and printer who established the first printing press in Puritan Boston and published the earliest illustrations in the New World of the Copernican system.

During the struggle for American independence, by contrast, a benign Father Time appeared in an engraving prepared in Nuremberg for multiple markets (the legend is written in three languages). The venerable elder, using a magic lantern, projects a slide showing the destructive consequences of the Stamp Act and the British tax on tea. America, represented

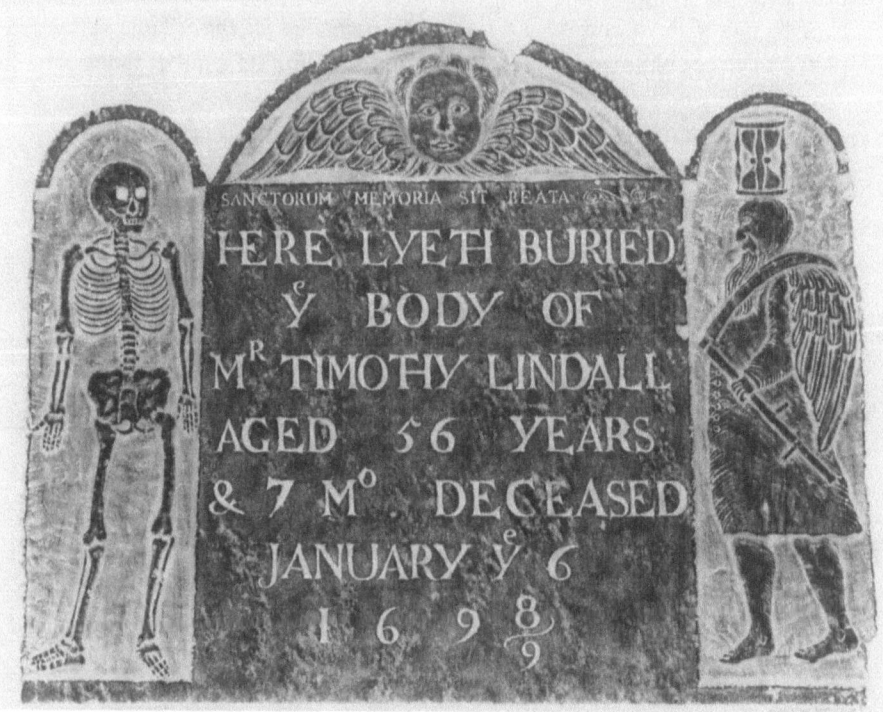

1-1. Timothy Lindall headstone, 1698/1699, Salem, Massachusetts. Stone rubbing by Ann Parker/Avon Neal (1963), 19 15/16 × 33 7/8 in. Amon Carter Museum, Fort Worth, Texas.

as an Indian, sits at the left while Europe, Asia, and Africa gaze upon the scene in dismay (fig. 1-4).

Contemporaneous with such political commentaries, Father Time was also a favorite figure on American-made tall case clocks. A prime example is supplied by Gawen Brown of Boston, who made an eight-day, weight-powered clock with brass works, a rack and snail strike, and a cherry case. Father Time has been cut on pewter and decorates the top (fig. 1-5). He, too, is comparatively benign.[9]

The same is true in a stipple engraving made at Philadelphia in 1802 by John James Barralet. Called *Apotheosis of George Washington*, it features the father of his country being gently raised from his sarcophagus and borne heavenward by Immortality, who is assisted by Father Time. Although Time is cast in the shadow of storm clouds, his scythe and hourglass rest near his feet. His appearance is that of a gentle soul, and he clearly is not

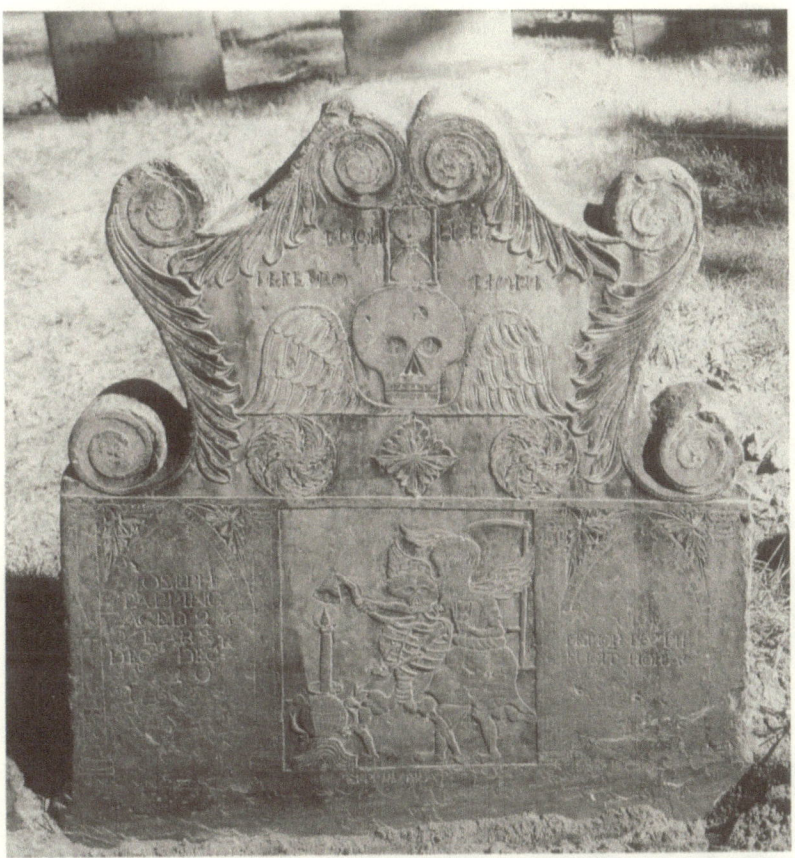

1-2. Joseph Tapping headstone, c. 1678, King's Chapel Burial Ground, Boston. Slate, attributed to the Charlestown stonecutter, 31 × 28 in. Photograph by Daniel Farber.

responsible for snuffing out Washington's life. Very swiftly this exact design appeared in oil-on-glass copies made by a Chinese artist, and on Liverpool pitchers for export to the United States.[10]

During the nineteenth century, representations of Father Time diminished, and the small number of residual invocations followed no coherent pattern. In 1846, for example, Thomas Cole wrote a poem, "The March of Time," in which the evangelical painter—obviously familiar with the changing relationship of Time and Death in Western iconography—asserted that everlasting life rendered Death nonthreatening. Time is designated as "God's servant" rather than Death's alter ego, and the poem closes with two positive lines:

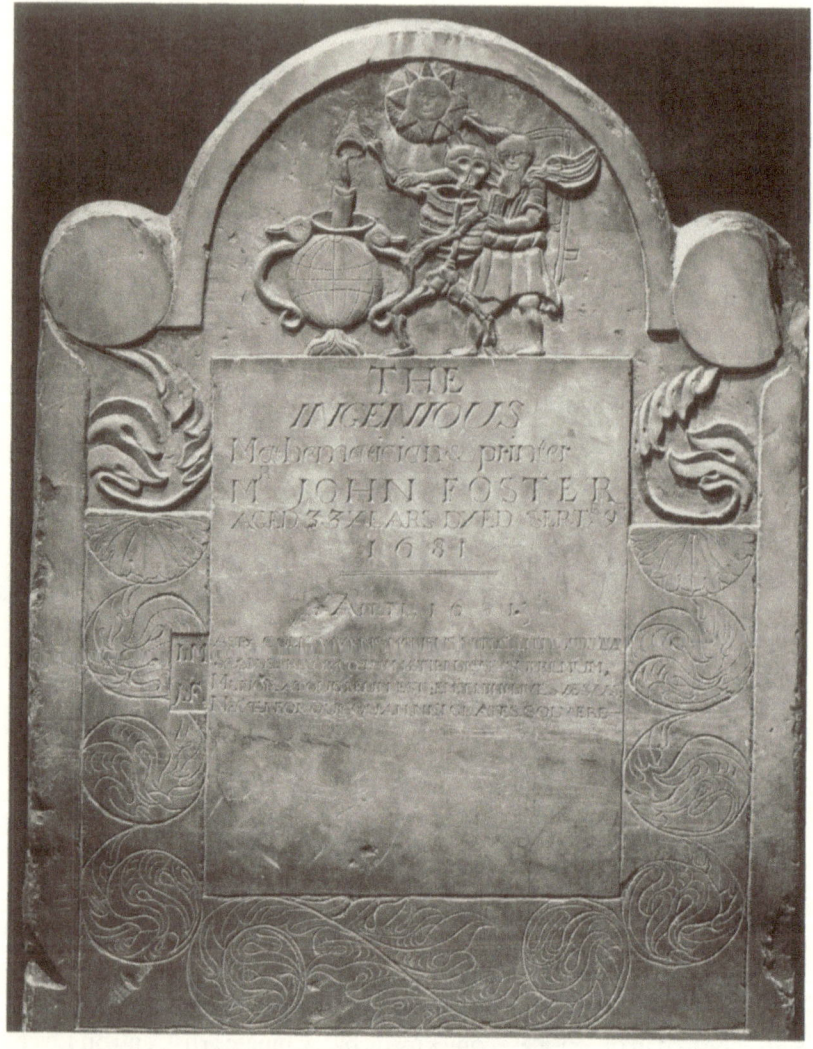

1-3. John Foster footstone, c. 1681, Dorchester Burial Ground. Slate, attributed to the Charlestown stonecutter, 15 1/2 × 17 in. Museum of Fine Arts, Boston, on loan from the Boston Parks and Recreation Commission.

Time shall, clasped by Death no more,
Take a new name—Evermore.[11]

At the close of Hawthorne's *House of the Seven Gables,* on the other hand, when Judge Pyncheon expires in the manner of his accursed ancestors, an "image of awful Death," we are told, filled the house and held

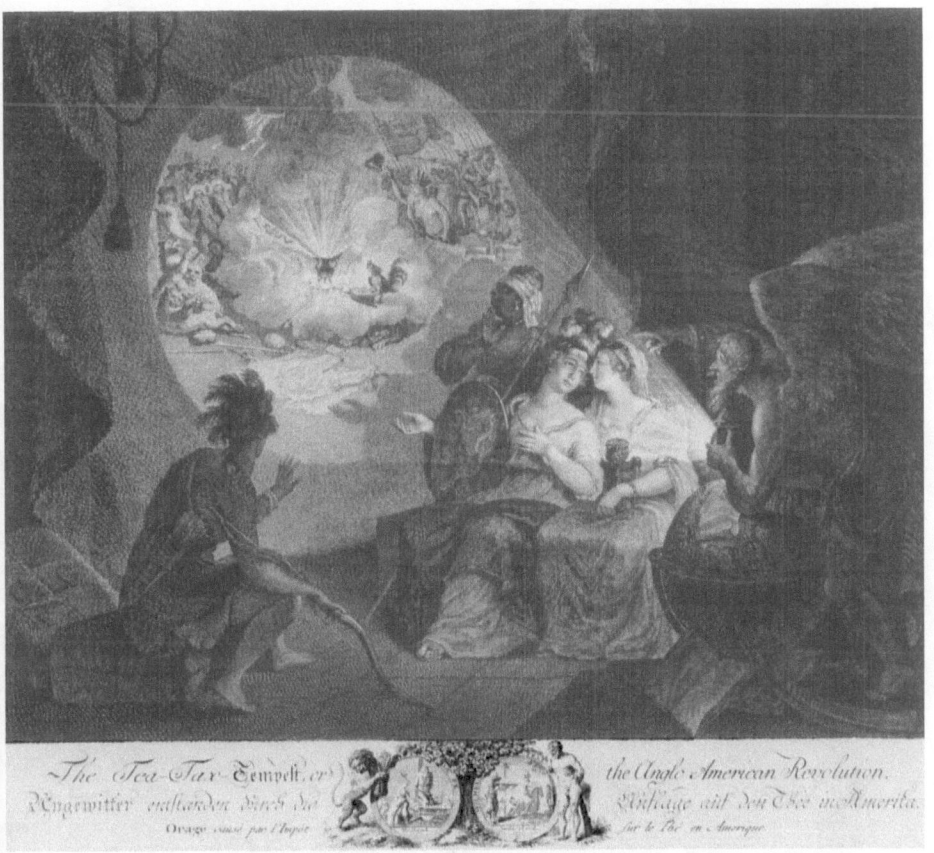

1-4. *The Tea-Tax Tempest or the Anglo-American Revolution*, 1779. Engraving, 13 × 17 in. John Carter Brown Library, Brown University, Providence, Rhode Island.

the family "united by his stiffened grasp."[12] The same tone is suggested in a wood engraving that appeared in *Harper's Weekly* on March 5, 1866. Entitled *Prepare!*, it combines Death and Father Time in a single reversionary figure: a skeleton draped in a sheet holds the customary scythe and hourglass.[13]

By the twentieth century, regardless of whether Death had lost his sting, the traditional imagery of Time had dissipated into an occasional, innocuous piece of folk sculpture or an accepting poem that put the most favorable face possible upon the inevitability that "Time remains at Best a flimsy line of credit."[14] That drift toward dissipation also occurred when it became Clio's turn to cross the Atlantic.

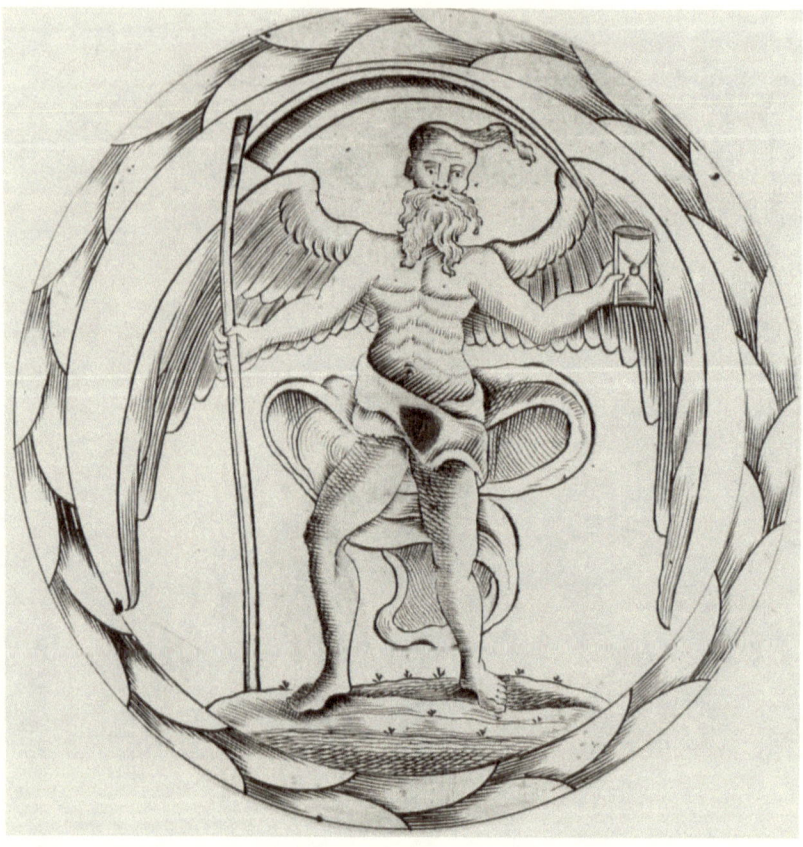

1-5. "Father Time" (detail) from *Eight-day clock* by Gawen Brown of Boston, c. 1762–1773. 90 in. high. Old Sturbridge Village, Massachusetts [57.1.132]. Photograph by Henry E. Peach.

Clio and the Muses in European Art

In a well-known seventeenth-century painting by Nicolas Poussin, *A Dance to the Music of Time*,[15] Father Time sits winged and nude, yet eunuchlike, at the right while four youthful muses dance in a circle and Apollo passes overhead in his cloud-supported chariot. These muses happen to be as nonspecific as the music that engages them, but the quartet of neoclassical lovelies serves to remind us that from the Renaissance through the Enlightenment, artists customarily portrayed the muses as a group, and more often than not, all nine of them together.

The principal tendency to be observed in this section involves the artistic transition from Clio found in a cluster to Clio seen as a solo act, so to

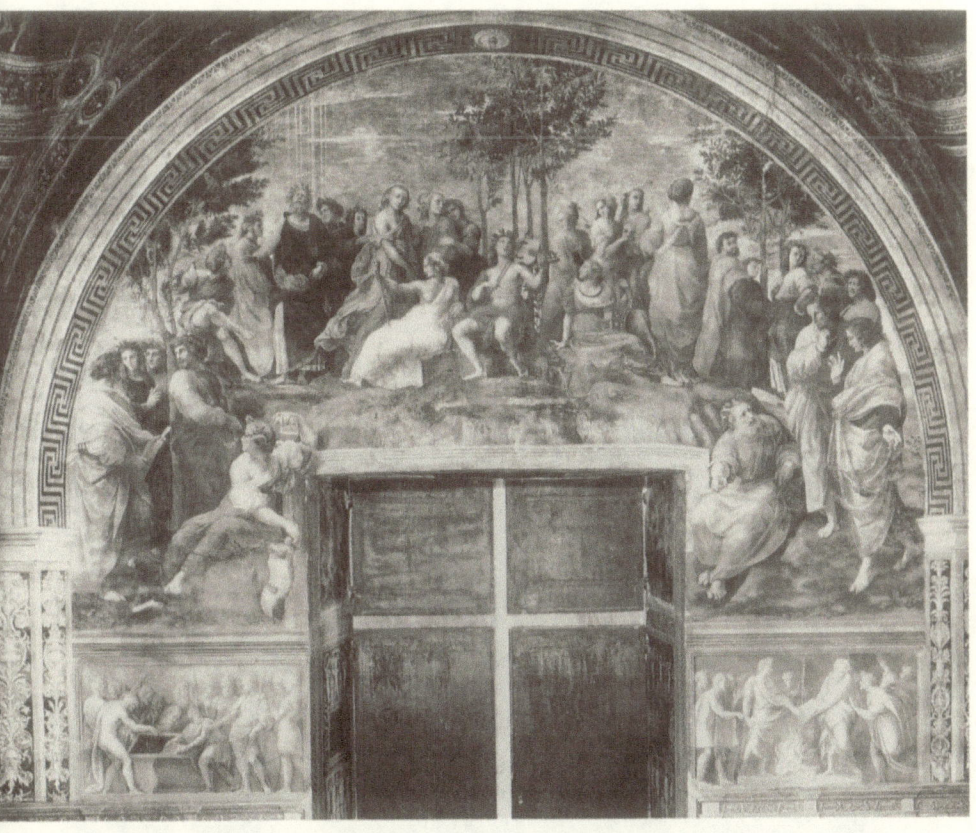

1-6. Raphael, *Parnassus*, 1508–1511. Fresco. Vatican Museum.

speak. Ever since the nineteenth century Clio is more likely to be found alone than in sorority, and Clio as an icon may owe more to Christian symbolism than we have hitherto acknowledged.

From the later fifteenth century to the early seventeenth, Italian artists seem to have been fascinated by the theme of Apollo with the muses. Most frequently they are shown dancing, as in several representations found at the Uffizi and two others at the Pitti Palace in Florence. In the best-known work of this genre, Raphael's *Parnassus* fresco in the Vatican, Apollo fiddles away in apparent ecstasy while the muses mingle with miscellaneous deities and poets (fig. 1-6).[16]

An occasional variation on this theme featured Hercules instead of Apollo, as in the work of Alessandro Allori, a sixteenth-century artist who also set his scene on Parnassus (fig. 1-7). Clio is clearly visible at the upper

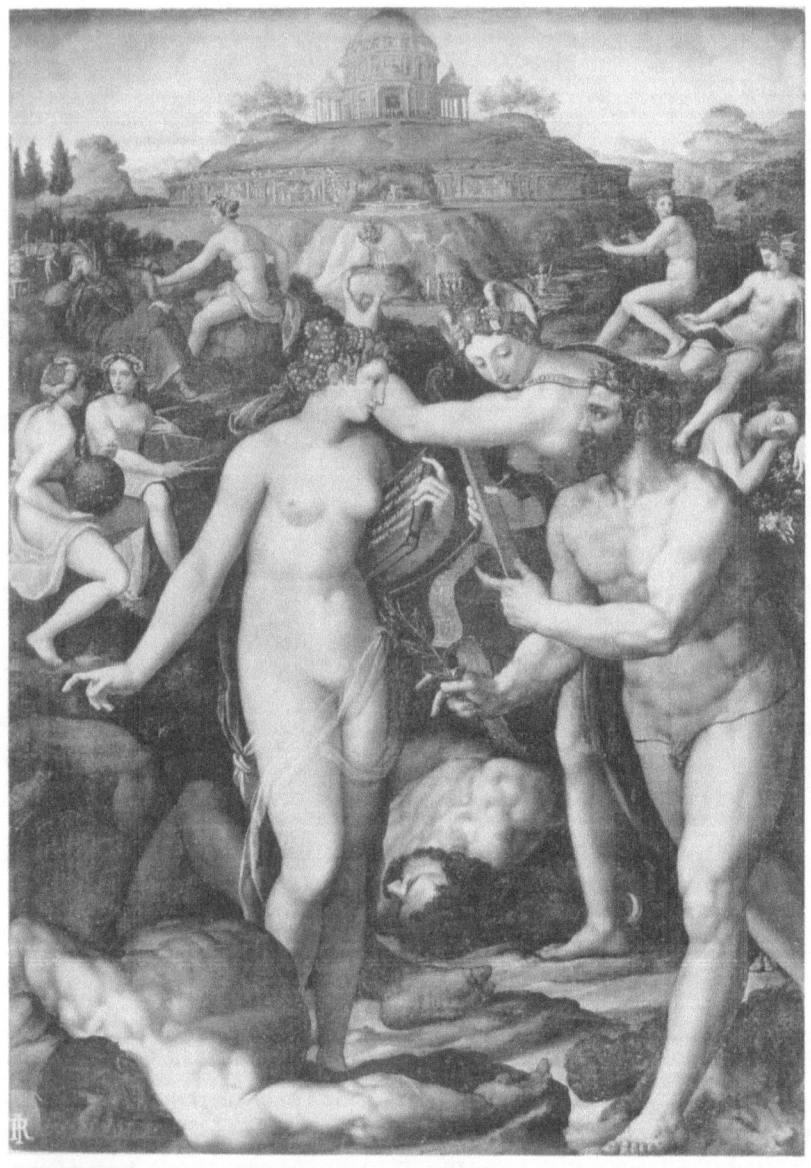

1-7. Alessandro Allori, *Hercules Crowned by the Muse*. Oil on copper, 39 × 29 cm. Uffizi Gallery, Florence, Italy.

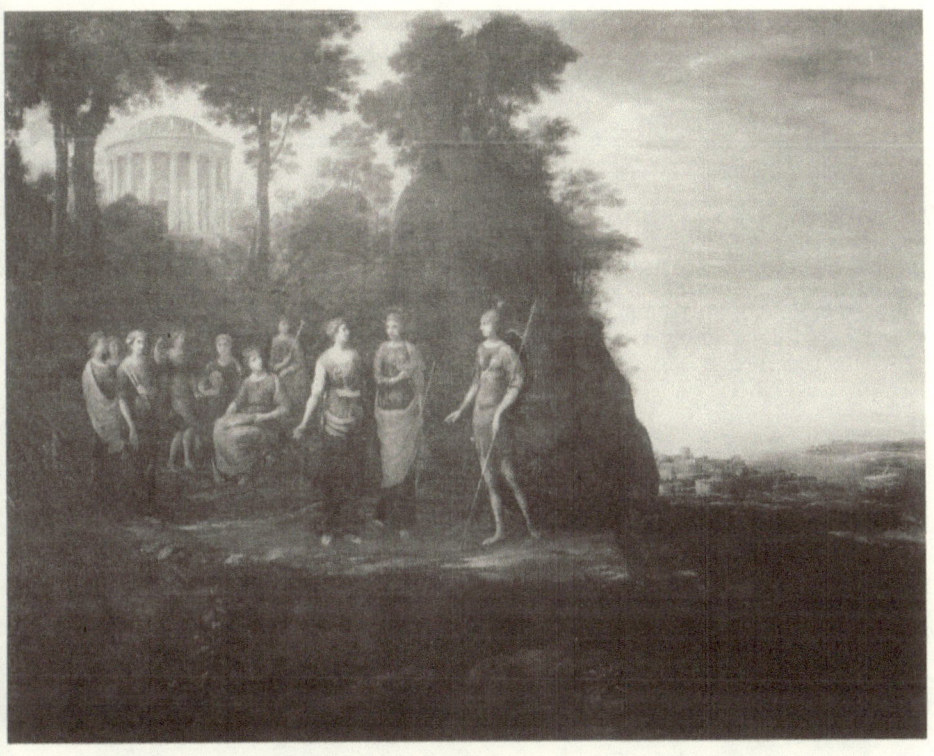

1-8. Claude Lorrain, *Parnassus with Minerva Visiting the Muses,* 1680. Oil on canvas, 57 × 76 in. Cummer Gallery of Art, Jacksonville, Florida.

right, reading an open book on her lap and holding her tablet for record-ing history beneath her left arm.[17]

During the seventeenth century this general subject became a special favorite of Claude Lorrain, who executed it in Arcadian landscape settings and occasionally substituted Minerva for Apollo (fig. 1-8).[18] Once again, Clio is seated in the center and holds an open book upon her lap. On this occasion, however, she appears to be more interested in Minerva, the god-dess of war, than she is in her book.[19]

A song written by William Byrd (1542–1623) sums up some of the senti-ments that this motif seemed to inspire and also carries it to England:

Thou poets' friend

Thou poets' friend that haunts Parnassus hill
And shroud'st in shade where Muses do abide,
Bedew'd with tears from Helicon's distil,

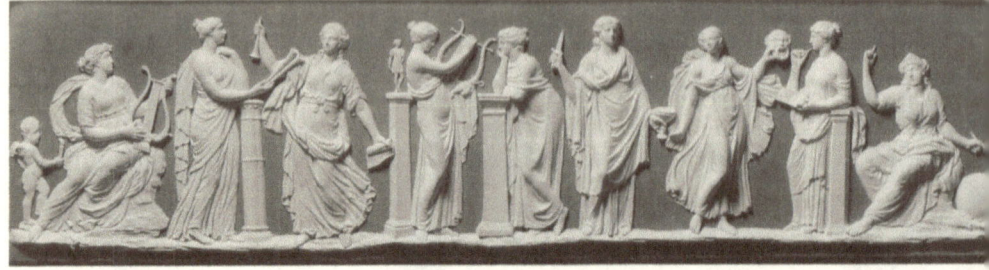

1-9. Probably John Flaxman, Jr., *Nine Muses*, c. 1775. White on blue jasperware made by Wedgwood and Bentley, 6 1/2 × 25 1/2 in. The Brooklyn Museum, The Emily Winthrop Miles Collection [60.198.1]. Photo by Patricia Layman Bazelon.

To skilless hand, fair Clio, be my guide,
And sing with me in praise of Music's Art,
Whose joyful sound doth salve the sighing heart.[20]

The motif of the muses flourished in English decorative art until the close of the eighteenth century. In the library at Osterley Park House, designed by Robert Adam in 1766, a Venetian artist named Antonio Zucchi painted *Apollo and Minerva on Mount Parnassus in the Company of the Muses*. The Brooklyn Museum owns several pieces of jasperware modeled in the mid-1770s by John Flaxman and produced by Wedgwood and Bentley. In one of them, *Nine Muses*, Clio stands second from the right holding a scroll and stylus (fig. 1-9). In another, *Five Muses*, Clio has been placed in the center. Such plaques enjoyed considerable popularity as friezes to be placed on chimney mantels.

I am not aware of many attempts during the past two centuries to depict all or most of the muses in any clustered or interactive manner. A notable exception is provided by *Les Muses* (1893), painted by Maurice-Denis and located in the Musée National d'Art Moderne in Paris. Clio is seated front and center in a heavily wooded setting, an open book in her lap and pen in hand.

For an alternative vision of History, therefore, we must turn from the clustered muses to a form that might be referred to as cloistered. At the simplest level that means isolated representations of Clio, an iconographic tradition that dates back to an ancient Roman statue of Clio with a scroll of parchment unfolded on her lap (fig. 1-10). In a brass plaquette (fig. 1-11) made at Nuremberg in about 1540, the standing muse points to four volumes arrayed on the ground, one of them lying open; and in the frontispiece for Sir Walter Raleigh's *History of the World* (1614), History, support-

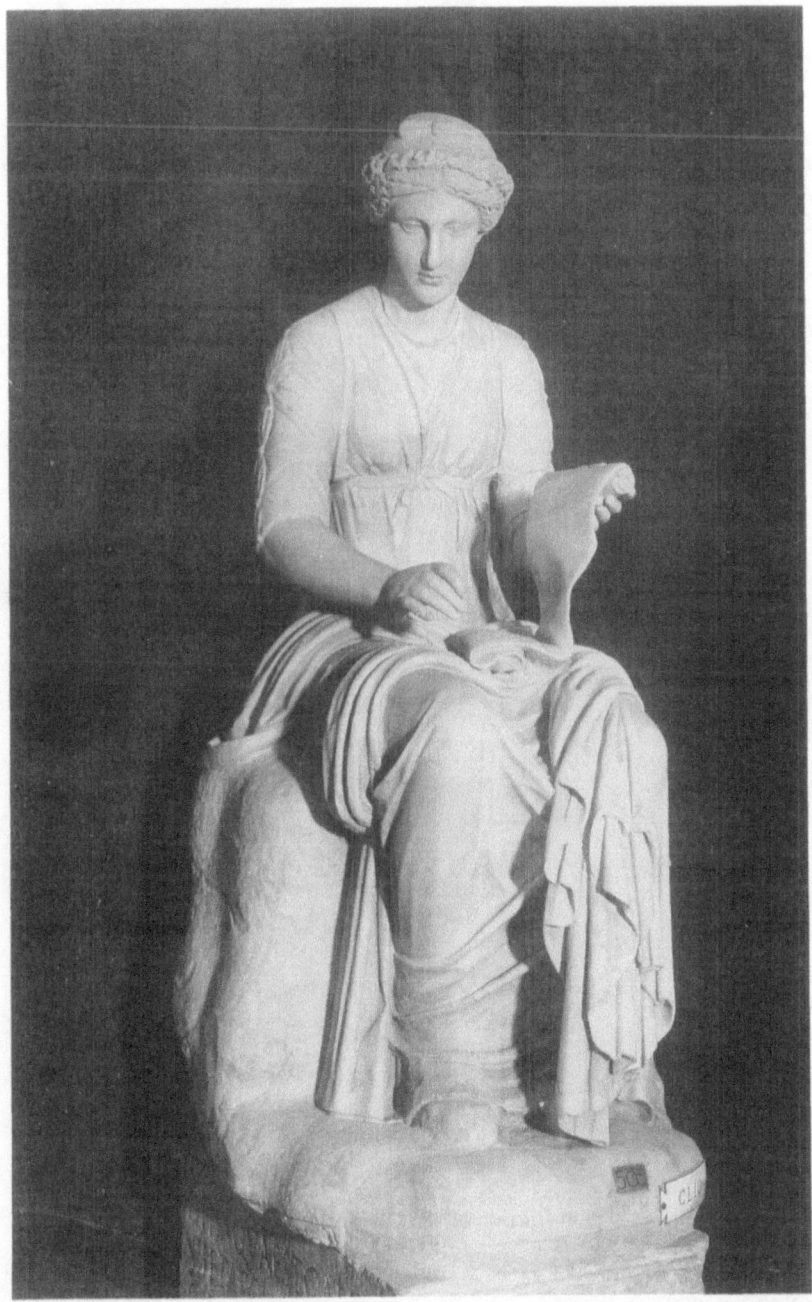

1-10. *Clio, Musa della Storia,* from Villa di Cassió near Tivoli; Roman sculpture, 2d century
A.D. Marble, 4 feet, 6 1/2 in. high. Vatican Museum.

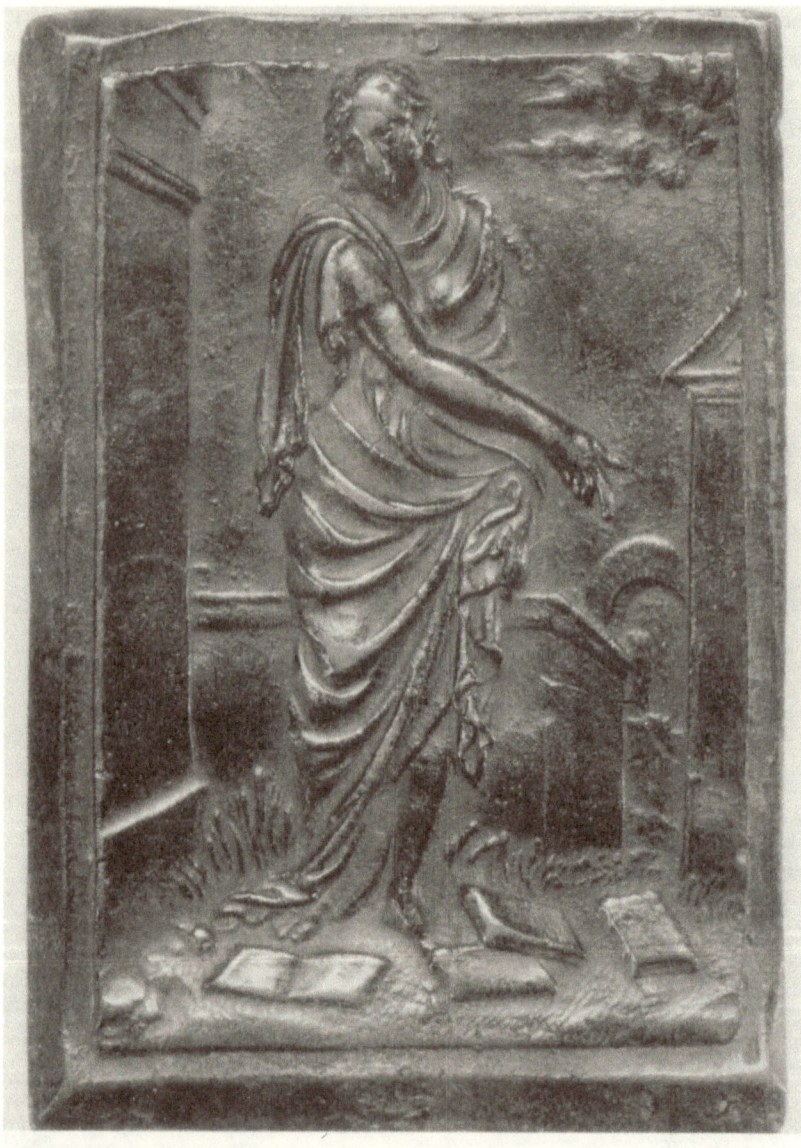

1-11. Peter Flötner of Nuremberg, *Clio* plaquette, c. 1540. Brass, 3 3/16 × 2 1/4 in. Heinz Schneider of Lakewood, Ohio.

ing the globe, flanked by Truth and Experience, treads upon Death and Oblivion (fig. 1-12).

Diverse other representations of Clio indicate an increasing tendency to depict her as a singular subject: Boucher did so during the 1750s, for ex-

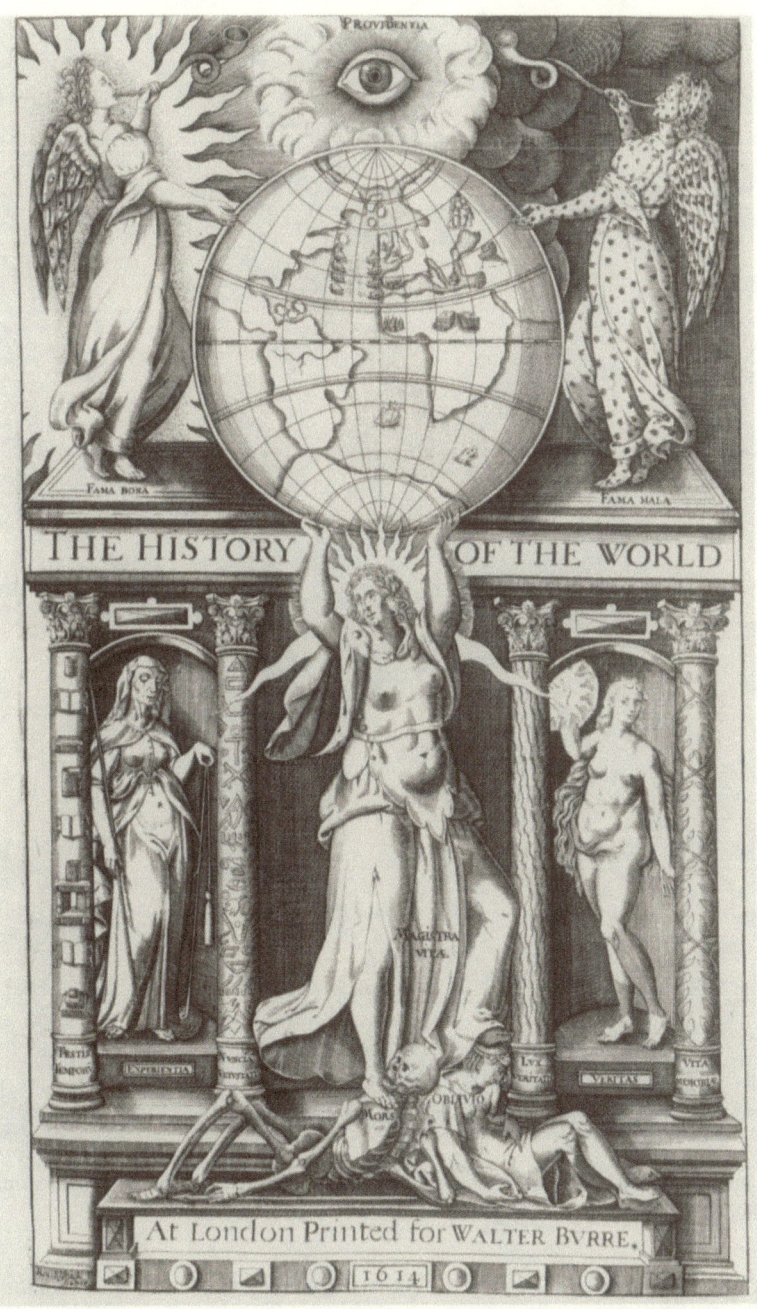

I-12. *History,* engraved frontispiece of Sir Walter Raleigh's *History of the World* (London, 1614).

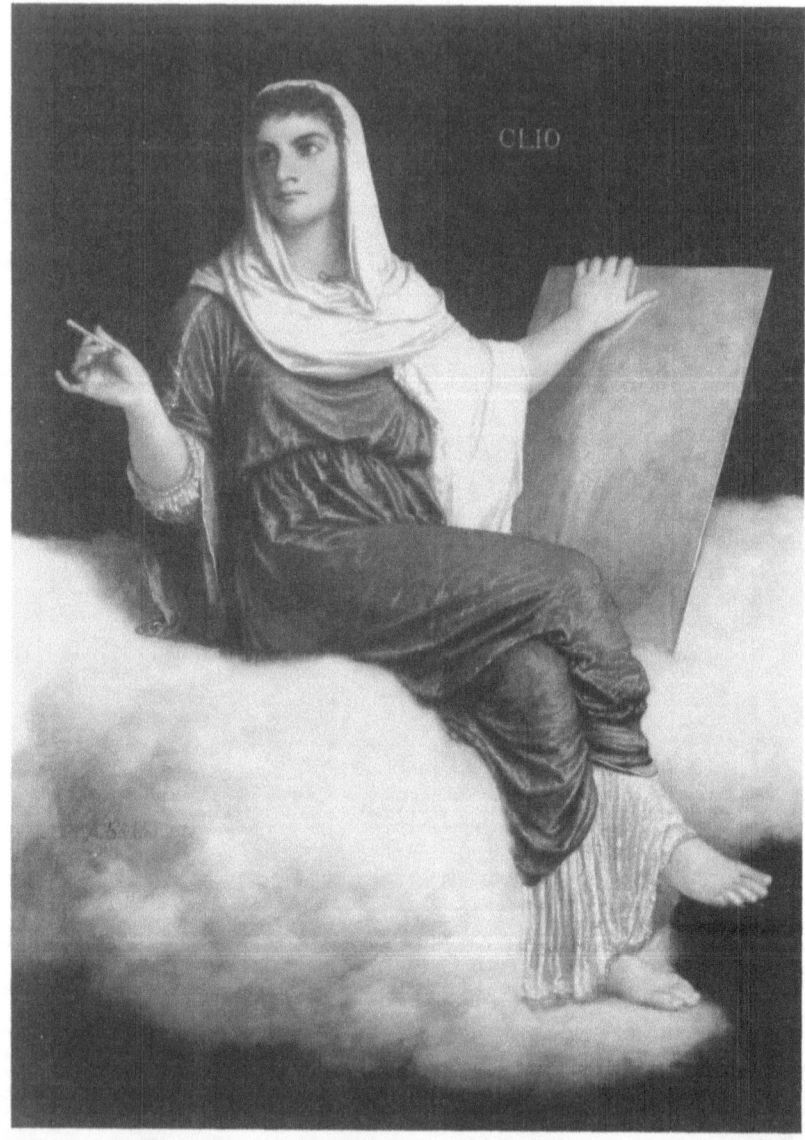

1-13. Arnold Böcklin, *Clio*, 1875. Oil on canvas, 41 1/2 × 30 3/4 in. Oeffentliche Kunstsammlung Basel, Kunstmuseum, Switzerland.

ample, in *La Muse Clio* (in the Wallace Collection); Gradiva, a variant or clone of Clio, was utilized in the nineteenth century as a symbol of memory as well as History;[21] and Arnold Böcklin, the Swiss expatriate who painted in Italy, created a shapely yet above-it-all *Clio* in 1875 (fig. 1-13).

Böcklin's Clio is poised to record events, just as so many of her predecessors had been represented as readers or, at least, as custodians of the
book. Although the logic of those functions may seem self-evident and
sufficient, I believe that we should also notice, at least suggestively, the recurrent tradition of women holding books in Christian iconology: in depictions of the Madonna and Child (fig. 1-14) or any of several saints, such
as Saint Elizabeth (fig. 1-15). One plausible response might be that the Vir-
gin or saint is simply holding scripture, which bears no relationship at all
to Clio's vocation; but a painting of Saint Anastasia (1490) in the Cathedral of Zadar, Yugoslavia, shows her with a book in her left hand and a
sturdy quill pen in her right.[22] The same is true of Saint Barbara in a superb
sixteenth-century Flemish work of stained glass located in the Burrell Collection at Glasgow. Her book is even open, as though she might contemplate writing in it. Just as M. H. Abrams has shown how writers of the
Romantic period reformulated Christian ideas and literary traditions for
new and secular purposes,[23] I simply wish to propose that Clio as we know
her may not be entirely derived from ancient mythology and then the
pagan revival in Renaissance Europe. If History's role is to read as well as
record, artists are likely to have acquired suggestive notions from spiritual
as well as from secular iconology.

Truth, Time, and History Interact

Having traced, however briefly, the separate imageries and trajectories of
Father Time and Clio, we want to return to those occasions—admittedly
infrequent—when the two actually interact. If Truth is the daughter of
Time, as we have noted, and Memory is the mother of the muses, including Clio, then there surely must have been some intimate moments between Father Time and Mother Memory.

The Elizabethans and Jacobeans liked to believe that history could transcend mortality (as in fig. 1-12). A related theme favored in literature and
art from the fifteenth to the eighteenth centuries was succinctly expressed
by the maxim *amor vincit tempus* (love conquers time), which helps to explain the numerous cupids filling the foreground in so many of the pictures that we have under scrutiny.[24]

With those contextual impressions in mind, we can at least contemplate
what might seem to be an inscrutable painting (in more ways than one):
Time Unveiling Truth (1745–1750) by Tiepolo (fig. 1-16). The question of
who is doing what to whom is draped in obscurity, though not exactly

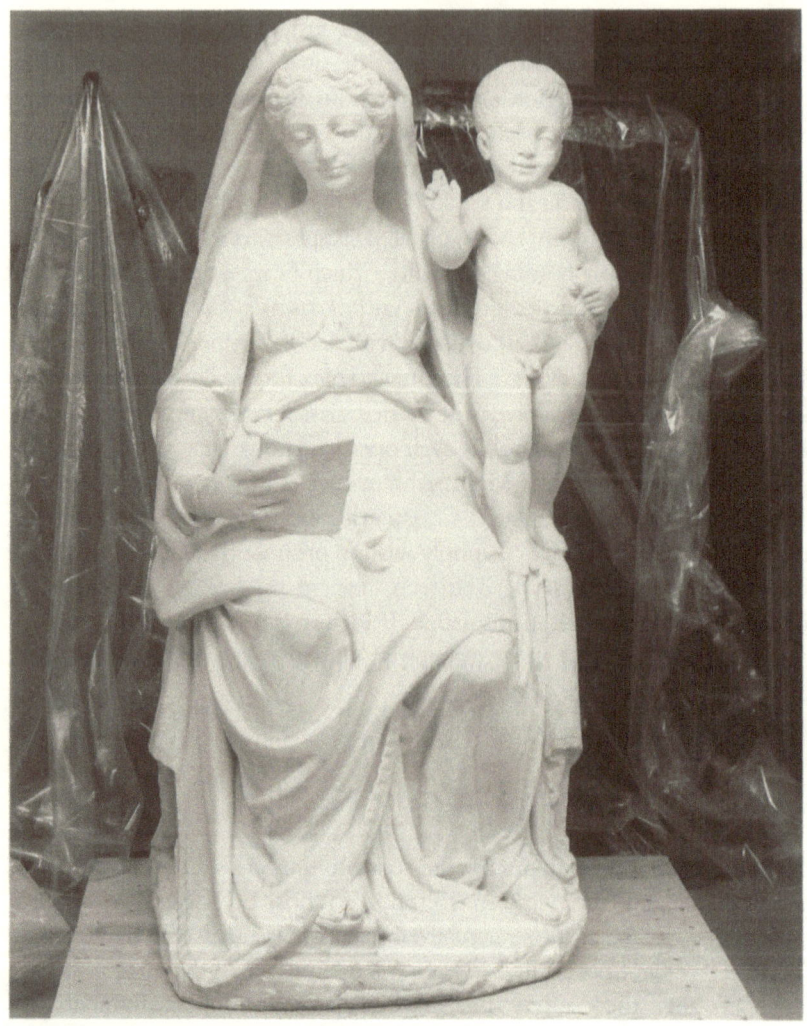

1-14. *Madonna and Child*, probably Lombard, first half of the sixteenth century. Marble, 49 × 22 3/4 in. The Fine Arts Museums of San Francisco, Museum Collection, 21981.157.

discreetly. Time may very well have unveiled Truth, and he has abandoned his accoutrements (scythe and sandglass) in order to hold her firmly. But she appears to be more self-possessed than he, and perhaps even more in control. Cupid certainly seems unconcerned on her behalf, and the blazing sun above her head bears a look of ecstasy about as intense as hers.

Whether Tiepolo recalled that Truth is the daughter of Time and intended this as an instance of incest, I do not pretend to know. Modern

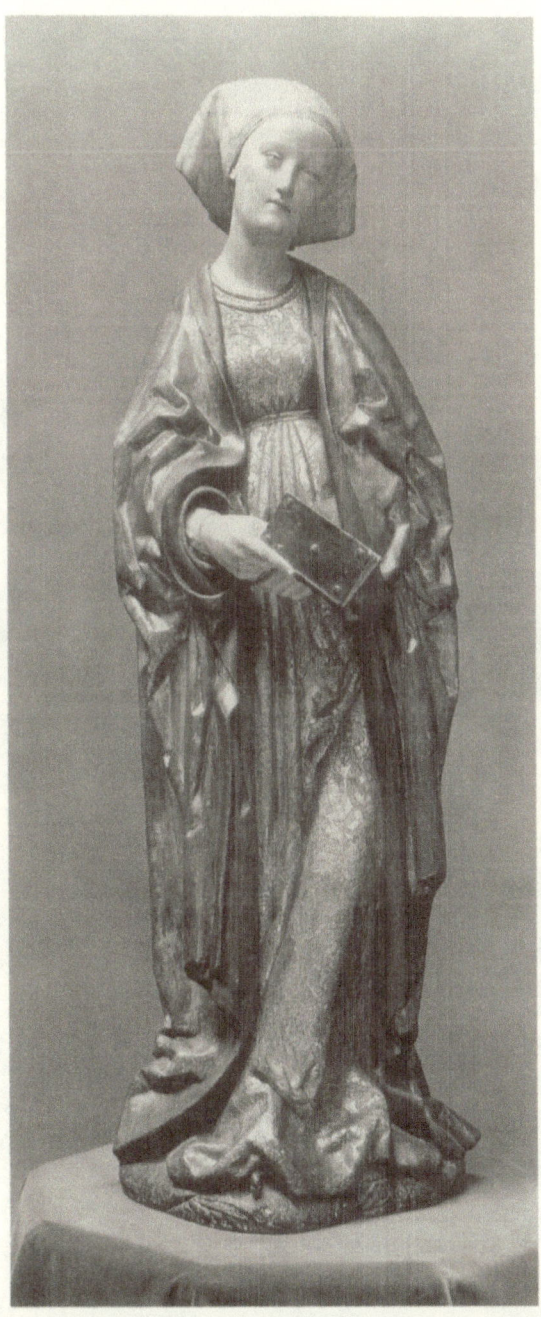

1-15. *Saint Elizabeth Holding a Book,* sixteenth-century German (Swabian). Linden wood
with polychrome and gilt decoration, 56 in. The Pierpont Morgan Library, New York.

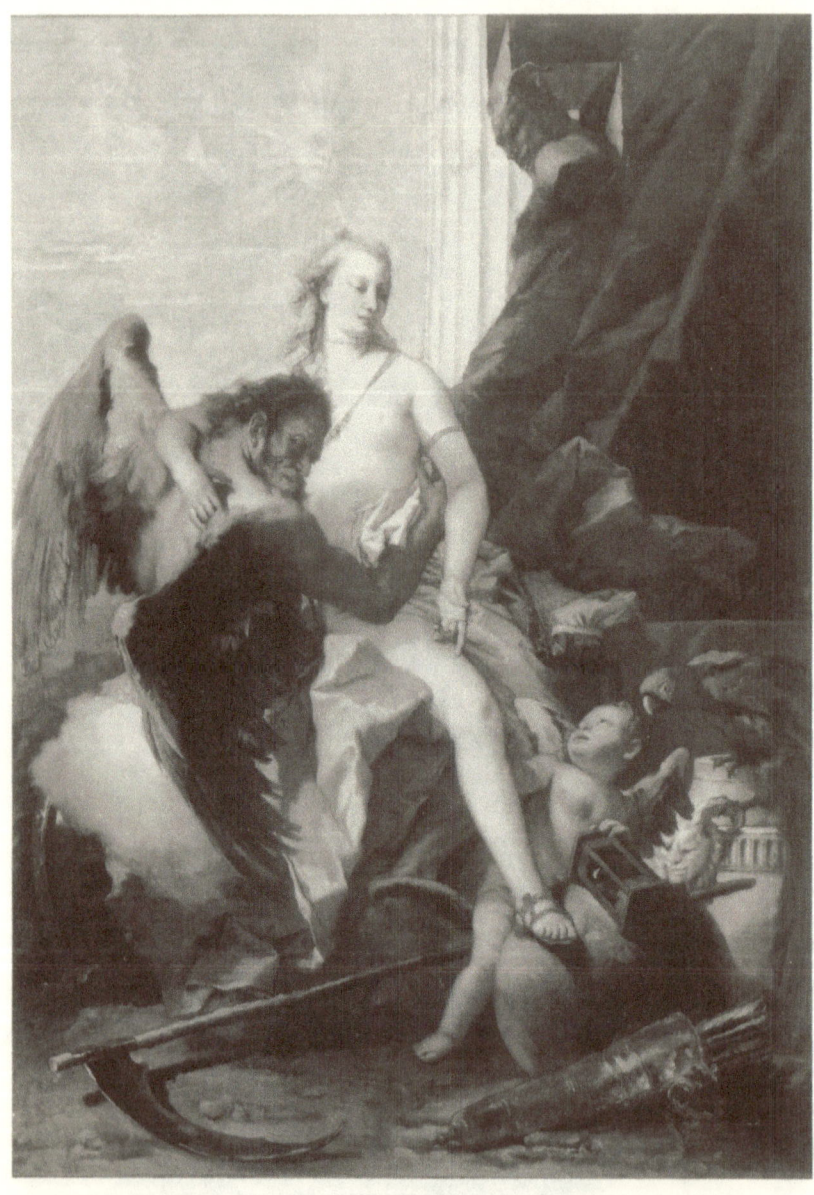

1-16. Giovanni Battista Tiepolo, *Time Unveiling Truth,* c. 1745–1750. Oil on canvas, 91 × 65 3/4 in. Museum of Fine Arts, Boston. Charles Potter Kling Fund.

notions of child abuse surely must be discarded here as anachronistic: the expression on her face is too sublime, and the fingers of her right hand are digging into Time's bare back with more passion than perturbation. Truth is riding high, so to speak, and the parrot just above Cupid can repeat what has happened even if he cannot record it. Tiepolo offers us the naked truth, and she may or may not be inscrutable.

Less enigmatic (and considerably more chaste) is Goya's *Truth, Time, and History* (fig. 1-17), which he painted in about 1797. Father Time clutches both his hourglass and Truth (or Spain), but his gaze is directed toward Heaven rather than the half-exposed bosom of Truth. Visionary matters have prevailed over venery. Truth, in turn, seems rather demure, despite her deshabille, and presents her book as a kind of counterbalance to Time's hourglass (note that all of his sand remains in the upper half; time is not yet running out). And cool Clio, her lips pursed, records with her right hand and secures a very big (and open) book firmly in place with her left foot. In this spectacular painting all three principals appear to be in control of the situation. Time has paused, History is poised, and Truth is, quite literally, posed. The symbolic transaction is a serene one.

What may be happening in these two pictures becomes a bit more complicated when we pay attention to two progenitors that provide us with some allegorical context. Ever since the eleventh century an allegory had developed in which Truth and Justice along with Peace and Mercy were widely perceived as daughters of the Judeo-Christian divinity.[25] The royal collection in Liechtenstein includes two bronzes by a Tuscan sculptor named Massimiliano Soldani (1656–1740). In 1694 he created *Peace and Justice,* the reconciliation of two great virtues, and for it a pendant called *Time Revealing Truth* in which Time is a bearded old man and Truth a nude and nubile female. The pendant relationship makes sense when we recall that Justice is one of the three sisters of Time's daughter, Truth.

The Art Institute of Chicago owns a *bozzetto* (a preliminary sketch for a larger and more finished work) by Pompeo Batoni (1708–1787) titled *Time Unveiling Truth* (1740–1745), which shows Justice with her symbolic scales standing beside Truth, who is revealed by Father Time. Discord and Envy cower at the right while Painting, Sculpture, and Architecture are featured in the foreground.

By the close of the eighteenth century, this theme of history being clarified by the passage of time seems generally to have worn thin, along with the theme's artistic potential. William Cowper, a pre-Romantic English poet, declared that

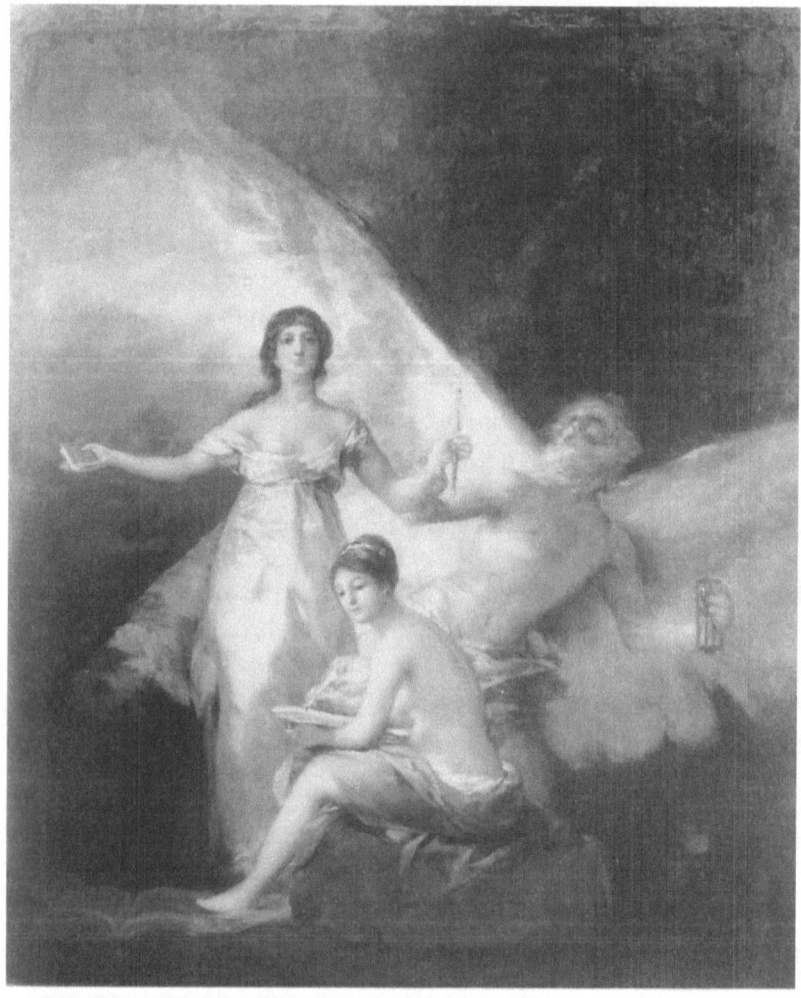

1-17. Francisco Goya, *Truth, Time, and History* (also known as *Spain, Truth, and History*), c. 1797. Oil on canvas, 115 3/4 × 96 in. The National Swedish Art Museums, Stockholm. A preliminary study for it is located at the Museum of Fine Arts in Boston.

> History, not wanted yet,
> Lean'd on her elbow, watching Time, whose course
> Eventful, should supply her with a theme.[26]

Early in the nineteenth century Benjamin West painted *Time Bringing Truth to Light*. Although the painting's location is no longer known, a sheet of six sketches for it, found in the British Museum, reveals a residual

affinity with Tiepolo's attitude toward the subject. A lecherous and apparently virile Father Time pursues, seizes, and roughly handles a Truth who
appears as vulnerable as she is voluptuous.[27] It is very hard to imagine that
these sketches were made by West!

Overall, in Europe and America, the customary domination of History
by Time seems to have diminished during the nineteenth century. The
frontispiece for *Monumental Effigies* (1811–1833), an extravagant enterprise
designed to publish British historical illustrations "from the Norman Con-
quest to the reign of Henry the Eighth," depicts a maiden (History) tram-
pling upon Father Time. She raises aloft a scroll that says RESCUED, and
the plate itself bears this caption: "Resurrecting the Past."[28]

Time and Death had once been allies and then adversaries. Now Time
and Clio alternately struggled, snuggled, disengaged, and finally History
(or Truth) triumphed. This trend seems to culminate not merely in the
United States but on its Pacific rim. During the third quarter of the nineteenth century a mill worker and folk sculptor named Erick Albertson
carved from a single block of redwood one of the most extraordinary
pieces of folk art in the United States. He placed it on top of the Masonic
Lodge in Mendocino, California, of which he was a charter member.

The work is known as *Father Time and the Maiden,* and their relationship could hardly be more amicable (fig. 1-18). He stands at ease behind her
and gently holds or braids her tresses, his hourglass at rest beside her. If
she feels any stress she does not show it because she is purposefully preoccupied with her quill pen; a lamp (or possibly an urn) rests on the pedestal
where she busies herself with a large book. The couple's platform is neoclassical, their inspiration mythological. Their relationship is platonic and
serenely compatible. Time seems to follow rather than precede History in
the American West. Mortality has given way to Memory.

It is possible that Albertson had seen a similar configuration and relationship in a drawing by Alonzo Chappel titled *Allegory of Time* (ca.
1848–1856) that does not seem to have been widely known then or since.
(Chappel's *Allegory* is in the Susan and Herbert Adler Collection of American Drawings and Watercolors, Scarsdale, New York.)

Although these images lingered on in American popular culture, their
relationship became even less intimate and more dutiful. In a political car-
toon from 1919, Clio still busily records, but a fairly frazzled Father Time
stands for a troubled year heading toward oblivion—the worse excesses of
1919 duly noted (fig. 1-19). Clio is not only ageless but seems almost judg-
mental despite her dispassionate visage. The old man is hoary, hopeless,
and allegorically best forgotten. Nevertheless, he has been duly noted by

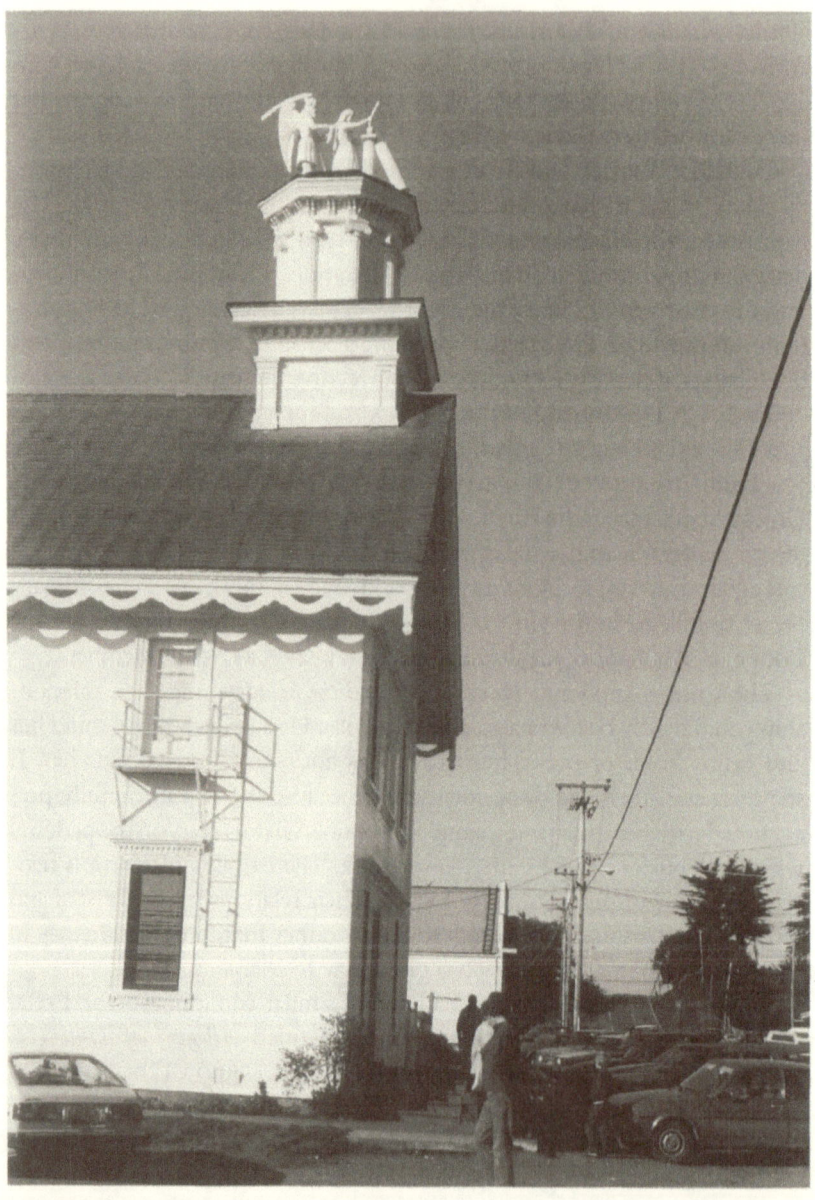

1-18. Erick Albertson, *Father Time and the Maiden*, c. 1870. Carved redwood. Photograph by Ro Peterson.

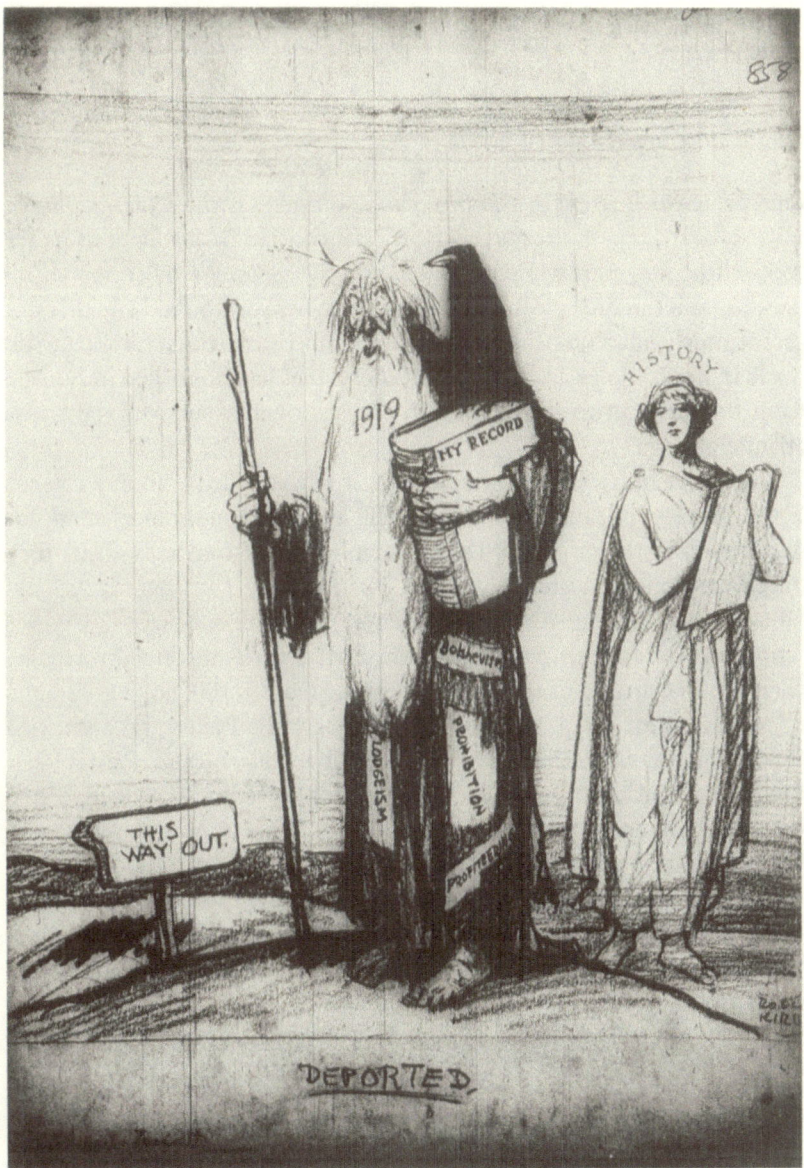

1-19. Rollin Kirby, *Deported*, 1919. Print Collection, Miriam and Ira D. Wallach Division of Art, Prints and Photographs. The New York Public Library. Astor, Lenox and Tilden Foundations.

the memory of society. She records the deeds committed in his time as well as his departure.

Clio Comes to the United States

Our principal interest in the preceding section was the iconography of History and Time as a reciprocal pair. That concern has brought us rather too swiftly, however, to Pacific shores and the 1870s. We must now move back just a bit in order to ask how Clio made her way to the United States pretty much unaccompanied. The answer, in brief, is that although she made it, her complex and symbolic contexts that had flourished in Europe from the fifteenth to the eighteenth centuries barely survived the transatlantic passage.

Let's start by seeking the tradition that I have called Clio in a cluster. Few examples appeared in America at all, and the circumstances are peculiar in each instance. In 1828 David Claypoole Johnston (1798–1865) produced an amusing watercolor called *The Heavenly Nine,* which was exhibited at the Boston Athenaeum (fig. 1-20). It is rather obviously a clever satire, and each of the muses is identified by an extreme, often grotesque, parody of the artistic or cerebral concern she represents. Clio, who is ugly, obese, and intoxicated, sleeps off her stupor while leaning on a stack of children's (childish?) histories. On top of a hill (Mount Parnassus?), Johnston has placed a walled-in "hospital" for the insane—Bedlam. Three years later Johnston prepared a variant of *The Heavenly Nine* to serve as an illustration in the *American Comic Annual.*

This parodic treatment really should not surprise us. Ralph Waldo Emerson's caustic yet positively received comments about History in his famous essay "Nature" (1836) were followed by a mildly conciliatory tone in "History" (1841):

> The student is to read history actively and not passively; to esteem his own life the text, and books the commentary. Thus compelled, the Muse of history will utter oracles, as never to those who do not respect themselves. I have no expectation that any man will read history aright who thinks that what was done in a remote age, by men whose names have resounded far, has any deeper sense than what he is doing to-day.[29]

When William Edward West thought seriously and visually about any of the muses in 1835, he chose to depict *Painting, Poetry, and Music.*[30] He simply ignored History.

The muses taken *en famille* have basically been relegated to academic

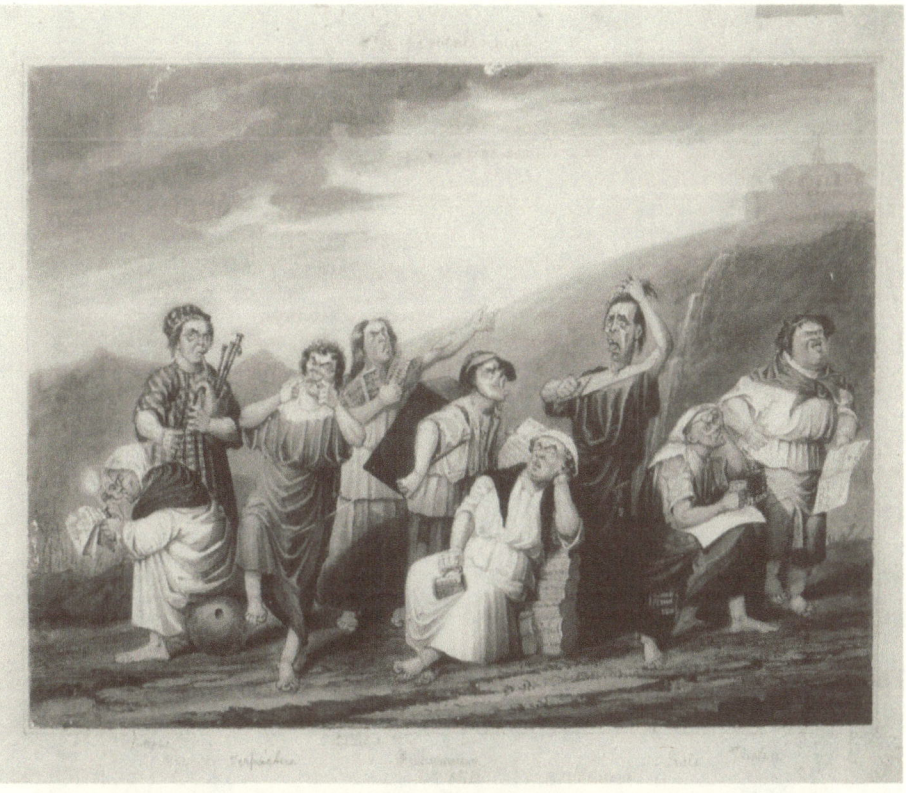

1-20. David Claypoole Johnston, *The Heavenly Nine*, 1828. Watercolor, 10 1/4 × 13 3/4 in. American Antiquarian Society, Worcester, Massachusetts.

treatment in a few tradition-oriented libraries. During the mid-1890s, for instance, the Boston Public Library commissioned a French muralist, Puvis de Chavannes, to decorate the building's grand staircase. He produced nine panels and described the pertinent one in this manner: "*History* attended by a Spirit [a seminude adolescent male holding a torch *and* a book] bearing a torch calls up the Past." [31] Similarly, the East Room of the Pierpont Morgan Library in New York has a series of lunettes surrounding the lower edge of the ceiling, and Henry Siddons Mowbray (1858–1928) included one of Clio. It is neither distinctive nor memorable. The tradition had been trivialized.

When the new Library of Congress was constructed late in the 1890s, its interior design provided for eight marble piers that would project into the rotunda, thereby defining the various precincts of the main reading room. The piers are capped by ivory-colored plaster figures representing Reli-

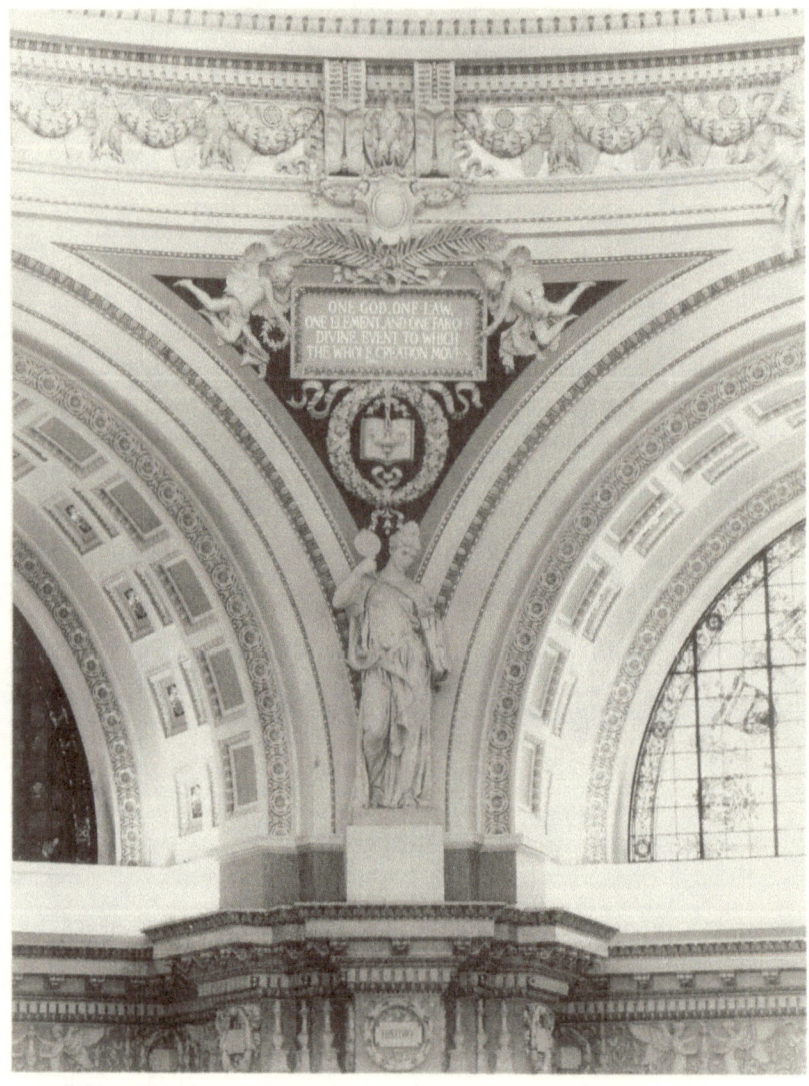

1-21. Daniel Chester French, *History*, 1896. Plaster, height 126 in. Library of Congress.

gion, Commerce, History, Art, Philosophy, Poetry, Law, and Science. The commission for *History* went to Daniel Chester French. Clio holds a mirror raised in her right hand and, like a teenager trudging home from high school, hefts a load of books in her left (fig. 1-21). Beneath her there are smaller bronze statues of Herodotus and Gibbon.[32]

The great clock above the entrance to the rotunda, as it happens, is sur-

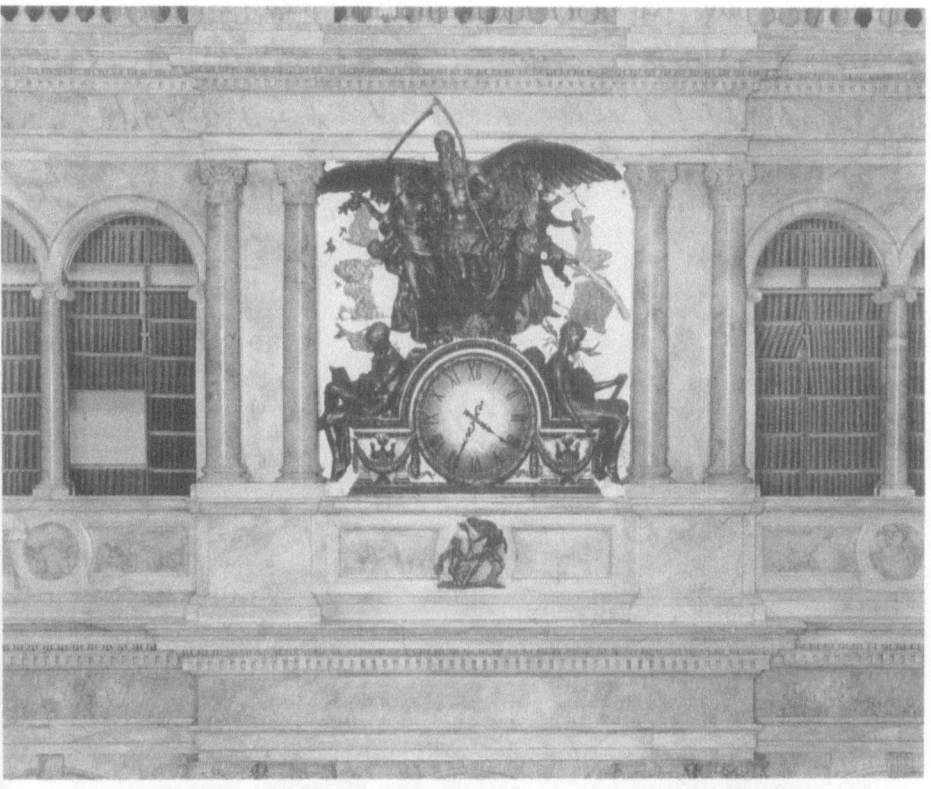

1-22. John Flanagan, marble rotunda clock with the figure of Father Time, 1902. Bronze. Library of Congress.

mounted by a bronze, life-sized figure of Father Time, who is striding forward with his scythe prominently in hand (fig. 1-22). I cannot tell whether or when he glances at History, but he is immediately surrounded by figures of maidens who represent the Four Seasons, a cyclical rather than a linear conception of time.

When we turn from Clio among her colleagues to History as a solo act, we achieve marginally better results, but only for the first two-thirds of the nineteenth century. The Lyman Allyn Art Museum owns a unique work, with the title *Mercy and Truth Are Met Together*, that dates from about 1810 (fig. 1-23). Mercy and Truth are mythological siblings, you will recall, and in this instance Truth, who is clearly the senior sibling, is really a Clio, replete with a large book and a bright sun brooch at her bosom.

The most distinctive and memorable Clio in the United States, from my point of view, is the so-called *Car of History*, a timepiece commissioned by

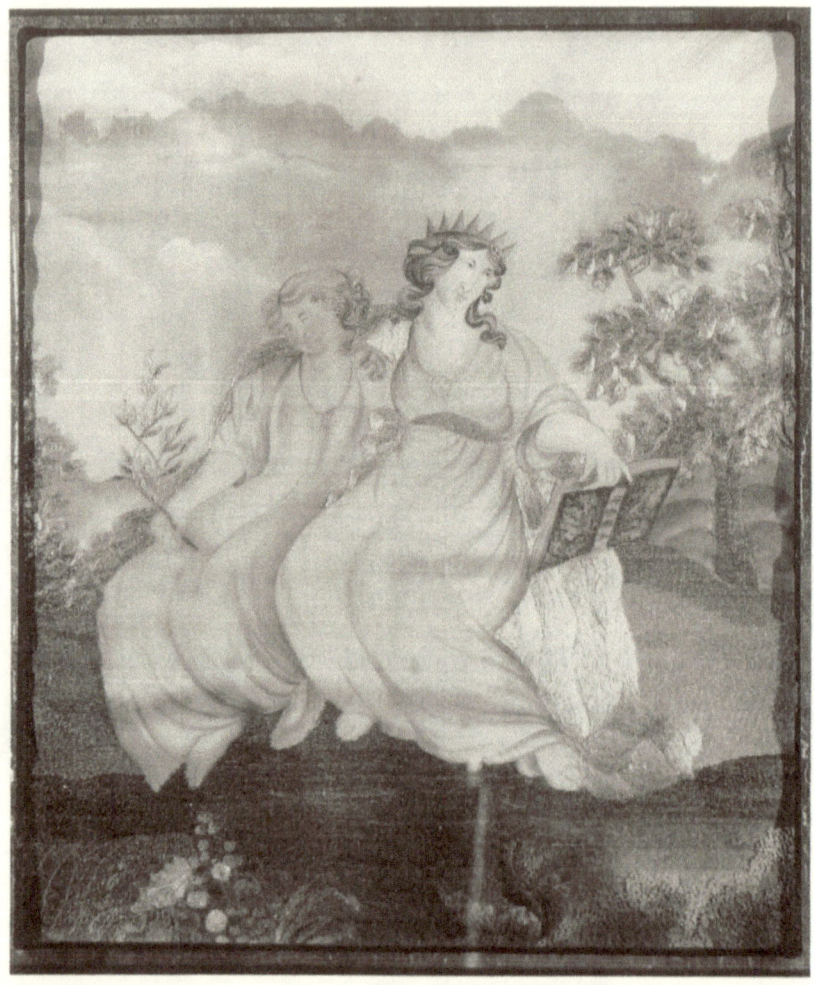

1-23. Anon. American, *Mercy and Truth Are Met Together*, c. 1810. Embroidery and water-color, 8 1/4 × 7 3/8 in. Lyman Allyn Art Museum, New London, Connecticut.

Congress and completed by the sculptor Carlo Franzoni in 1819 (fig. 1-24). The muse of history stands in a winged Car of Time, ready to record great events as they occur. (She is, in a figurative sense, our earliest public historian.) The car rests upon a marble globe on which the zodiac signs have been carved in relief. The chariot wheel also serves as the clock's face, with the mechanism made by Simon Willard. All in all, it is a stupendous piece of work.

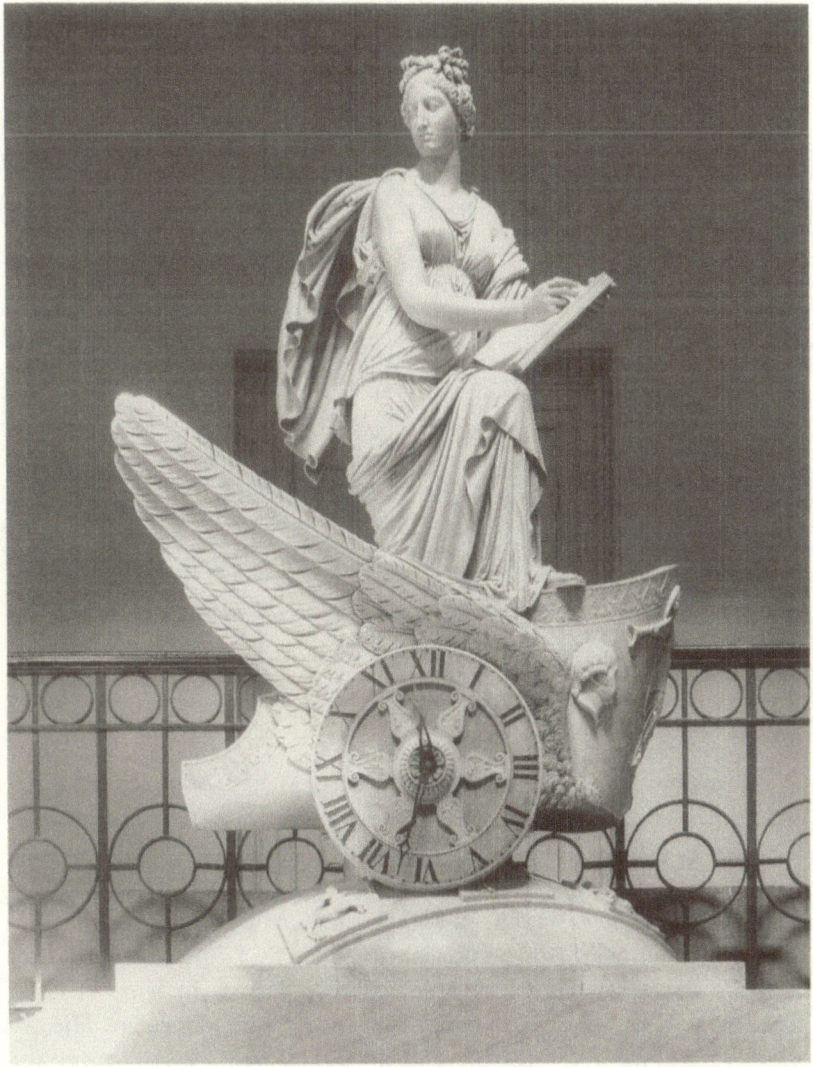

1-24. Carlo Franzoni, *Car of History,* 1819. Marble. Statuary Hall, the United States Capitol. Architect of the Capitol. Sculptures are in the United States Capitol Art Collection.

On the other side of the Capitol, above an entrance to the Senate, recumbent figures representing those mythological siblings, History (left) and Justice (right), were carved during the early 1860s by Thomas Crawford (fig. 1-25). History's scroll reads "History. July 1776."

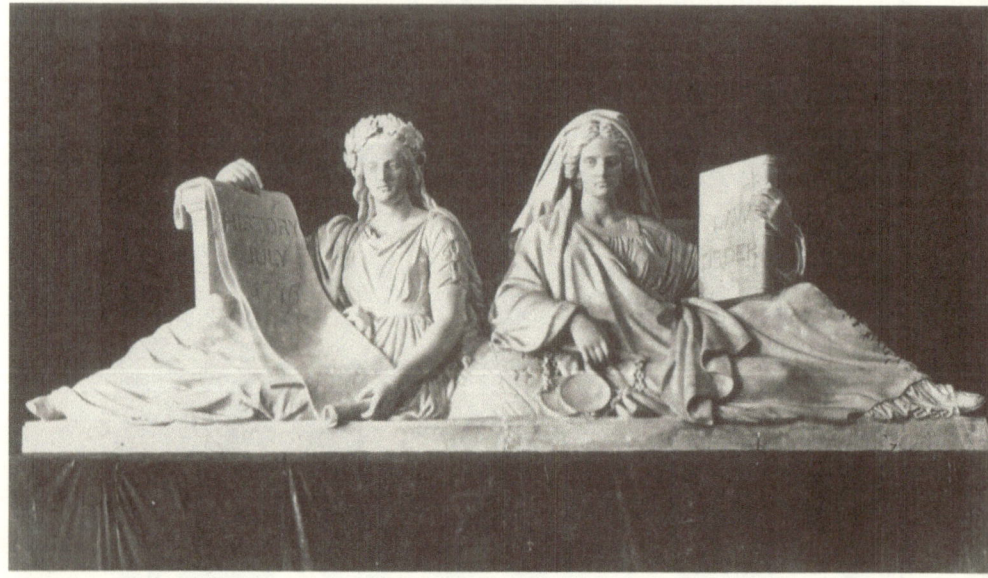

1-25. Thomas Crawford, *Justice and History*, 1863. Marble, 11 ft. 2 in. long ×3 ft. 10 in. high × 2 ft. 2 in. deep. Architect of the Capitol. Sculptures are in the United States Capitol Art Collection.

The image of History actually recording notable events materialized occasionally, but not often, during the nineteenth century. There is, for example, an obscure oil painting attributed to John Archibald Woodside (1781–1852) called *History Inscribing Washington's Fame,* in which Clio sits front and center, writing in a huge tome, while Washington is apotheosized above her.[33] At the Old Courthouse in St. Louis, Missouri, there are four allegorical figures designed by Carl Wimar in 1862: History, Knowledge, Law, and Instruction. The female embodiment of History stands on a cloud and records events on a long scroll. At the base of the Soldier's National Monument, erected in 1865 at Gettysburg Cemetery, four statues represent War, Peace, History, and Plenty. History rests her foot on two books and, in a third volume which lies upon her lap, inscribes the epic battle's action as well as the names of those heroes who lost their lives (fig. 1-26). Edward Valentine's statue of Jefferson Davis, unveiled in Richmond in 1907, portrays Davis lecturing from a history book with his arm outstretched.[34]

Otherwise the nineteenth century supplies us with scant and highly idiosyncratic vestiges of a tradition that had once been pervasive. In 1827, when

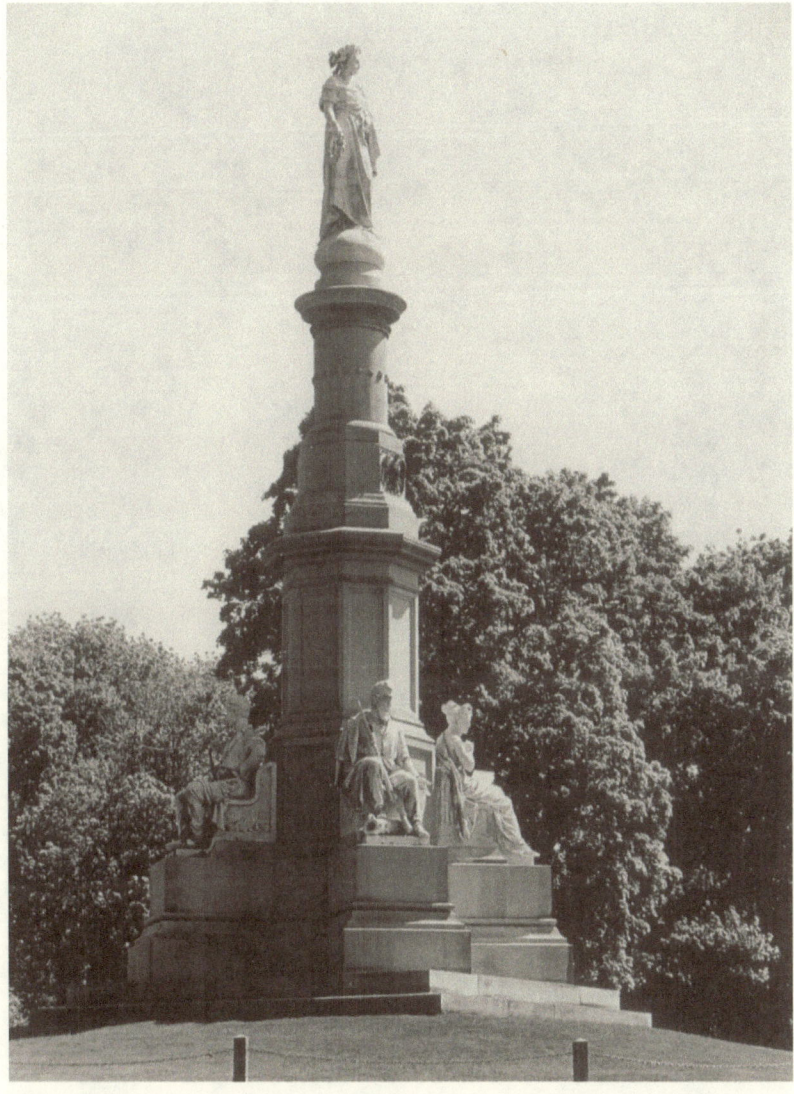

1-26. Soldier's National Monument at Gettysburg, Pennsylvania, 1865. Marble sculptures on granite, designed and modeled for James G. Batterson by George Keller and Randolph Rogers. Photograph by Milo V. Stewart, Cooperstown, New York.

James G. Percival published a collection of poems, many of them commemorative odes for events of the American Revolution (for example, "Ode, Concord, April 19, 1825"), he called the volume *Clio*. When Cecil B. Hartley published a biography of Daniel Boone in 1865, the frontispiece

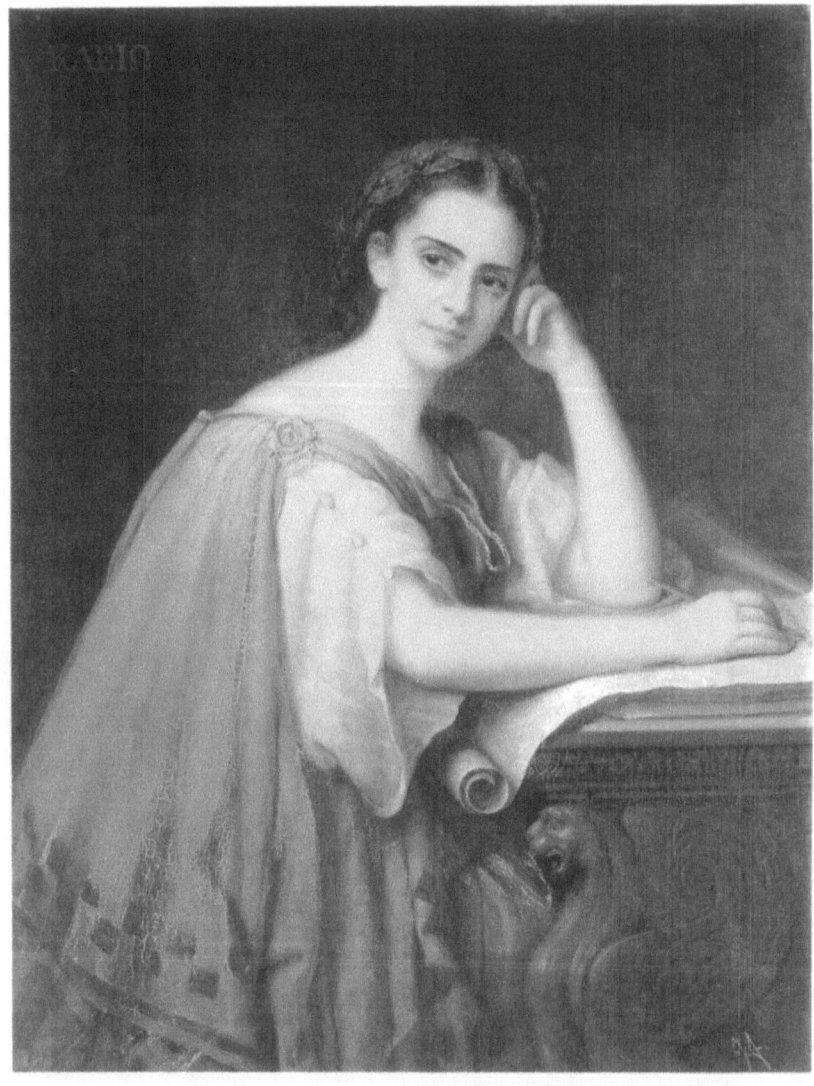

1-27. Joseph Fagnani, *American Beauty Personified as the Nine Muses: Clio: Mrs. William M. Johnson*, 1868–1869. Oil on canvas, 43 1/2 × 33 1/2 in. The Metropolitan Museum of Art, Gift of an Association of Gentlemen, 1873 [74.42].

presented a portrait of Boone accompanied by Clio, who has a scroll enumerating the names of Columbus, Americus (Vespucci), Cabot, and Raleigh. In History's judgment, Boone is the "Columbus of the Woods." And in 1882 William Bradford, the marine and seascape specialist, painted

Schooner Yacht Clio because a schooner of that name had been brought to New Bedford in 1881 by Horatio Hathaway, a figure from a family long prominent in the China trade.[35]

As American portraiture developed during the nineteenth century, suggestive associations with history that presumably had some purpose, such as the prominence of history books in the family's possession, were supplanted by titles such as "Clio" that were intended simply to flatter the sitter by identifying her with an inspirational muse. Ammi Phillips's portrait of Mrs. John Vincent Storm (c. 1835–1840) includes two books, both of which have "History" lettered on their spine.[36]

On the other hand, Joseph Fagnani, who came to the United States from Naples in 1849 and painted portraits of the rich and powerful until his death in 1873, called his portrait of Mrs. William M. Johnson *Clio* for bizarre reasons (fig. 1-27). As a contemporary booklet titled *American Beauty Personified as the Nine Muses* explains, Fagnani heard "a foreigner remark that America afforded no examples of the purely classic face so often encountered in the Old World. To demonstrate the fallacy of this assertion, the artist conceived the plan of painting the portraits of nine American ladies of acknowledged beauty, idealizing them no further than to give them the accessories with which the daughters of Mnemosyne [Memory] are commonly represented."[37] The booklet subsequently supplies this description of Clio: "A parchment scroll lies before her, and the trumpet of fame. A brunette, whose face is cold and passionless, but wears an expression of deep and earnest thought."

Had the representation of History finally reached its nadir in American culture? Almost, but not quite. According to a tale that appeared in the *Saturday Evening Post* in 1922, called "Mr. Pottle and Pageantry," Mrs. Blossom Pottle insisted that her husband put on a cheesecloth toga when impersonating the "Spirit of History" in a local community pageant because "spirits never wear pants."[38] That, I think, must surely have been the nadir.

Occasional pieces of sculpture over the past century have ranged from a diminutive porcelain Clio (fig. 1-28) to a full-scale reproduction, commissioned by Miss Ima Hogg, of the Vatican Museum's ancient Roman Clio (fig. 1-10)—to serve as the centerpiece of Miss Hogg's Clio Garden at her Bayou Bend estate in Houston—to a droll neoclassical Clio carved in 1982 by the American sculptor Victor Colby (fig. 1-29).

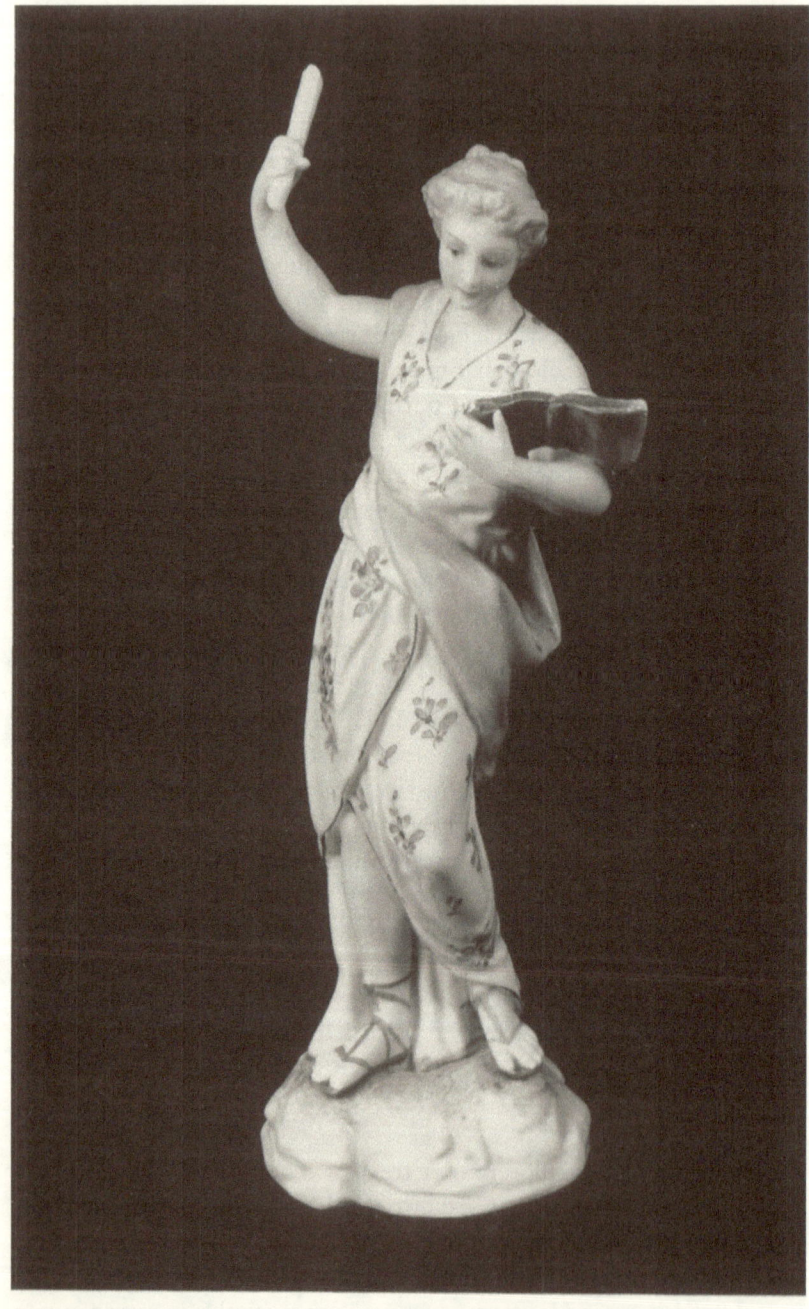

I-28. Anon. American or English, *Clio*, late nineteenth century. Porcelain, 7 1/2 in. high. Collection of the author.

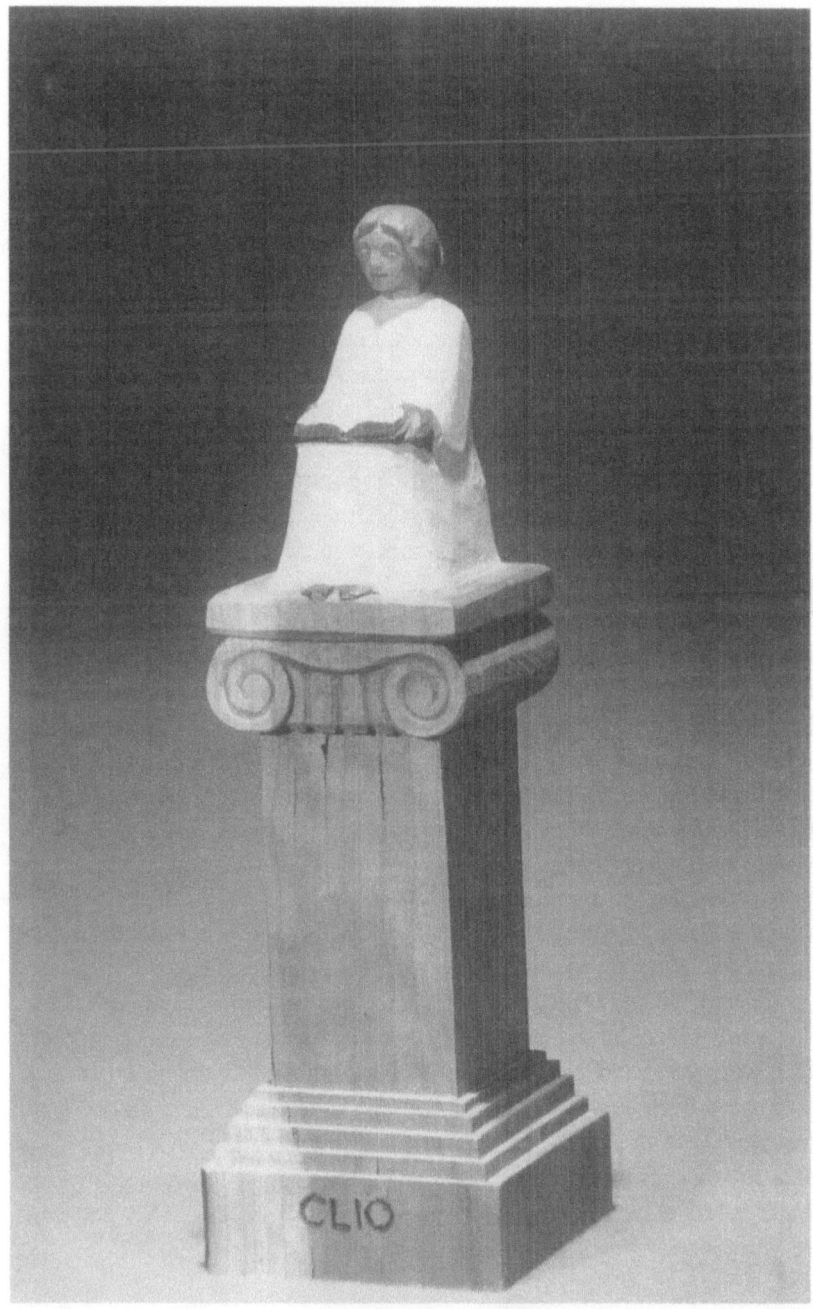

1-29. Victor Colby, *Clio*. 1982. Carved cherry wood, 11 3/8 in. high. Collection of the author.

Time's Pulse: Clocks, Watches, and Memory

Have we now essentially exhausted the imaginative possibilities for envisioning and discussing Truth, Time, and History? Not exactly, as I hope to show in the next two chapters. Not quite, as I want to suggest in the remaining sections of this one. It does seem clear, however, that most of the customary images—many of them dating back centuries—have long since lost their appeal, their meaning, even their recognition value.

One set of symbols lingers on in curious ways, however, and cannot be altogether ignored: clocks and watches. Hawthorne, for instance, used the timepiece as an ominous mechanism. In *The House of the Seven Gables*, Judge Pyncheon's watch ticks in a "fearful" manner when it becomes manifest that he is a doomed man: "this little, quiet, never-ceasing throb of Time's pulse . . . has an effect of terror" (p. 403).

During the later seventeenth century, Dutch and British artists depicted watches by using techniques that anticipated the trompe l'oeil still-life paintings of William Harnett and John Peto. Their psychological intent, in large measure, was to assert the transitory nature of human life.[39] Others, though, preferred to affirm human progress and the Calvinist preoccupation with industry. William Penn had said that "a man, like a watch, is to be valued for his going," and Poor Richard improvised variations on that sentiment during the mid-eighteenth century.[40]

Permutations and combinations of those themes have persisted in nineteenth- and twentieth-century American art, but in fairly straightforward ways, such as John Haberle's *Time and Eternity* (c. 1890), in which a stopwatch hangs with assorted other objects on a board, or Betty Parson's *Clocks of Time* (1968), in which circular clocks (more or less) enclosing triangles are interspersed and partially separated by irregular rectangles.[41] I might have called it "the geometry of time," but then I am not the artist.

Expressionism and surrealism provided such painters as Magritte and Dali with wonderful opportunities to create all sorts of startling fantasies. Magritte's *Time Transfixed* ingeniously puts a clock on a locomotive coming directly from a wall (Art Institute of Chicago), and Dali's *Persistence of Memory* presents that unforgettably bleak landscape in which three melting watches rest in weird ways upon three different sorts of surfaces (Museum of Modern Art).[42]

Although Dali's wiggly and wavy watches must surely be sui generis as a composition, his chosen title brings us at last to the motif that has increas-

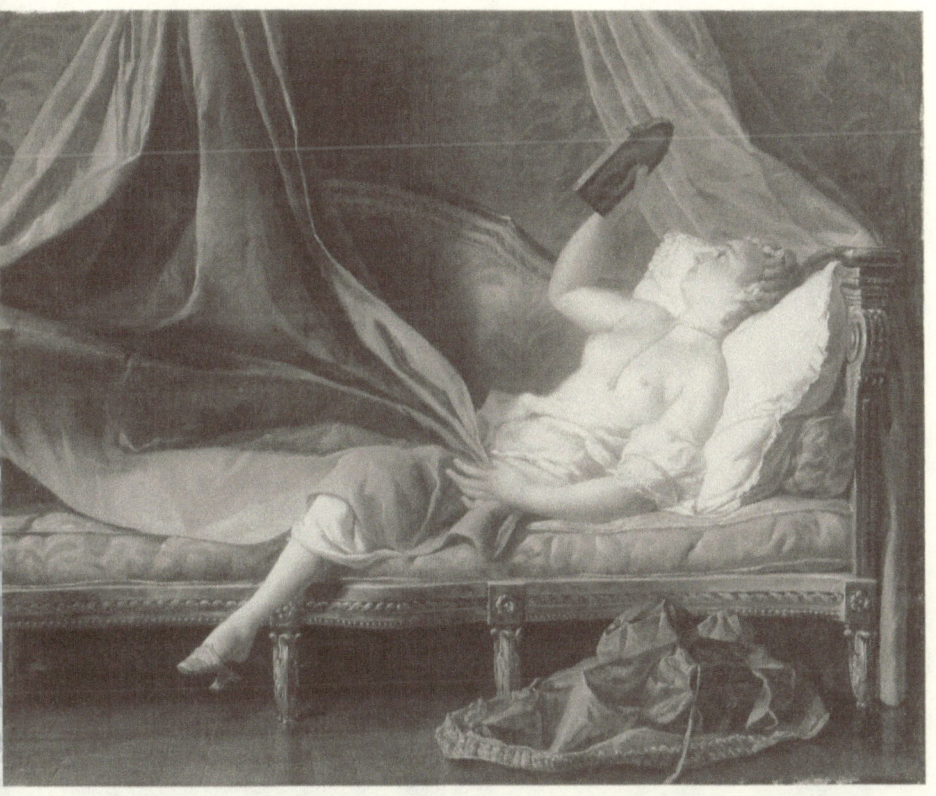

1-30. Charles André van Loo, *Woman on a Couch*, c. 1760. Oil on canvas, 21 × 27 in. The Metropolitan Museum of Art, Gift of Forsyth Wickes, 1957 [57.152].

ingly become an American surrogate for the traditional iconography of Time and History—Memory. There are even two transitional links, moreover, and we will find one of them in figure 1-12, the engraved frontispiece from Raleigh's *History of the World*. On the base of the column at the extreme right, next to Veritas, we see the words *Vita Memoriae*.

Even more prescient, however, was the customary practice for representations of History to hold a hand mirror.[43] (I note only in passing the convention in European art of lovely ladies, usually located in boudoirs, checking their cheeks with a hand-held mirror [fig. 1-30].) The most notable linkage of that sort to American artistic statements about the importance of knowing the past is the beautiful marble sculpture titled *Memory*, made by Daniel Chester French (fig. 1-31). This work was a labor of love for which he had no commission, and that may explain why he started sketches

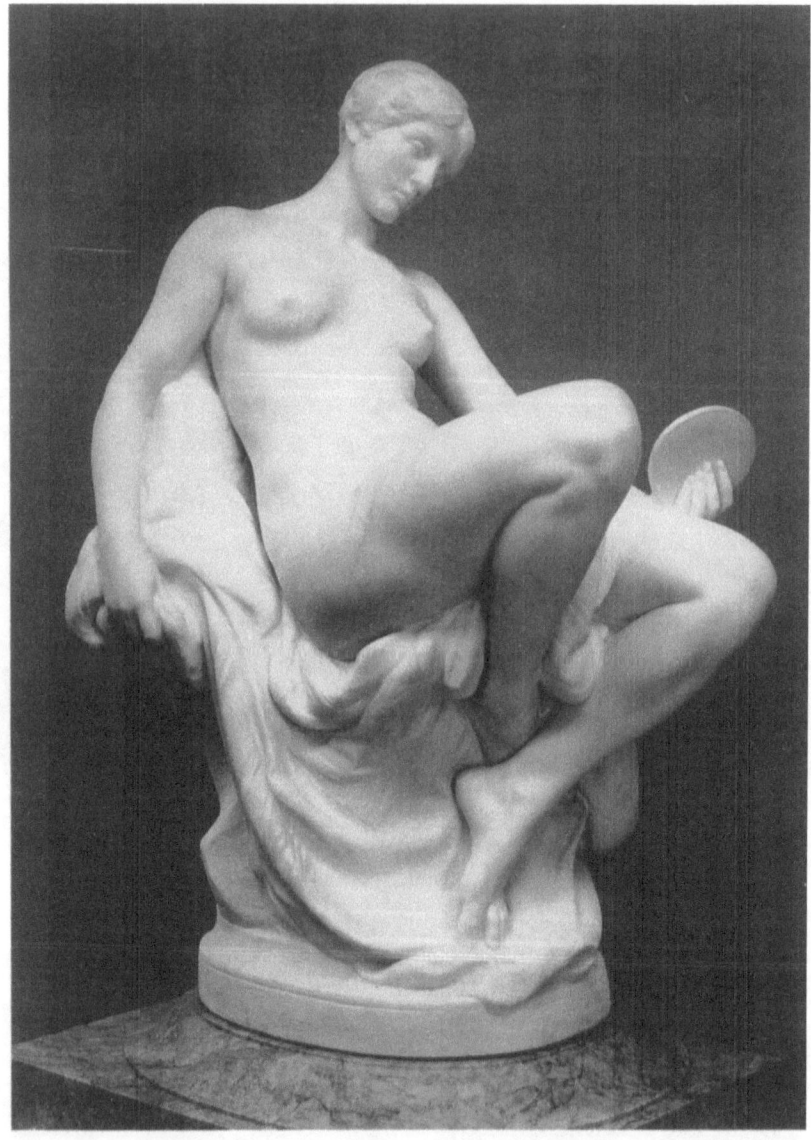

1-31. Daniel Chester French, *Memory,* 1886–1911. Marble, 57 in. high. The Metropolitan Museum of Art, Gift of Henry Walters, 1919.

for it in 1886 but did not complete the piece until 1911. In a letter that he wrote in 1919, French explained that "reflecting in the mirror which she holds [is] not her own face, but what is behind her."[44] She looks retrospectively to the past. French had abandoned Clio's familiar accoutrements, but *Memory* is most clearly an assertion of the significance to society of historical knowledge.

Memory had emerged as a compelling personal theme early in the 1870s. We have Elihu Vedder's seascape titled *Memory*, for example (fig. 1-32), which brings to mind Ishmael's words in *Moby Dick* that "meditation and water are wedded forever." In an undated oil painting called *Old Memories* by John George Brown (1831–1913), an elderly couple sit beside their hearth; the woman holds an old scrapbook of some sort.[45]

Between 1872 and 1880 Emily Dickinson composed at least three poems explicitly concerned with memory, and for Dickinson they all seem remarkably direct, even didactic at times. My favorite is the third one, apparently written around 1880:

> You cannot make Remembrance grow
> When it has lost it's Root—
> The tightening the Soil around
> And setting it upright
> Deceives perhaps the Universe
> But not retrieves the Plant—
> Real Memory, like Cedar Feet
> Is shod with Adamant—
> Nor can you cut Remembrance down
> When it shall once have grown—
> It's Iron Buds will sprout anew
> However overthrown—[46]

Around 1880 American artists seem to have acquired an obsession with notions of "real memory" and "remembrance," as though currents in the culture had thrown a switch. That year Thomas Eakins painted his *Retrospection*, in which a pensive young woman wearing an old-fashioned dress sits in a homely chair, thereby becoming, perhaps, both the subject as well as an object of memory.[47]

Variations on that motif persisted during the following half-century, some (like Eakins's picture) concentrating on personal memories and the process of remembrance in individuals,[48] but others recalling aspects of the collective past, such as triumphant or tragic events in the nation's history.

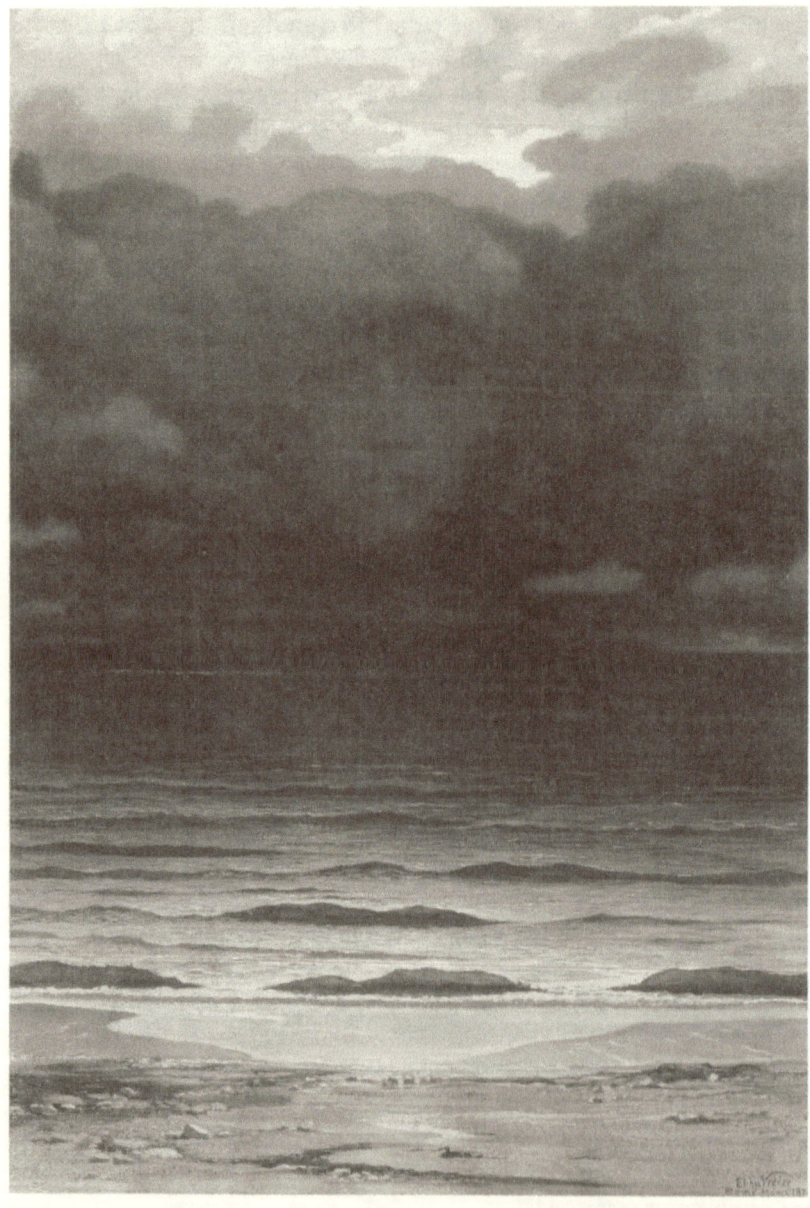

1-32. Elihu Vedder, American, 1836–1923, *Memory*, 1870. Oil on mahogany panel, 21 × 16 in. Los Angeles County Museum of Art, Mr. and Mrs. William Preston Harrison Collection [33.11.1].

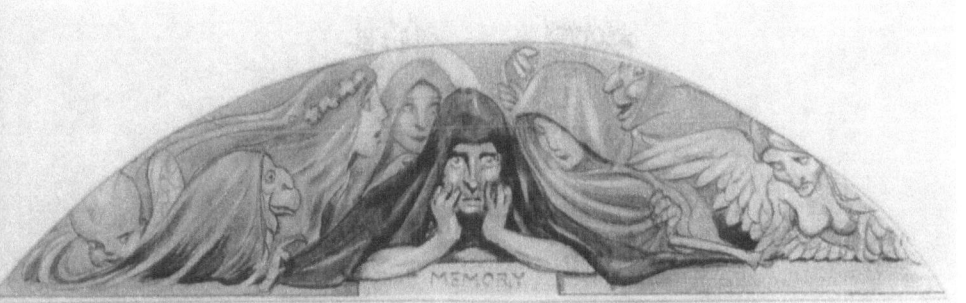

1-33. Oliver Herford, *Memory*, 1919. Pencil and wash drawing, 1 3/4 × 7 in. Courtesy of the Prints and Photographs Division, Library of Congress.

John F. Peto's affectionate and deceptively folksy recollections of Abraham Lincoln, painted late in the nineteenth century, supply several choice examples. They typically bore such titles as *Reminiscences of 1865*.[49]

We seem to have forgotten that "memory," used in various modes, virtually became a cultural buzzword. When *Harper's* decided to publicize Frederic Remington's illustrations during the 1890s, he was likened to "a camera with a memory" because he rendered "bits of his past" so skillfully.[50] Oliver Herford prepared *Memory* as an illustrative headpiece for "Because She Died," which appeared in *Everybody's* in March 1919 (fig. 1-33). And Wendell Jones, a muralist who was active during the Great Depression—he painted *First Pulpit in Granville* [Ohio] in 1938, a shrewd work of historical imagination—observed that "the spiritual reservoir of society has countless memories which have given man faith, courage, strength, and a sense of the abiding goodness of life."[51]

Two fine works of art created early in the twentieth century best exemplify the varied aspects of this vision of memory as a melding of truth, time, and perhaps even history into a singular notion. The first is an etching by John Sloan called *Memory*, which he made in 1906 (fig. 1-34). Fundamentally pictorial rather than allegorical, it illustrates the manifold ways in which memory is exercised: through reading, writing, drawing, and, quite obviously, reverie.

Meadows of Memory (fig. 1-35) is an undated and attractively mysterious landscape by Arthur Bowen Davies (1862–1929). A woman who is perhaps in early middle age moves rather briskly across a meadow while an older woman proceeds more deliberately in the middle distance. Are they mother and daughter or simply representatives of two distinct generations, one remembering another? Or, equally possible, is it the very same person

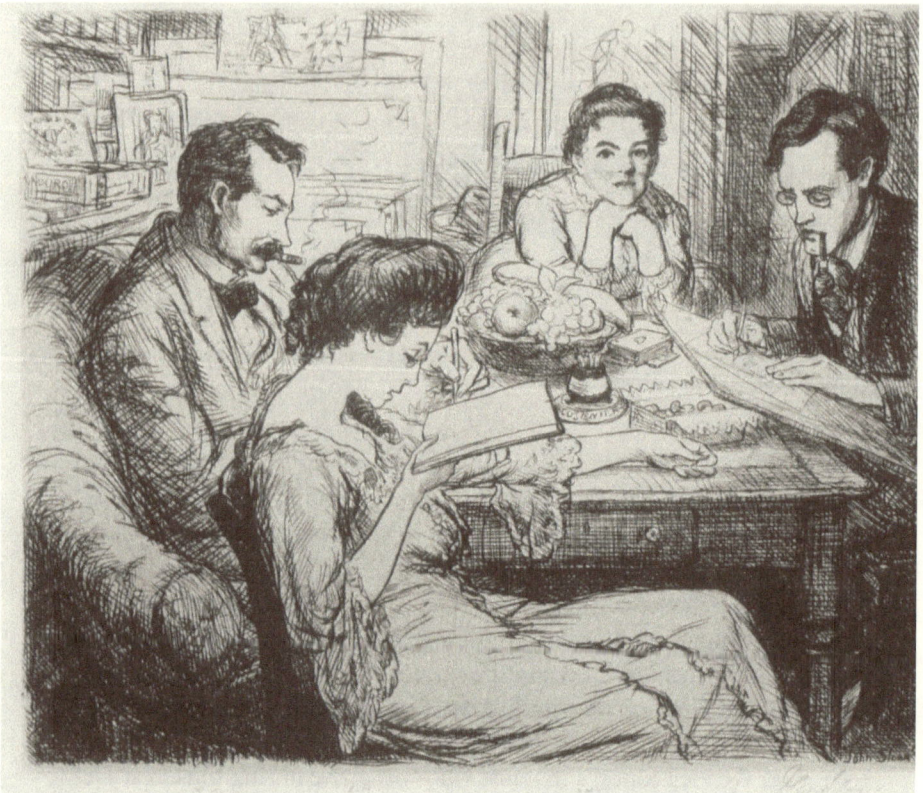

1-34. John Sloan, *Memory*, 1906. Etching, 7 1/8 × 8 5/8 in. Amon Carter Museum, Fort Worth, Texas.

in two different phases of her life?[52] I cannot say with assurance, but this enigmatic painting, with its alliterative title,[53] is highly symptomatic of Clio having been supplanted by alternative visions of pastness in the United States at the start of our century. Clio came to be displaced by Memory, her own mother. American culture, one might say, was growing matronly.

Truth, at least in any literal sense, may very well elude us, but the presence of time past and passing is almost palpable. A set of images that once seemed timeless—Goya's *Truth, Time, and History*—has given way to an alternative vision: movement through space as a wistful means of conveying the poignant passage of time.

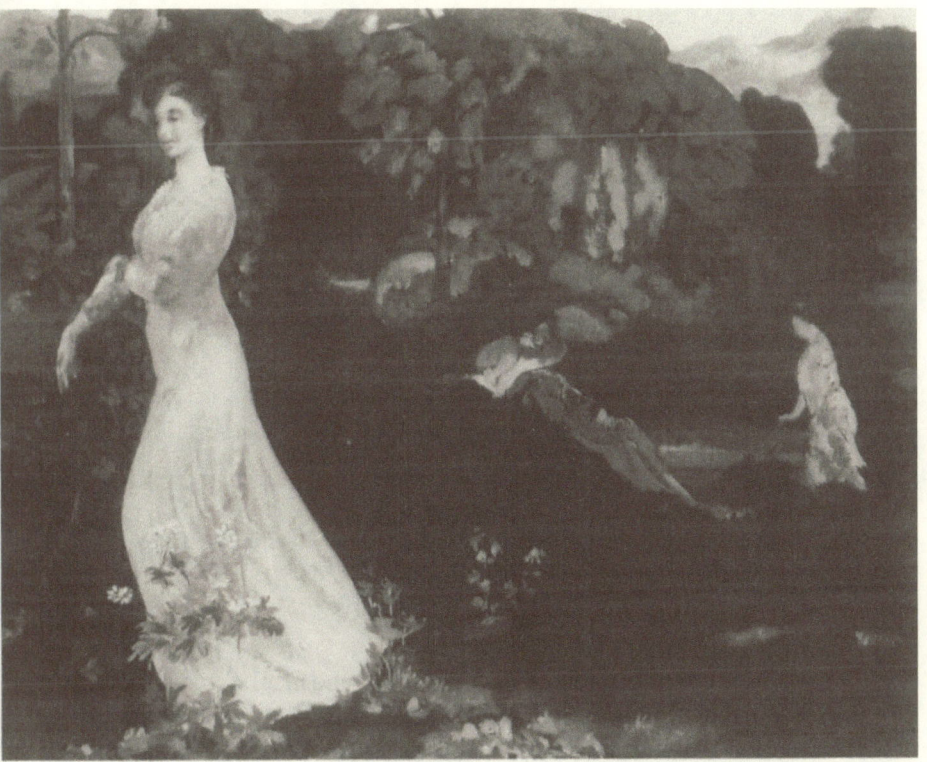

1-35. Arthur Bowen Davies, *Meadows of Memory*, n.d. Oil on canvas, 18 × 23 1/2 in. Cincinnati Art Museum. Edwin and Virginia Irwin Memorial.

Coda: Mortality and Memory in the American Landscape

A particular subgenre of American art connects this chapter with the one that follows—burial paintings, or more particularly, burials that take place in a landscape setting. The motif is germane to this chapter, obviously, because it involves the melancholy subject of mortality. (Re-enter Death and Father Time.) The motif is equally germane to the next chapter, however, because its focus, fundamentally, will be landscape art viewed as a means of describing movement through time as well as through space. When a person died while crossing the Great Plains, for example, it seems fair to say that the poor soul had done both: namely, moved quite permanently through time as well as space.

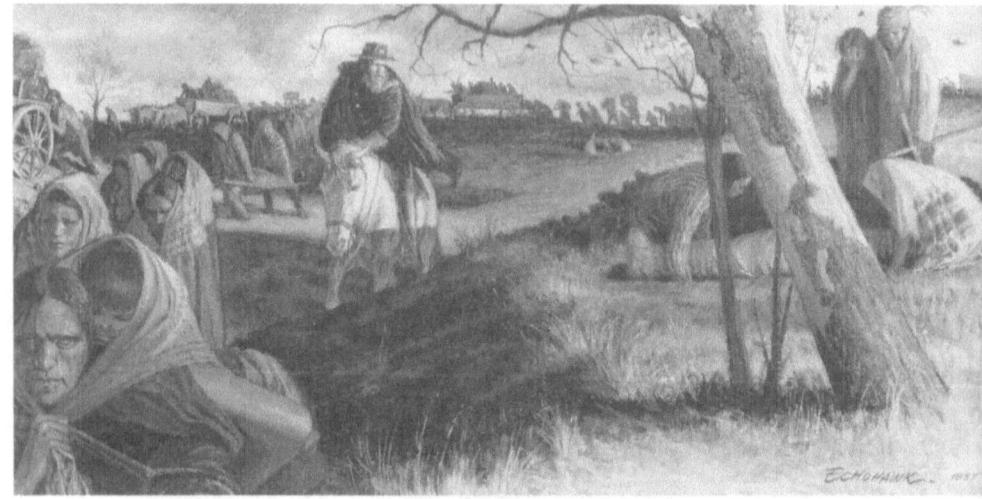

1-36. Brummet Echohawk, *Trail of Tears*, 1957. Wash on paper, 9 × 20 in. The Thomas Gilcrease Institute of American History and Art, Tulsa, Oklahoma.

A relatively recent example of what I have in mind may be seen in *Trail of Tears,* painted by Brummet Echohawk (1922–), a Pawnee Indian (fig. 1-36). The title alone tells us that the topic is historical, one among several forced migrations that took place during the nineteenth century. Those primitive wagons that line the background also harken back much more than a century. And the bearded federal officer astride his plodding nag could almost be Father Time in uniform—his flowing cape a substitute for the familiar wings. Behind the long dead tree to the right, an Indian is being wrapped in a shroud. The trail is finished for him or her. Tears remain, however, for those who face us in the left foreground.

This particular rendering of grief is less stoic than many others of the subgenre. What it shares in common with its predecessors, though, is that it *is* historical, and the artist's way of conveying a compelling historical quality as well as authenticity is to use the immediacy of movement through space as a means of establishing movement through time—which is what history is all about.

Because I know of no exhibition or literature that has been devoted to this theme, it might be instructive simply to list a diverse range of examples, bearing in mind all the while that plaintive line: "Bury me not on the lone prairie-e-e." Among them:

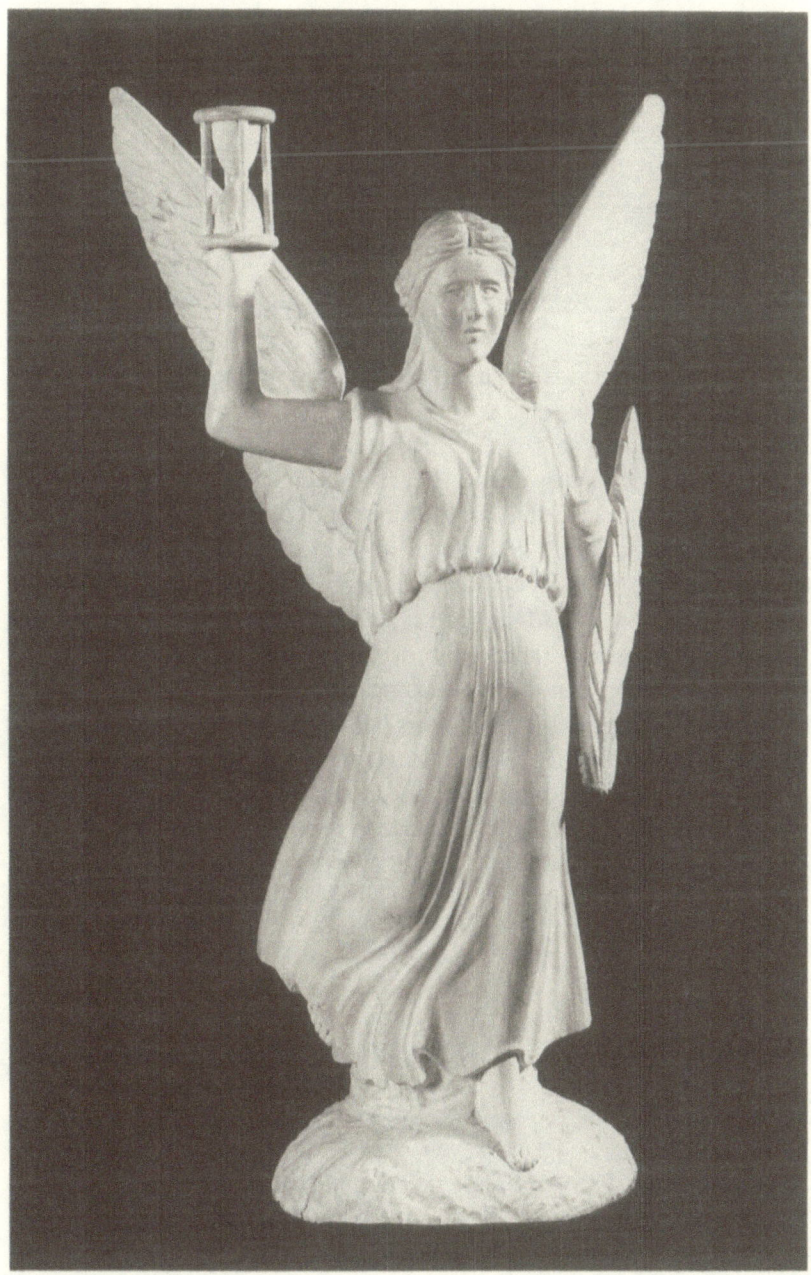

1-37. Anon. American, *Personification of Time*, mid-nineteenth century. Carved wood, 21 × 11 × 9 in. Private collection.

John Antrobus, *Plantation Burial,* c. 1860, in which almost all of the twenty-five or so persons depicted are African-Americans. The plantation master and mistress stand apart, to the right, between two huge trees.[54]
William T. Ranney, *Prairie Burial* (1848).[55]
Richard Lorenz, *Burial on the Plains* (no date).[56]
Johann M. Culverhouse, *Burial of DeSoto* (1875).[57]
Louis Eilshemius, *The Funeral* (1916).[58]
Bert G. Phillips, *Penitente Burial Procession* (no date).[59]

One last observation—for a touch of irony as well as transition to chapter 2. Maxim Karolik, that unconventional and self-assured collector of American art, loved to say that "Father Time takes care of Mother Nature." His distinctions by gender may have been traditional yet excessively clear-cut. During the first half of the nineteenth century, at least, American hearses were commonly decorated with carved wooden figures holding hourglasses (fig. 1-37). The figures had large, open wings, as you would expect. They wore a wistful or sad expression, as you would expect. And they wore neoclassical drapery. But they were youngish *female* personifications of time rather than hirsute and ancient males.[60]

Somehow, American folk sculptors had economically managed to conflate Clio and Father Time into a single figure. Somehow the gender of American Memory emerged from an unplanned and unaccountable collaboration of Truth and Time. *Cherchez la femme?*

Notes

1. Samuel L. Macey, *Patriarchs of Time: Dualism in Saturn-Cronus, Father Time, the Watchmaker God, and Father Christmas* (Athens, Ga., 1987), pp. III, 168–171; Macey, "The Changing Iconography of Father Time," in *The Study of Time,* ed. J. T. Fraser (New York, 1978), 3:540–575.
2. See Fritz Saxl, "Veritas Filia Temporis," in *Philosophy and History: Essays Presented to Ernst Cassirer,* ed. Raymond Klibansky and H. J. Paton (New York, 1963), pp. 197–222; Donald Gordon, "Veritas Filia Temporis," *Journal of the Warburg and Cortauld Institute* 3 (Apr. 1940): 228–240.
3. Macey, *Patriarchs of Time,* pp. 36, 47–49.
4. Denver Art Museum.

5. Both in the Museum of Fine Arts, Boston. In the latter painting Time wears an hourglass on his head, like a helmet.

6. See Frantisek Ignác Weis (Bohemian), *Chronos* (polychromed gilt and wood, c. 1740), Museum of Fine Arts, Boston; Ignaz Günther, *Chronos* (c. 1765–1770), Bavarian National Museum, Munich; Robert Darnton, *The Great Cat Massacre and Other Episodes in French Cultural History* (New York, 1984), p. 84; Macey, *Patriarchs of Time*, pp. 41–42, 169. For the perpetuation of an older iconographic tradition, however, see George Frederick Watts, *Time, Death, and Judgment* (pre-1865), Art Institute of Chicago.

7. The motif was taken from a seventeenth-century English emblem book.

8. See David E. Stannard, *The Puritan Way of Death: A Study in Religion, Culture, and Social Change* (New York, 1977); Charles O. Jackson, ed., *Passing: The Vision of Death in America* (Westport, Conn., 1977).

9. There are several other instances of Father Time on New England clocks in the J. Cheney Wells Clock Gallery at Old Sturbridge Village. For a handsomely carved Father Time made of wood, c. 1790, used as a store sign by Samuel Thaxter on State Street in Boston, see Robert Bishop, *American Folk Sculpture* (New York, 1974), p. 25.

10. Phoebe Lloyd Jacobs, "John James Barralet and the Apotheosis of George Washington," *Winterthur Portfolio* 12 (1977): 116, 134. A marble mantle at the Georgetown mansion called Tudor Place (c. 1810) in Washington, D.C., features a seated Father Time holding a broken scythe.

11. Marshall B. Tymn, ed., *Thomas Cole's Poetry* (York, Pa., 1972), pp. 164–165.

12. Nathaniel Hawthorne, *The House of the Seven Gables: A Romance* (1851: Boston, 1900), p. 446.

13. *Harper's Weekly*, Mar. 3, 1866, p. 144. See also Christopher Kent Wilson, "Winslow Homer's *The Veteran in a New Field:* A Study of the Harvest Metaphor and Popular Culture," *American Art Journal* 17 (Autumn 1985): 16–19.

14. See *Father Time*, c. 1910, an anonymous folk sculpture from New York's Mohawk Valley, Museum of American Folk Art, New York; "Timepiece (For Chronos)," an uncollected poem by Harold Corbin of Salisbury, Connecticut, June 1987. For cultural context generally, see Philippe Ariès, *Western Attitudes toward Death: From the Middle Ages to the Present* (Baltimore, 1974), esp. chap. 4, "Forbidden Death."

15. One version is located in the Wallace Collection, London.

16. For an engraving based upon Raphael's complex work, see Marcantonio Raimondi, *Apollo on Parnassus, Surrounded by the Muses and Poets*, Art Institute of Chicago (1944.621). The Uffizi's *Apollo and the Muses* by Maerten Van Heemskerck, executed late in the 1550s, is an example of the impact of this theme upon the northern Renaissance. The New Orleans Museum of Art has yet another version by the same artist.

17. The exhibition titled "Liechtenstein: The Princely Collections" (Metro-

politan Museum of Art, New York, Oct. 1985 to May 1986) included a North Italian work (oil on wood), c. 1515–1530, called *Apollo and the Muses,* in which Clio is seated and holds an open book.

18. See also Claude Lorrain, *Landscape with Apollo and the Muses* (1652), National Gallery of Scotland, Edinburgh, in which Clio sits in the center of the group and holds a book; and Claude Lorrain, *Apollo and the Muses on Mount Helicon* (c. 1680), Museum of Fine Arts, Boston, in which Clio sits toward the right and holds her oversized volume vertically on her lap.

19. At one juncture in *The House of the Seven Gables,* Hawthorne refers to "the contemplation of a landscape by Claude, where a shadowy and sunstreaked vista penetrated so remotely into an ancient wood" (p. 295). At another point Hawthorne evokes the traditional attributes of Cronus: "the very emblem of old Father Time, both in respect of his all-devouring appetite for men and things, and because he, as well as Time, after engulfing thus much of creation, looked almost as youthful as if he had been just that moment made" (pp. 165–166).

20. Philip Brett, ed., *The Collected Works of William Byrd* (London, 1970), 15:84–86.

21. See David Lowenthal, *The Past Is a Foreign Country* (Cambridge, Eng., 1985), pp. 254–255; and especially Stephen Bann, *The Clothing of Clio: A Study of the Representation of History in Nineteenth-Century Britain and France* (Cambridge, Eng., 1984), p. 1, for Clodion's bas-relief of History ("Maternal sustenance and grave example"). A recumbent Clio holds a stylus in her right hand and an open scroll in her left, while an attentive cherub keeps a large slate ready for her use.

22. A fascinating permanent exhibition of ecclesiastical art at the convent in Zadar includes numerous examples of saints who bear a resemblance to Clio. For an explicit connection made between the iconography of Historia (Clio) and an episode in the life of Christ, see Cesare Ripa, *Baroque and Rococo Pictorial Imagery: The 1758–60 Hertel Edition of Ripa's 'Iconologia',* ed. Edward A. Maser (New York, 1971), plate 122 and facing page. For an important allegorical painting by Johannes Vermeer, titled *An Artist in His Studio,* in which the female figure is believed to be Clio, see Lawrence Gowing, *Vermeer* (London, 1952), pp. 139–143 and plates 50–51. The other large allegory of Vermeer's later years represents the Catholic faith.

23. M. H. Abrams, *Natural Supernaturalism: Tradition and Revolution in Romantic Literature* (New York, 1971), pp. 339–341.

24. See Macey, *Patriarchs of Time,* pp. 47, 60–62. For context, see Elizabeth Eisenstein, "Clio and Chronos: An Essay on the Making and Breaking of History-Book Time," in *History and the Concept of Time* (Middletown, Conn., 1968), Suppl. 6 of *History and Theory,* pp. 36–64.

25. Macey, *Patriarchs of Time,* p. 52; José López-Rey, *A Cycle of Goya's Drawings: The Expression of Truth and Liberty* (London, 1956), p. 134 and plate 133. See also Ripa, *Baroque and Rococo Pictorial Imagery,* plate 122 (first published in 1603).

26. Cowper, "Yardley Oak," quoted in Bann, *The Clothing of Clio,* p. vi.

27. Helmut von Erffa and Allen Staley, *The Paintings of Benjamin West* (New Haven, 1986), pp. 404–405.

28. Bann, *The Clothing of Clio*, pp. 64–66.

29. Ralph Waldo Emerson, "History," in Brooks Atkinson, ed., *The Complete Essays and Other Writings of Ralph Waldo Emerson* (New York, 1940), pp. 125–126. In Melville's *Mardi* (1849), the historian is named Mohi (or Braid-Beard). At one point the poet, Yoomy, declares: "I deal in pure conceits of my own; which have a shapeliness, and a unity, however unsubstantial; but you, Braid-Beard, deal in mangled realities. In all your chapters, you yourself grope in the dark. Much truth is not in thee, historian." Herman Melville, *Mardi and a Voyage Thither* (Boston, n.d.), 1:253. See also David Bradley, *The Chaneysville Incident* (New York, 1981), p. 200.

30. Donelson F. Hoopes, *American Narrative Painting* (Los Angeles, 1974), p. 43. See also Bartley Campbell, *Clio: A Romantic, Spectacular Drama, in Five Acts* (New York, n.d.), which is set in twelfth-century Venice.

31. Handout, Boston Public Library.

32. See Herbert Small, *The Library of Congress: Its Architecture and Decoration* (New York, 1982), pp. 91–97; "The National Library," *Munsey's Magazine* 18 (Feb. 1898): 706–713; William A. Coffin, "The Sculptor French," *Century Magazine* 59 (Mar. 1900): 871–879.

33. Sotheby Parke Bernet auction catalogue, no. 4338 (Feb. 2, 1980), vol. 1, fig. 219. For an illustration from 1788, see the frontispiece to Michael Kammen, *Sovereignty and Liberty: Constitutional Discourse in American Culture* (Madison, Wis., 1988).

34. Wayne Craven, *The Sculptures at Gettysburg* (Gettysburg, 1982), pp. 16–17; Gaines M. Foster, *Ghosts of the Confederacy: Defeat, the Lost Cause, and the Emergence of the New South, 1865 to 1913* (New York, 1987), p. 158. In 1892 Senator David Bennett Hill of New York offered this pearl in a speech at Charlotte, North Carolina: "It is the credulity of opposing partisans, sectarians, bigots, which the muse of history now mocks with her wise smile." Quoted in Richard N. Current, *Arguing with Historians: Essays on the Historical and the Unhistorical* (Middletown, Conn., 1987), p. 21.

35. The painting belongs to the Whaling Museum, New Bedford, Massachusetts. For Clio as a neoclassical figure used as a small decorative design in popular American magazines, see James Russell Lowell, "Francis Parkman," *Century Magazine* 45 (Nov. 1892): 44; Woodrow Wilson, "On the Writing of History," *Century Magazine* 50 (Sept. 1895): 787. Clio is perched alone on top of a neoclassical column. Her legs are crossed and a large tablet rests on her lap. She holds a quill but seems to gaze off into space.

36. The painting is located in the Brooklyn Museum.

37. The booklet is unpaginated and lacks a place and date of publication. But see the useful information in Natalie Spassky et al., comps., *American Paintings in the Metropolitan Museum of Art* (Princeton, 1985), 2:110–113.

38. Richard Connell, "Mr. Pottle and Pageantry," *Saturday Evening Post,* Jan. 14, 1922, pp. 10–11, 34–36.

39. See Edwaert Colyer (Dutch, 1662–1702?), *Still Life,* Hunterian Art Gallery, University of Glasgow, Scotland; and Thomas Warrender (Scottish, active 1673–1713), *Still Life* (c. 1692), National Gallery of Scotland, Edinburgh.

40. Macey, *Patriarchs of Time,* chaps. 4–5; Penn is quoted in George W. Pierson, *The Moving American* (New York, 1973), p. 48.

41. For Haberle see *The New Britain Museum of American Art: Catalogue of the Collection* (New Britain, Conn., 1975), pp. 39, 40; for Parsons see *The American Painting Collection of the Montclair Art Museum* (Montclair, N.J., 1977), p. 207, fig. 254. See also John Haberle, *Clock* (n.d.), a painting in the trompe l'oeil style of an old-fashioned case clock, in Alfred Frankenstein, *After the Hunt: William Harnett and Other American Still Life Painters, 1870–1900,* 2nd ed. (Berkeley, 1969), p. 114.

42. See also John Covert, *Time* (1919), Yale University Art Gallery, New Haven, Connecticut; William Johnstone, *A Point in Time* (1929–1937), Scottish National Gallery of Modern Art, Edinburgh; and Max Ernst, *Time and Duration* (1948), Denver Art Museum.

43. See Robert A. Ferguson, *Law and Letters in American Culture* (Cambridge, Mass., 1984), p. 13. The basilica of San Marino in Italy contains a larger than life-size statue of a standing woman who is holding a mirror and looking at herself. Although she appears to be a Memory figure, she is identified (perhaps incorrectly) as Prudenza (apparently a seventeenth- or eighteenth-century copy of a Roman original). A snake is twined around one arm, and she holds her looking glass with the other.

44. Michael Richman, *Daniel Chester French: An American Sculptor* (New York, 1976), pp. 152–153. The full-size plaster model for *Memory* is located at Chesterwood, French's summer studio near Stockbridge, Massachusetts, in the Berkshires.

45. Sotheby Parke Bernet auction catalogue of Americana, no. 4408 (July 10, 1980), fig. 12.

46. Thomas H. Johnson, ed., *The Poems of Emily Dickinson* (Cambridge, Mass., 1955), 3 : 1040. See also pp. 863, 885–886. For the impact of Wordsworth upon the Victorians regarding the "sanctity of memory," see Jerome Hamilton Buckley, *The Triumph of Time: A Study of the Victorian Concepts of Time, History, Progress, and Decadence* (Cambridge, Mass., 1966), p. 107.

47. Lloyd Goodrich, *Thomas Eakins: His Life and Work* (New York, 1933), plate 21; Theodore E. Stebbins, Jr., and Galina Gorokhoff, comps., *A Checklist of American Paintings at Yale University* (New Haven, 1982), p. 46 and fig. 471. See also William Merritt Chase, *Memories* (1885–1886), in the Munson-Williams-Proctor Institute, Utica, New York.

48. See Frederick Carl Frieseke, *Memories* (1915), in *Survey of American Painting, October 24–December 15, 1940: Department of Fine Arts, Carnegie Institute* (Pitts-

burgh, n.d.), no. 227; Richard Emil Miller, *Reminiscence* (c. 1915–1920), exhibited at Grand Central Art Galleries, Inc., New York, April–May 1988; Frank Weston Benson, *Reflections* (1921), in the Virginia Steele Scott Gallery of American Art, Huntington Collections, San Marino, California; Minetta Good, *Retrospection* (1938), located in Dresden, Tennessee, cited in Karal Ann Marling, *Wall-to-Wall America: A Cultural History of Post-Office Murals in the Great Depression* (Minneapolis, 1982), p. 137.

49. John Wilmerding, *Important Information Inside: The Art of John F. Peto and the Idea of Still-Life Painting in Nineteenth-Century America* (Washington, D.C., 1983), pp. 193–204.

50. Peggy and Harold Samuels, *Frederic Remington: A Biography* (Garden City, N.Y., 1982), p. 134.

51. Wendell Jones, "Article of Faith," *Magazine of Art* 33 (Oct. 1940): 557–559; Marling, *Wall-to-Wall America*, pp. 213–222. See also Arthur G. Dove, *Reminiscence* (1937), in the Phillips Gallery, Washington, D.C.; and Ernest Lawson, *Retrospection* (1937–1938), in the Hirshhorn Museum, Washington, D.C.; the latter is a seascape like fig. 1-32.

52. There is a very poignant moment in A. B. Guthrie's classic novel *The Way West* (New York, 1949) when Dick Summers, a moody mountain man who had successfully led his group across the Oregon Trail, becomes pensive and silently thinks back to his life twenty-five years earlier in the 1820s. Lije Evans, heroic "captain" of the pioneering party, speculates that Summers "was just shaking hands with the man he had been" (p. 230). For other instances of memory as a primary motif in *The Way West*, see pp. 217, 262, 263. "The dreams dreamed and the hopes hoped and the hurts felt and the jolts suffered, they all got covered by the years. They buried themselves in memory" (p. 262).

53. John Steinbeck favored the phrase "mothballs of memory" in *Travels with Charley* (New York, 1962), p. 183, a book about movement through the changing American landscape. For an anonymous American painting, perhaps mid-nineteenth century, titled *Meadows*, see *American Painting Collection of the Montclair Art Museum*, p. 53, fig. 12. See also William L. Lathrop, *The Meadows* (1897), in Doreen Bolger Burke, comp., *American Paintings in the Metropolitan Museum of Art* (Princeton, 1980), 3:368–369.

54. Patricia Hills, *The Painters' America: Rural and Urban Life, 1810–1910* (New York, 1974), pp. 62–63.

55. Richard J. Boyle et al., *In This Academy: The Pennsylvania Academy of the Fine Arts, 1805–1976. A Special Bicentennial Exhibition* (Philadelphia, 1976), p. 116; *Masterpieces of the American West: Selections from the Anschutz Collection* (Denver, 1983), plate 6.

56. *Masterpieces of the American West*, plate 35.

57. Stebbins and Gorokhoff, comps., *American Paintings at Yale University*, p. 37, no. 364.

58. *American Art in the Newark Museum: Paintings, Drawings and Sculpture* (Newark, N.J., 1981), p. 319.

59. Oil on canvas (0137.2083), located in the Thomas Gilcrease Institute of American History and Art, Tulsa, Oklahoma.

60. See Bishop, *American Folk Sculpture*, p. 41, no. 52.

2.
Time
and
Space

*The American space-sense, the
American time-sense, the
American sense of personal
identity are not those of
Europeans.*
—THORNTON WILDER (1952)

This essay takes its title from a painting of the same name by William S.
Schwartz (fig. 2-1). Although the curious perspective of that picture and
the artist's focus could not be more apropos, the nature of my presentation
needs to be even more dimensional than Schwartz's bleak perspective because the subject has numerous aspects and is deeply situated in the historical development of American culture. In 1952 Thornton Wilder observed: "From the point of view of the European an American is nomad
[*sic*] in relation to place, disattached in relation to time, lonely in relation
to society . . . . the American space-sense, the American time-sense, the
American sense of personal identity are not those of Europeans. . . ."[1]
Wilder's assertions are startlingly sweeping and consequently require care-
ful qualification. Even so, they sum up quite succinctly much that I want
to suggest about various works of American landscape painting as historical statements or interpretations. In these prefatory paragraphs I offer the
reader a few indications of what to look for in the pages that follow.

First of all, I shall sidestep some of the most familiar landscape and history paintings, partially because they are so accessible in recent works like
Grand Illusions: History Painting in America (1988) by William H. Gerdts
and Mark Thistlethwaite, but even more because I hope to expand the evi-
dentiary base for my contentions by calling attention to a diverse range of
less canonical pictures. Mainly, however, my motive is to broaden our customary criteria, and hence our perception, of what qualifies as "historical"
art. In order to achieve that aim, my organizational strategy will be roughly
chronological, but within selected themes and topics. The latter convey
the substantive interpretations that I seek to offer, whereas chronology is a
matter of secondary significance.

Because mystical or mythical moments of early discovery, European ar-

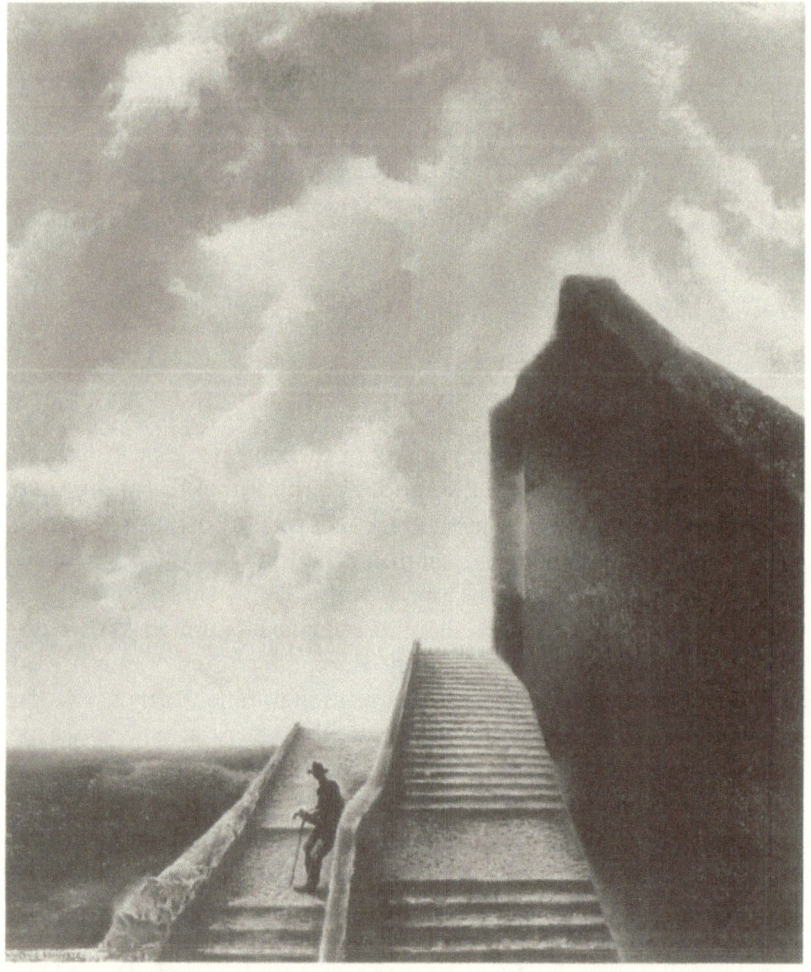

2-1. William S. Schwartz, *Time and Space,* 1945. Oil on canvas, 31 1/2 × 27 in. Collection of The Montclair Art Museum, Montclair, New Jersey.

rival, and exploration have long been familiar themes in American histori-cal art,[2] I have chosen instead to call attention to subsequent passages through public life and space and to illustrate those passages with some lesser-known yet equally revealing works.

One motif that the reader will encounter involves purposeful movement through space and time by nonheroic, mostly anonymous people. The de-piction of transportation and migration by common folk has not exactly been an inconsequential theme, and it offers the opportunity to observe and think about Americans engaged in routine yet highly representative activities. Some of those activities occurred repetitively, such as traversing the wilderness for worship or for trade. Others, however, were the sorts of activities that most people performed only once, such as crossing the continent in an era when doing so consumed a long period of time and perhaps even courted oblivion.

We will also look at and think about history as a process of change over time: social, economic, technological, and intercultural change. Transformation through time has preoccupied "regular" historians considerably more than it has historians of American art. Many of the pictures that demonstrate this dynamic process are themselves necessarily static. The viewer may infer historical change, however, either by comparing one painting with another to which it is related or by identifying the artist as an individual cognizant of the gap between what had once been and what was in the course of becoming. In some masterpieces, moreover, such as *Boston Harbor* by Fitz Hugh Lane (fig. 2-39), evidence for the process of change is entirely internal to the painting itself.

My last major motif, called "migratory emotions," derives its name from personal notes written in 1861 by Emanuel Leutze when he was schematizing *Westward the Course of Empire Takes Its Way,* his very large mural for the U.S. Capitol. "Migratory emotions" as a category of artistic expression enables us to contemplate, *pari passu,* such historical themes in American iconography as leaving home, immigration, the anxieties felt by fugitive slaves, and the experience of being attacked or captured by Indians.

This essay, like the first, also contains a coda, one devoted to artists themselves moving through American space and time, in some instances deliberately to undergo physical relocation, like Marsden Hartley, Georgia O'Keeffe, or Jackson Pollock; and in other cases in quest of experience, or material, or even the meaning of America itself. The chronological locus of my coda will primarily be the 1920s and 1930s.

Ultimately, however, the reader should bear in mind that these categories of analysis are not neatly self-contained. Migratory emotions must, inevitably, recur hither and yon. The same is true of history conceived as a process of change over time. My purpose in differentiating those topics as formal categories for analysis is to highlight them and, I hope, make them a more memorable and persuasive part of the ways in which we think about interconnections between history and art in American culture.

Much of our myopia, in my view, is the consequence of manmade wonders that have long since become commonplace. Alfred Lord Tennyson conveyed this point in two lines of "Locksley Hall Sixty Years After" (1886), when the marvels of travel by rail and steamship had become so familiar that people took them for granted.

> Half the marvels of my morning, triumphs over time and space,
> Staled by frequence, shrunk by usage into a commonest commonplace! [3]

Seeing History in the American Landscape

Several matters require clarification or explication before we get to the heart of this essay. First, although travel through the countryside has long been a popular subject for European as well as American art, movement through pictorial space is not necessarily a statement about movement through time.[4] I gratefully recognize that everything is not grist for my mill. In *The Mountain Ford* by Thomas Cole (1846), for instance, in which a man is about to cross a ford on horseback, the action portrayed takes place in an allegorical landscape rather than a historical landscape in any sense. The obverse obtains as well. *Plains of Abraham*, a watercolor by Winslow Homer (1895), has a historical site as its subject, but there is no movement whatever (the composition is architectural and static). I see no historical statement there.[5]

In the year 1850 the Pennsylvania Academy of the Fine Arts sponsored a competition in which there were two categories: first, historical, scriptural, and dramatic works; and second, landscape or marine painting. The first category enjoyed greater professional prestige and was accompanied by higher monetary awards.[6] I submit that that distinction, which has been with us for so long, is excessively arbitrary and that numerous landscapes have historical content intentionally incorporated. Sometimes the content involves time-specific historical events, such as *Hooker and Company Journeying through the Wilderness from Plymouth to Hartford in 1636* by Frederic E. Church (fig. 2-2).[7] At other times the content is derived from what historians now call latent events: namely, an entire historical process, transformation, or *type* of event. A good example would be *Over the Mountains* by Thomas Hart Benton (fig. 2-3), part of his "American Historical Epic," an immense series that preoccupied him for much of the 1920s. Although both modes of historical presentation require our attention, this second type may very well be the more interesting of the two. It certainly is one that has been largely overlooked.

With a few striking exceptions, we have had a tradition of defining his-

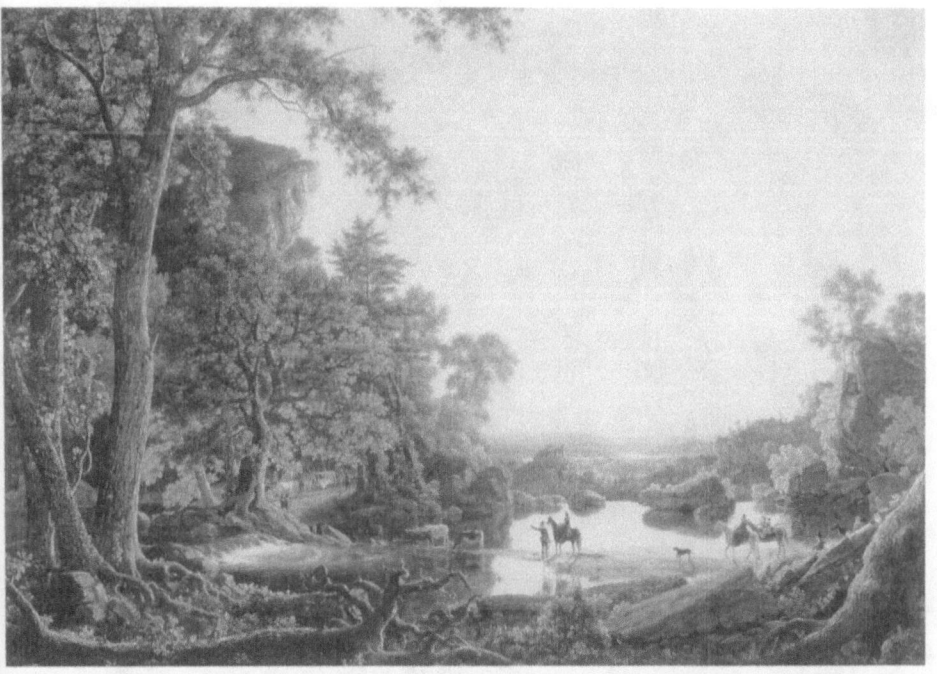

2-2. Frederic Edwin Church, *Hooker and Company Journeying through the Wilderness from Plymouth to Hartford in 1636*, 1846. Oil on canvas, 40 1/4 × 60 3/16 in. Wadsworth Atheneum, Hartford [1850.9].

tory painting in needlessly narrow ways. The text for an 1851 exhibition asked rhetorically: "After taking out the Indians and the Puritans, what is there left besides the contentions of deliberative assemblies and the mathematical evolutions of the wars of Great Britain and Mexico?"[8] Washington Allston did not believe that American civil history could sustain serious art. James Jackson Jarves echoed that view in 1864, albeit even more expansively as a discernible phenomenon that seemed to be simultaneously lamentable and laudable. On the one hand, we had "no history more poetical or fabulous than the deeds of men almost of our own generation, too like ourselves in virtues and vices to seem heroic"; on the other, we were happily "not overborne by the weight of a glorious past, disheartening the weak of the present, and rendering many, even of the strong, servile and mind-ridden."[9]

Ever so gradually, however, a few voices began to speak of broader possibilities for history. Contemplating courageous yet semisuccessful figures like DeSoto, William Gilmore Simms insisted that his was "a story to burn

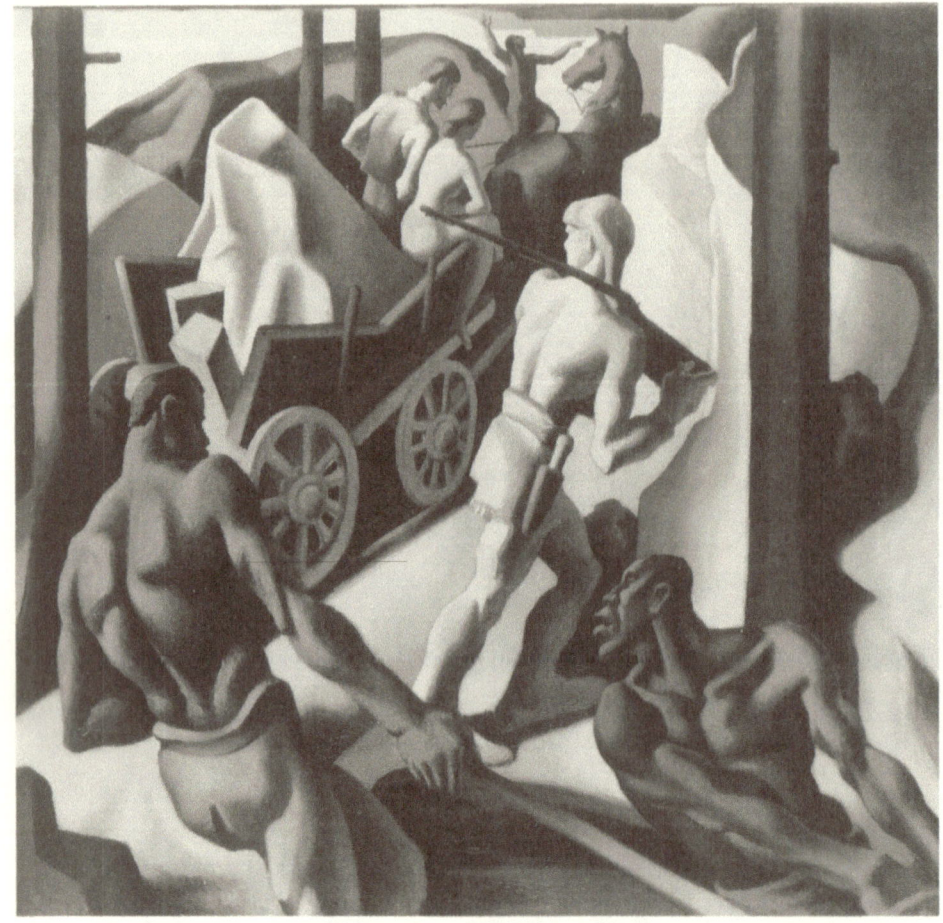

2-3. Thomas Hart Benton, *Over the Mountains (American Historical Epic)*, 1924–1926. Oil on cotton duck on aluminum honeycomb, 65 7/8 × 71 7/8 in. The Nelson-Atkins Museum of Art, Kansas City, Missouri (Bequest of the artist) F75-21/7.

upon the canvas, and breathe in life and beauty from the chiselled lips of stone!" An anonymous essay that appeared in 1866, moreover, boldly redefined historical art in a manner at once mundane and strikingly democratized—using criteria commonly neglected that I wish to revitalize. Historical art, according to this critic, "is good when the artist is at home in, and strongly impressed by, the scenes he delineates; the truest and therefore the most valuable historical art being the record of what the artist sees and knows in his own time,—events that happen around him, events of which he makes part." [10]

In 1878 George Inness offered an extraordinary critique of orthodox European criteria for historical painting. He faulted J. M. W. Turner quite harshly because of his inability to narrate a story within a landscape setting. Inness then complained of excessive literary stimuli affecting American painters: "the influence upon us of what we have heard or read of things we have not seen." What sort of solution did he propose? Moving away from particular events in the past which artists could not have witnessed toward more generic historical phenomena that in some sense they might have experienced, such as westward migration or encounters with Indians. "Things that were," Inness declared, "can be properly represented only in things that are." [11]

Four years later Fairman Rogers would remark: "Some care will have to be exercised in defining what historical painting is, which it strikes me is not an easy thing to do." [12] A comparable challenge might very well have been put to landscape painting because a deep devotion to the concept of Nature's Nation, to mysteries of the American wilderness, and above all to notions of the picturesque had paralyzed what was said as well as much of what was done in landscape art. It tended to consist of beautiful but static vignettes in which human activity took place on a minuscule scale when it appeared at all. [13]

Those artists who established the initial guidelines for American landscape painting viewed it, first of all, as an alternative to historical art, and they believed that landscape lent itself to their contemporary social and environmental situation in a way that history did not. John Vanderlyn, Thomas Cole, and Asher B. Durand all said so, in diverse ways, between 1818 and 1855. As Durand declared: "It is the province of art, then, and all the license that the artist can claim or desire, to choose the time and place where she [Nature] displays her chief perfections, whether of beauty or majesty, repose or action." [14]

Most American landscape art sought to record the distinctiveness of American scenery in general and to identify the beauty of particular places as well. It emphasized the inherent drama or even theatricality of nature, and only cautiously at first—in works that sang the praises of progress— did it depict human "improvements" upon nature. This remained especially true during the middle third of the nineteenth century, and historical episodes were paradoxically implied yet suppressed. [15] What else can we conclude about Albert Bierstadt's breathtaking vista in *Donner Lake at the Summit* (1873)? The tragic and notorious cannibalism episode that occurred there in the winter of 1846 is left entirely to the viewer's imagination (and sources of information). Here we have a prime example of antihistorical art. There is no movement or historicity. An awesome sense of space is conveyed, but no touch of time at all.[16]

Less obvious and less familiar, by contrast, is a comparatively neglected American custom of combining recent and contemporary history with landscape art. It was well launched with George Catlin, for instance, who in 1832 asserted his mission of recording the "anecdotes, traditions, and history" of the various Indian "nations." He makes explicit his awareness that they moved continuously through space and time, and that he would have to do the same if he wished to succeed as their visual historian.[17] In 1847 the *Missouri Republican* wrote in praise of George Caleb Bingham that he had "struck out for himself an entire new field of historic painting, if we may so term it."[18] And in 1871 Bingham himself explained in correspondence with a close friend that such works as *The Jolly Flatboatmen* "assure us that our social and political characteristics as daily and annually exhibited will not be lost in the lapse of time for want of an art record rendering them full justice."[19] Recognizing that landscape art had a historical dimension for Bingham makes the subjects of some of his pictures more meaningful in terms of movement through time as well as space. I have in mind, for example, *Fur Traders Descending the Missouri* (1845) and *Halt in the Forest: Emigrants Resting at Night* (1852).[20]

In 1852 Henry T. Tuckerman prepared an essay that he called "Over the Mountains, Or the Western Pioneer" in which he explicitly linked the American landscape with a sense of history being made. Perhaps, he speculated, "it is this very succession of 'moving accidents' and lonely quiet, of solemn repose and intense activity, that constitutes the fascination which the sea and the wilderness possess for imaginative minds."[21]

How then can we reconcile, if at all, this apparent disjuncture between nineteenth-century artists who, on the one hand, differentiated sharply between historical and landscape art and regarded the latter as a logical American surrogate for the former, and those like Tuckerman and Bingham, on the other, who viewed landscape art as an opportunity to record and recall history? An adequate response to that question will require the remainder of this essay, but a more particular part of the explanation may appropriately close this section. For diverse reasons, many Americans who fit into the Tuckerman-Bingham category subscribed to Courbet's belief that "historical art is by nature contemporary."[22] Works by Benjamin West, for example, were filled with allusions to contemporary events.[23] Some of the historical art produced during the middle decades of the nineteenth century seems obsessed with Columbus and Cortez,

DeSoto, LaSalle, and Hudson; and scholars have shown that these were thinly veiled attempts to provide validation for American continental expansion. Zachary Taylor and Winfield Scott were depicted as latter-day embodiments of Columbus and Cortez. As the *Washington National Intelligencer* observed in 1855: "The present is emphatically the age of discovery. At no period since the days of Columbus and Cortez has the thirst for exploration been more active and universal than now." [24]

The attractive challenge is that historical art in the United States requires a multifaceted explication, even though one fairly prominent facet can be explained by the impulsive superficiality of a society bent upon self-indulgent expansion necessitating self-justification. Be that as it may, our nexus of time and space has more to do with mobility than it does with hypocrisy. Tocqueville recorded in his diary on June 7, 1831, that the American "has lived in twenty different places and nowhere found ties to detain him." Sixteen years later Domingo Sarmiento, an Argentine visitor, quipped that "if God were suddenly to call the world to judgment He would surprise two-thirds of the American population on the road like ants." [25]

If historian George W. Pierson is correct in claiming that "few if any societies have absorbed spatial mobility as profoundly into their way of life as we have done in this country," then we are obliged to explore the implications of that tendency for our understanding of American landscape and historical art. [26]

Passages through Public Life and Space

For the sake of spatial economy and perhaps enhanced freshness, I am essentially going to pass over two subgenres of historical art that are pertinent to my argument but have already been much treated by scholars. The first, as I previously mentioned, is the art of arrival: discovering, landing, and exploring. [27] The second, which I have discussed elsewhere, is art inspired by the American Revolution, which was easily the most popular subject for historical painting between 1790 and 1860. [28]

Because we cannot ignore the Revolution entirely, I shall briefly call attention to two neglected works that, in different aesthetic ways and from different political perspectives, mark the momentous events that occurred near Boston, Massachusetts, in April 1775. First there is *View of Concord*, painted by a naive artist early in the nineteenth century (fig. 2-4). The stiff

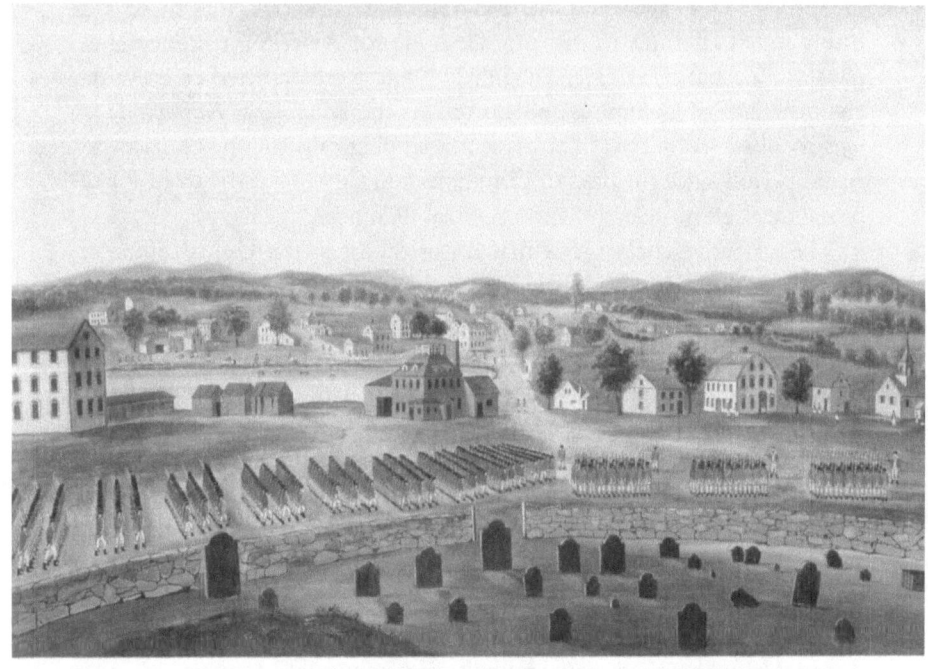

2-4. Anon. American, *View of Concord*, c. 1830. Oil on canvas, 26 × 39 1/8 in. National Gallery of Art, Washington, D.C. Gift of Edgar William and Bernice Chrysler Garbisch.

movement of Redcoats dominates the landscape, but one's eye is also drawn to tombstones in the foreground; (presumably) patriot soldiers form a dark line in the middle distance. Contrast the static quality of that "primitive" painting with the marvelous sense of urgent movement conveyed by Thomas Ball's bronze, *Paul Revere* (fig. 2-5). The work was surely inspired by Longfellow's immensely popular poem, published during the Civil War in *Tales of a Wayside Inn*.[29]

I really want to start, however, with a category that I call passages through public policy, public life, and public space. Two of the earliest examples derive in historical terms from bitter disputes, and each one achieved resolution, in part, because of the availability of and access to American space. *The Banishment of Roger Williams* (fig. 2-6) depicts an event that occurred in the dead of winter, 1636, when authorities in the Massachusetts Bay Colony decided that Williams posed too great a threat to good order. Williams promptly migrated in a southerly direction and founded the colony of Rhode Island and Providence Plantations, a place regarded by the rest of New England as Bedlam incarnate.

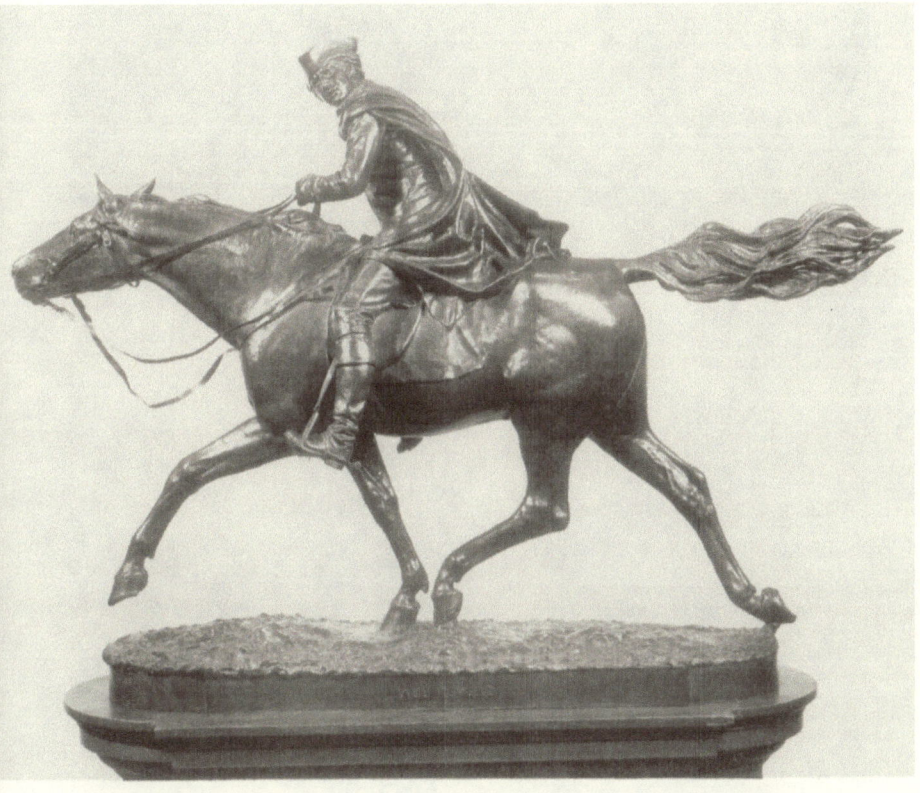

2-5. Thomas Ball, *Paul Revere*, 1883. Bronze. Cincinnati Art Museum. The Edwin and Virginia Irwin Memorial.

Next we have *The Paxton Boys* (fig. 2-7), an engraving that conveys the commotion and concern that occurred at Philadelphia in 1763–1764 when a group of frontiersmen known as the Paxton Boys became distressed by the bloodiness of Pontiac's Rebellion and the belief that Pennsylvania's legislators, secure in their provincial capital, were not sufficiently concerned about frontier defense. The Paxton Boys massacred a group of peaceful Indians and then marched on Philadelphia to demand governmental action, by force if necessary. They were mollified at a conference held in Germantown, however, at which Benjamin Franklin played a prominent role as conciliator.[30]

The successful public impact in 1851 of Emanuel Leutze's *Washington Crossing the Delaware* eventually sparked several derivative works, such as *Washington and Gist Crossing the Allegheny* (1863) by William Sidney Mount.[31] More interesting in our context, however, is a Philadelphia

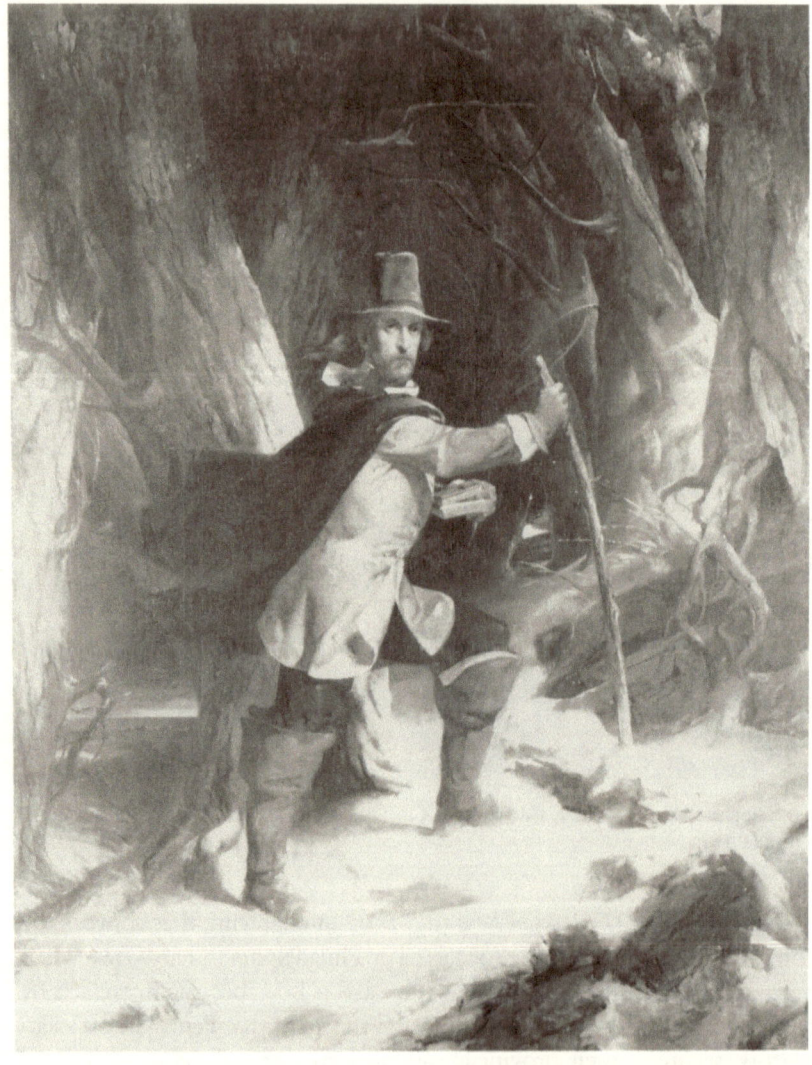

2-6. Peter Frederick Rothermel, *The Banishment of Roger Williams*, c. 1850. Oil on canvas, 35 1/2 × 28 1/2 in. Courtesy of The Rhode Island Historical Society.

cityscape engraved to commemorate ceremonies following the death of George Washington in 1799 (fig. 2-8). The thronged procession moves deliberately through a very crowded space because the father of his country had been overtaken by Time. Time surely must have been in the forefront of many minds in Pennsylvania: the century was winding down, the nation's

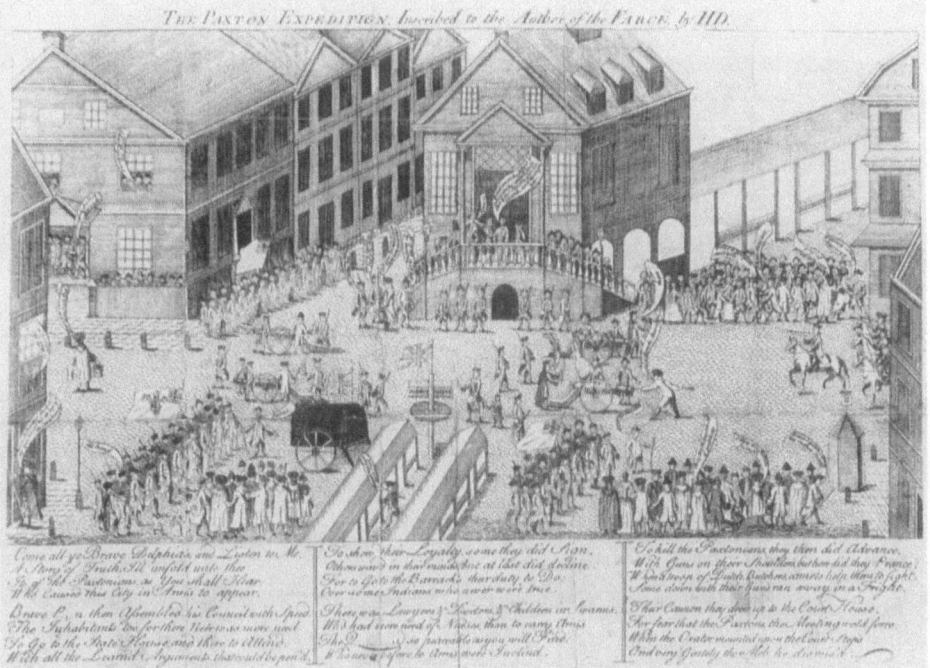

2-7. Henry Dawkins, *The Paxton Boys*, 1764. Engraving, 9 1/4 × 13 3/4 in. The Library Company of Philadelphia.

capital would soon remove to the Federal District on the Potomac, and social as well as economic transformations were visible at every turn.[32]

One of the most astounding passages in our entire history involving public policy and American space, yet one of the most neglected by artists, is Lewis and Clark's expedition across the continent between 1803 and 1806 (fig. 2-9). Perhaps it failed to have very much iconographic impact because Lewis and Clark's journals, which comprise a genuine American epic (they total five thousand printed pages) were not published until 1814, eight years after the expedition returned and five years after Lewis had died.[33]

Early in 1803 President Jefferson sent Congress the confidential "Message on Expedition to the Pacific," in which he revealed the rationale for this awesome undertaking as well as his sense of its historic importance:

> While other civilized nations have encountered great expense to enlarge the boundaries of knowledge by undertaking voyages of discovery, and for other literary purposes, in various parts and directions, our nation seems to owe to

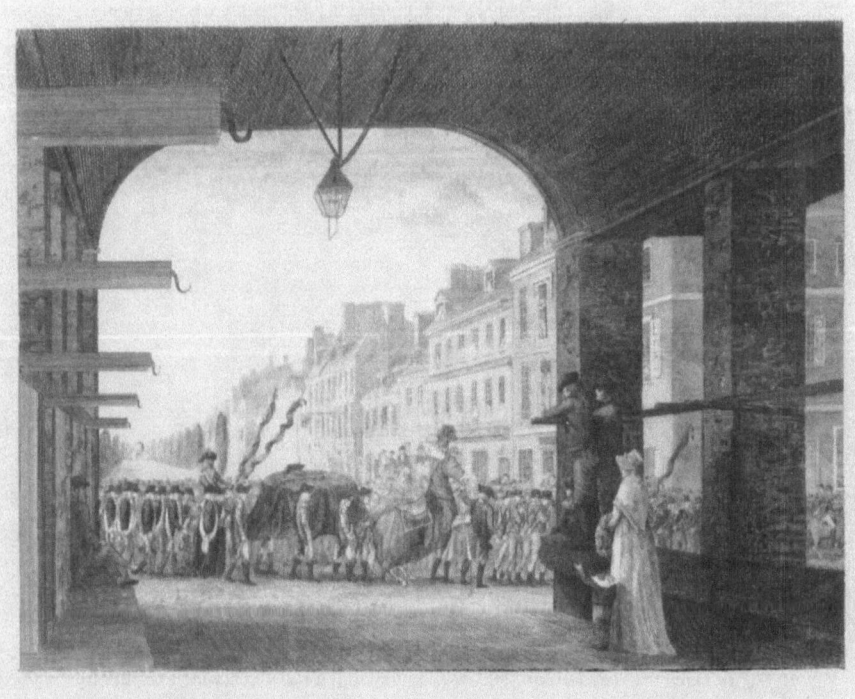

2-8. William Birch, *High Street, from the Country Market-place Philadelphia: With the Procession in Commemoration of the Death of General George Washington, December 26th, 1799,* 1799. Engraving, 8 1/4 × 11 1/8 in. The Library Company of Philadelphia.

the same object, as well as to its own interests, to explore this, the only line of easy communication across the continent, and so directly traversing our own part of it.[34]

Jefferson's written instructions to Meriwether Lewis concerning the conduct of the expedition are notable for their comprehensiveness and precision. There can be no doubt of the president's awareness that this unprecedented venture could transform the American understanding of space and time as well as topography and landscape:

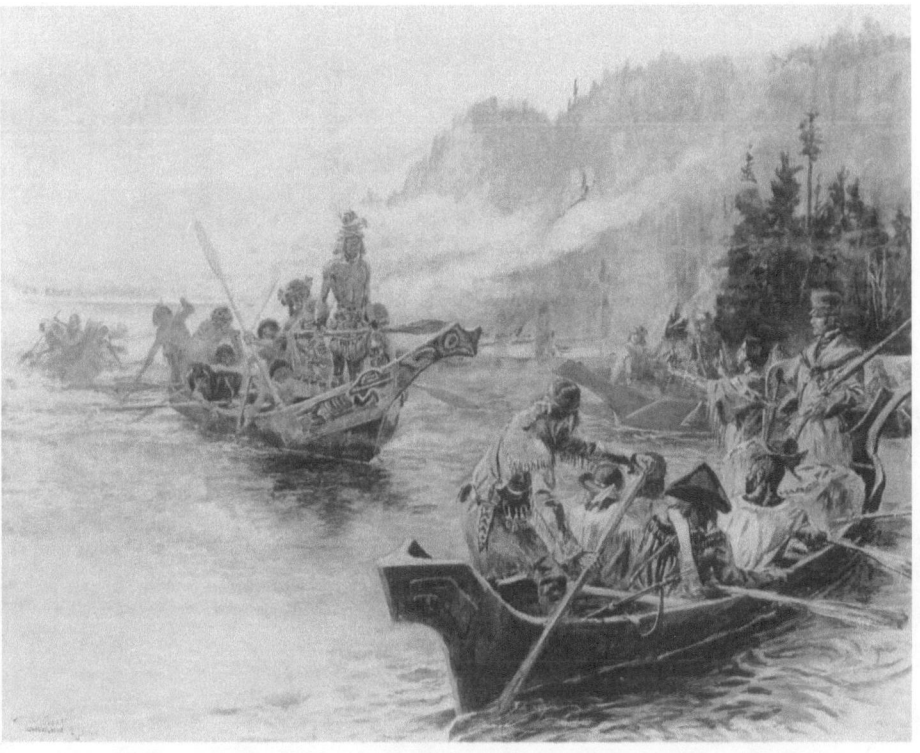

2-9. Charles M. Russell, *Lewis and Clark on the Lower Columbia*, 1905. Watercolor, 18 7/8 ×
23 7/8 in. Amon Carter Museum, Fort Worth, Texas.

The object of your mission is to explore the Missouri river, & such principal
stream of it, as, by it's course & communication with the waters of the Pacific
Ocean, may offer the most direct & practicable water communication across
this continent, for the purposes of commerce.[35]

In encounters with Native Americans (Jefferson called them natives), he
urged Lewis to "endeavor to make yourself acquainted . . . [with] their
language, traditions, monuments; . . . peculiarities in their laws, customs
& dispositions. . . ." Jefferson knew full well that the journey would be
historic. He hoped that it might be historical as well: a journey into ethno-
graphic time as well as an exploration of contemporary space.

If the momentous trek by Lewis and Clark has been comparatively
neglected by artists, quite the opposite is the case with Daniel Boone.
George Caleb Bingham's striking composition, *Daniel Boone Escorting*

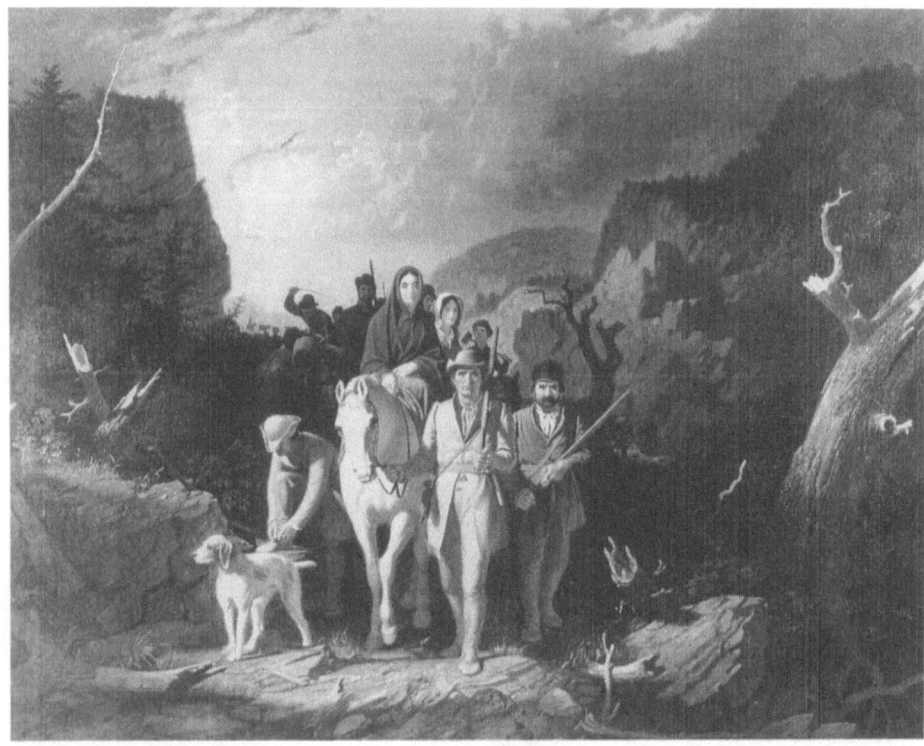

2-10. George Caleb Bingham, *Daniel Boone Escorting Settlers Through the Cumberland Gap,*
1851–1852. Oil on canvas, 36 1/2 × 50 1/4 in. Washington University Gallery of Art, St. Louis.

Settlers through the Cumberland Gap (fig. 2-10), may be the most familiar,
but there are dozens of others and hundreds of reproductions of various
sorts. One of the most attractive in terms of symmetrical composition,
plausible coloration, and involvement of the viewer, who can *imagine*
the vast space being admired by Boone and his five companions, is by
William T. Ranney, *Boone's First View of Kentucky* (1849).[36]

Writers interested in American history, folklore, and art, incidentally,
commented endlessly upon Boone's whole narrative as the most poignant
story of historical movement through the American wilderness. Henry
Tuckerman stressed the sad finale to this saga on the banks of the Missouri
River, where Boone had been driven by despair:

> Overmatched by the conditions of the land law in Kentucky, and annoyed by
> the march of civilization in the regions he had known in their primitive beauty,
> he had wandered here, far from the state he founded and the haunts of his

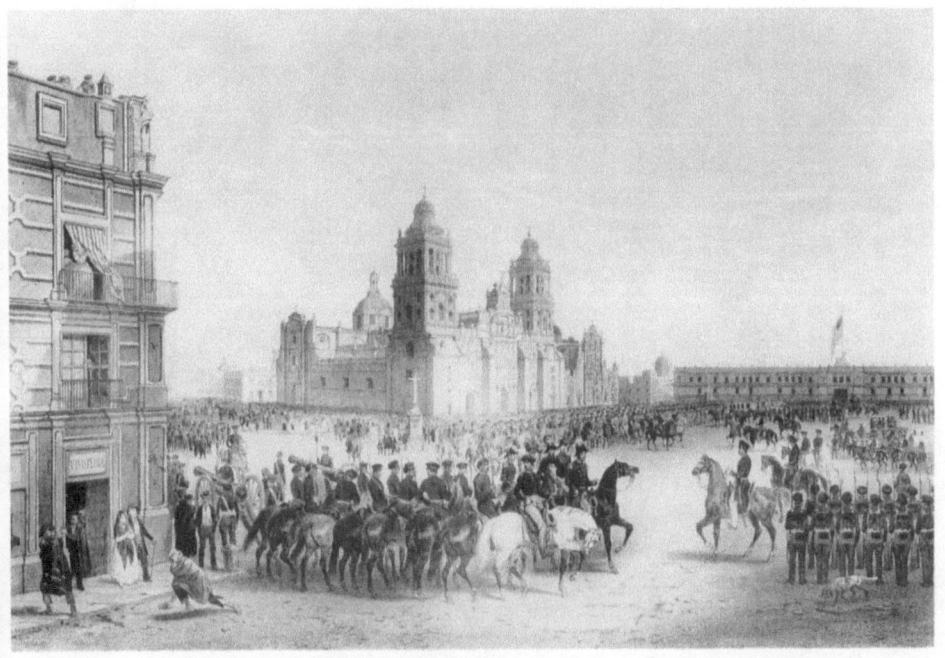

2-11. Carl Nebel, *General Scott's Entrance into Mexico,* c. 1851. Hand-colored lithograph, 17 3/8 × 23 3/16 in. Amon Carter Museum, Fort Worth, Texas

manhood, to die with the same adventurous and independent spirit in which he had lived.[37]

Although they were less intensely personalized, major military conflicts became increasingly prominent in these passages through public life and space, especially episodes from the American Revolution, the War of 1812,[38] the Mexican War of 1846–1847 (fig. 2-11), and subsequently even the brief Spanish-American War. One thinks of *The Scream of Shrapnel at San Juan Hill* by Frederic Remington (1898), which evokes one of the best-known (though perhaps inconsequential) movements through space in all of American history.[39]

Among the most persistent yet least explicable generalizations that I encounter is the view that the Civil War had little impact upon American art. That assertion began with James Jackson Jarves in 1864 and has been perpetuated by some of the leading scholars of our own time.[40] I regard such pronouncements as unacceptable, particularly if we acknowledge that many Americans subscribed to Courbet's belief that "historical art is by nature contemporary." One observer summed up the national scene very

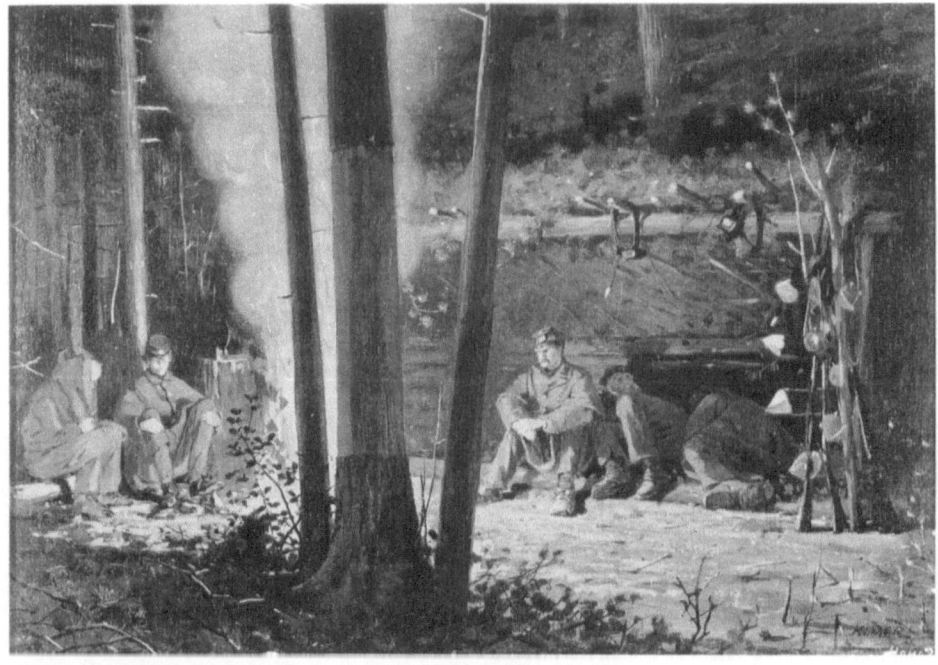

2-12. Winslow Homer, *In Front of Yorktown*, 1862. Oil on canvas, 13 1/4 × 19 1/2 in. Yale University Art Gallery. Gift of Samuel R. Betts, B.A. 1875.

well in the 1860s. We were, he noted, "a bivouac rather than a nation, a grand army moving from the Atlantic to the Pacific, and pitching tents by the way."[41] Inevitably one thinks of Winslow Homer and such paintings as *In Front of Yorktown* (fig. 2-12),[42] but that is just for starters. What about James Walker, who depicted diverse Civil War scenes; or William MacLeod's *Maryland Heights: Siege of Harper's Ferry 1863*; or Bingham's *Martial Law or Order No. 11* (concerning a violent episode in Missouri-Kansas history); or the Civil War art of James Madison Alden?[43]

Let's look at two very different yet highly representative works of art. During the summer of 1864 General Grant moved from Fort Monroe and seized City Point, Virginia (fig. 2-13), which provided him with a superb convergence of transportation facilities: a harbor, rail lines, and numerous wagons. Note the African-Americans hard at work in the foreground and the Union cavalry beyond. The convergence of three modes of transportation makes this busy historical landscape rather decidedly a study in space, time, and (by dint of sheer traffic congestion) the critical need for movement.

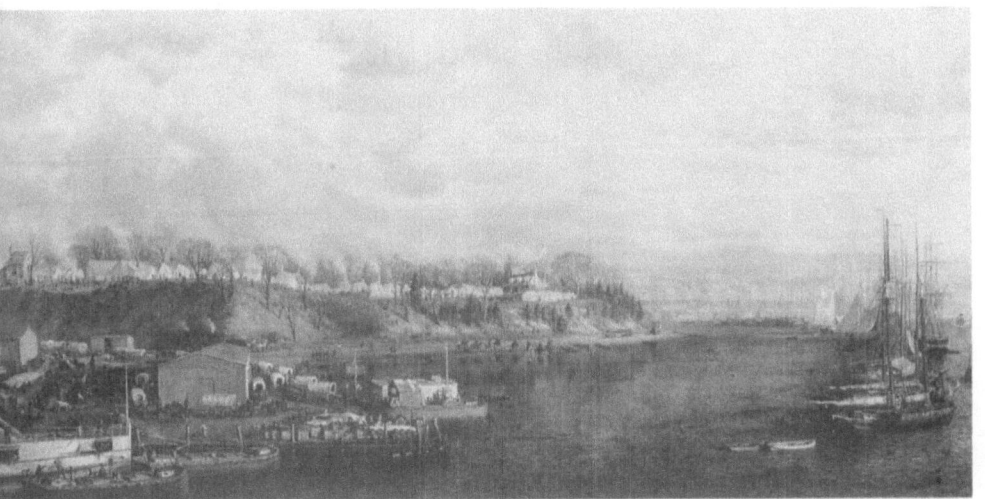

2-13. Edward Lamson Henry, *City Point, Virginia, Headquarters of General Grant,* 1865–1873. Oil on canvas, 30 × 61 in. © Addison Gallery of American Art, Phillips Academy, Andover, Massachusetts. All Rights Reserved.

Sheridan's Ride (fig. 2-14) brings to mind quite a contrasting setting, the Shenandoah Valley of Virginia, where Grant sent his ablest cavalry commander, General Philip Sheridan, to deal with Jubal Early in September 1864. Sheridan fought a series of twenty-six successful engagements, made a quick trip to Washington for consultation with Lincoln, and returned only to find that his troops had been driven back and were in disarray as a result of Confederate counterattacks. Then, according to James G. Randall,

> Hearing the noise of distant battle at Winchester, where he had stopped overnight, he rode to meet his retreating force and succeeded in rallying his unhurt but demoralized men who gave him a wild cheer as they re-formed their lines for a new attack which reversed the tide of battle and brought Union triumph. Inevitably this ride was magnified and embroidered in song and story. The spectacle of one commander turning defeat into victory by a rush to the rescue, a timely arrival, and the electric effect of his sudden appearance on the battlefield, caught the imagination.[44]

One additional illustration may help to indicate the scope and diversity of passages through public life and space as a useful means of defining and perceiving American historical art. Following his retirement from the

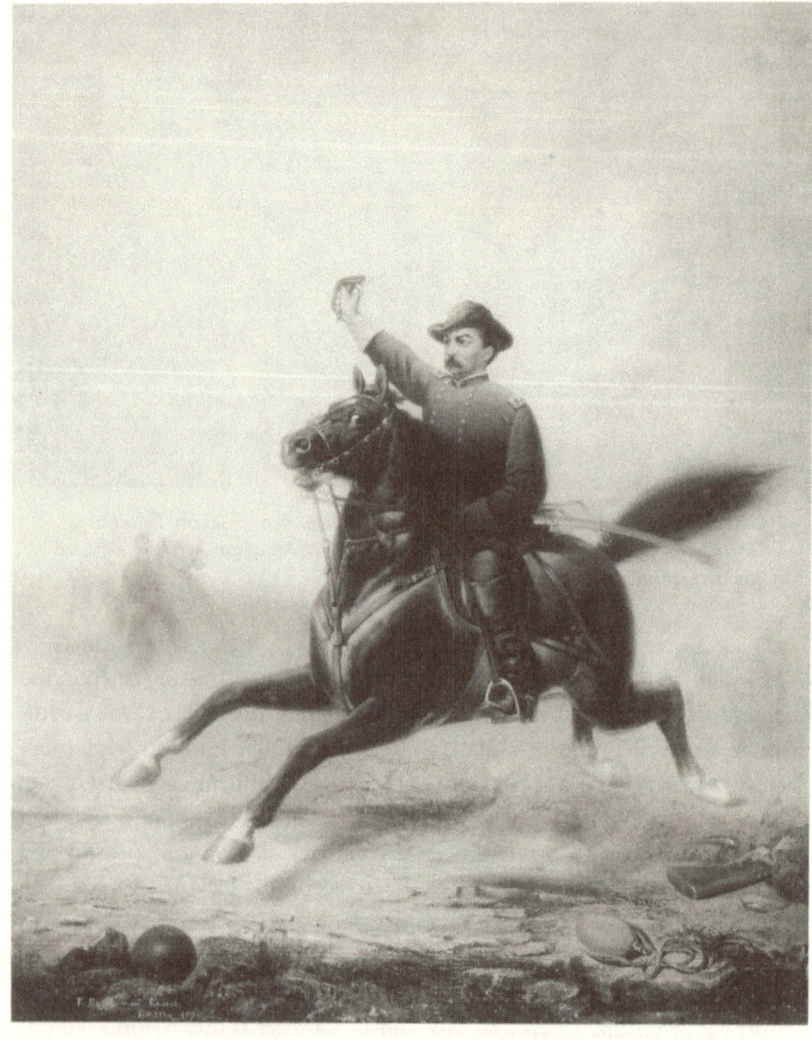

2-14. Thomas Buchanan Read, *Sheridan's Ride,* 1870. Oil on canvas, 29 1/2 × 24 1/2 in. Collection of The Newark Museum. Marcus L. Ward, Jr. Bequest, 1921.

presidency in 1877, Ulysses S. Grant and his wife, Julia, made a triumphant tour around the world in which they were enthusiastically received by great throngs.[45] Grant's historic and unprecedented voyage was immortalized on canvas: in Coulter's *The Arrival of President Grant* (fig. 2-15) we see the Grants completing their circumnavigation of the globe in Septem-

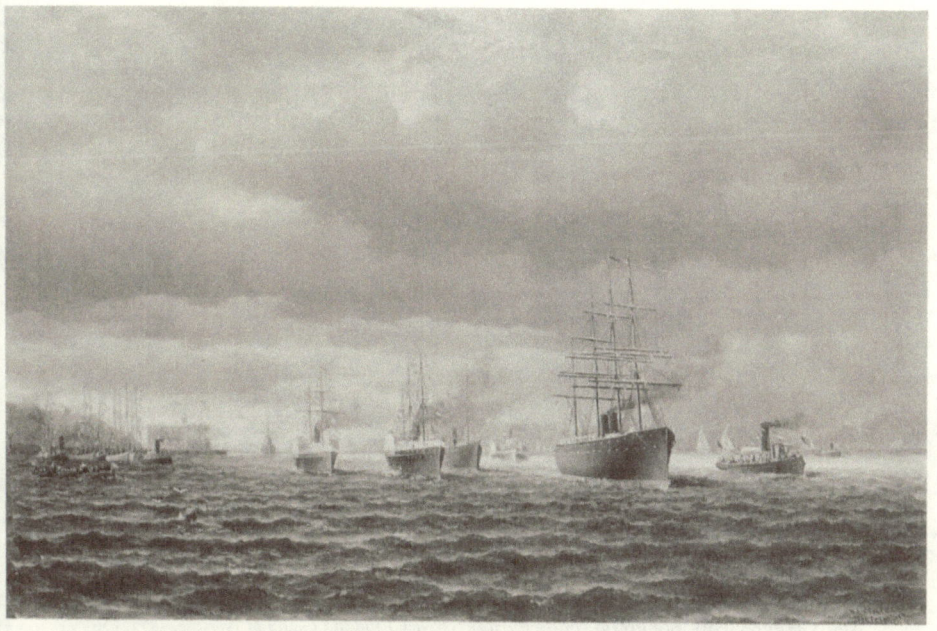

2-15. William A. Coulter, *The Arrival of President Grant*, 1879. Oil on canvas, 40 1/2 × 26 in. San Francisco Maritime National Historical Park, San Francisco, California.

ber 1879, as they reach San Francisco on a Pacific steamer called *City of Tokio*. Municipal officials have gone out on a tug, the *Millen Griffeth*, to meet the popular ex-president. (The tug chugs to the right of the black, iron-hulled steamer.)

Other sorts of American harbor scenes would convey different modes of meaning, as we shall see in the section on implied narrative below.

Mastering Nature: Historical Modes of Migration and Transportation

I turn next from prominent figures and public life to meaningful movement, mostly by ordinary Americans—movement for purposes of transportation and migration, commercial advantage, and spiritual rejuvenation. We will encounter six modes of travel: on foot and on horseback, by ferry and canal boat, by wagon and by railroad. Although transportation underwent a remarkable revolution by the end of the nineteenth century, it

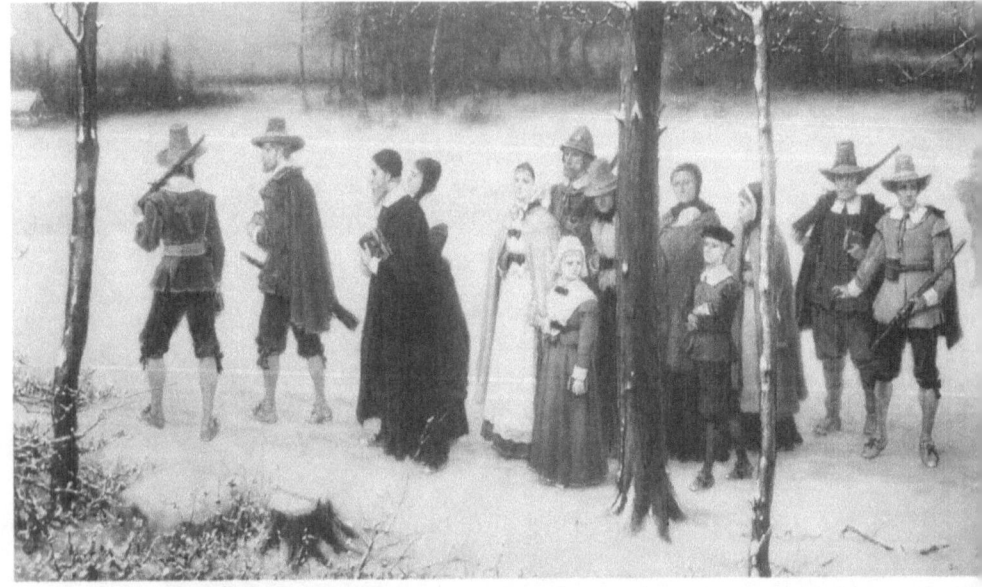

2-16. George Henry Boughton, *Early Puritans of New England Going to Worship,* 1872. Oil on canvas, 14 3/16 × 25 1/4 in. The Toledo Museum of Art; Gift of Florence Scott Libbey. (A larger version [1867] located at the New-York Historical Society is titled *Pilgrims Going to Church.*)

had been unreliably slow for a great many Americans; travel required patient waiting. Much of the art that we will now examine concerns the *possibility* of movement along with ambivalent responses to civilization's augmented mastery over nature.

I should begin by acknowledging that some presentations of motion through the American landscape concern activities that were, in diverse ways, repetitive, such as processions through the woods to attend worship (fig. 2-16),[46] or fording a stream on horseback (fig. 2-17), or crossing a river by ferry only to recross it at some subsequent time (fig. 2-18).[47] Here we have goings and comings—some of them historical, but most of them not. Artists have also been interested in pictorial crossings of the landscape that are primarily local and domestic, and therefore scarcely historical in any sense of the word.[48]

Then there are works depicting situations that permit two-way traffic, so to speak, in a setting that is historical in terms of the site itelf, or the type of activity, or the means of transportation.[49] *The Coming and Going of*

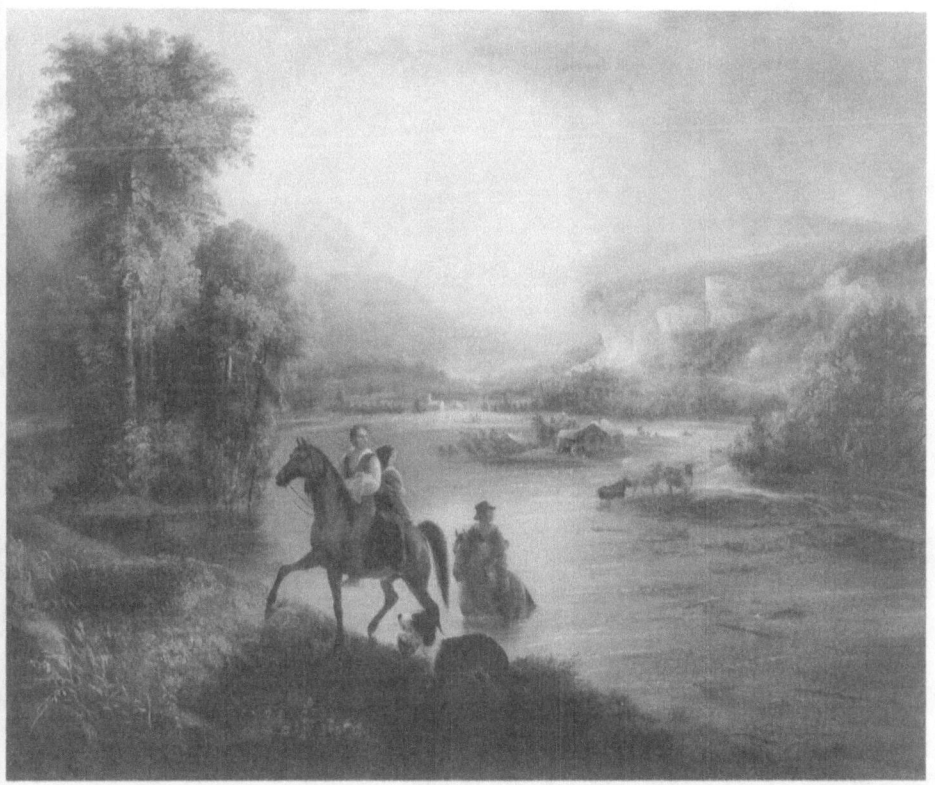

2-17. Alvan Fisher, *The Freshet*, 1837. Oil on canvas, 32 3/4 × 43 in. The Baltimore Museum of Art. Gift of Mrs. Thomas G. Machen, in memory of her husband, Thomas G. Machen, BMA 1979.169.

the Pony Express by Frederic Remington (1900), located in the Gilcrease Institute, provides a prime example. Or consider a wonderfully naive watercolor of Lockport, New York, on the newly completed Erie Canal (fig. 2-19), in which a canal boat is being hauled by three gallant horses. Although it is all happening in slow motion, we are looking at an important icon of the transportation revolution.

Or look at a detail section of the large and complex piece of folk art called *Land and Sea Quilt* (fig. 2-20). It includes every mode of transportation known when it was made in New Jersey around 1830: sailboats and steamships, rowboats and horse-drawn wagons, not to mention long-distance hikers with rucksacks and walking sticks. The point seems to be that Americans are on the go: some will return, but others may not.

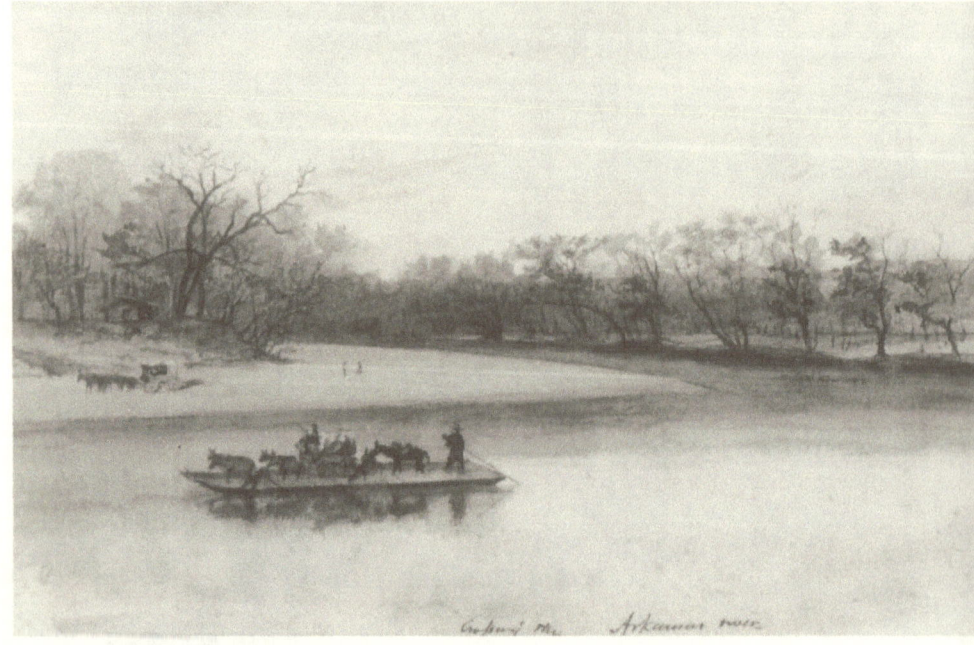

2-18. Vincent Colyer, *Ferry Crossing Arkansas River*, 1867. Watercolor on paper, 6 × 9 1/2 in. The Thomas Gilcrease Institute of American History and Art, Tulsa, Oklahoma.

Because there has recently been so much show-and-tell regarding the railroad's impact upon American art, I shall only pause long enough to make a few points. First, some "train pictures," like Inness's well-known *Lackawanna Valley* (fig. 2-21), convey a sense of the *allez-retour*, so to speak: these trains come and go because they have been tamed like the very landscape they cut diagonally across.[50]

Others, however, such as Rossiter's *Opening of the Wilderness* (fig. 2-22) or Benton's *Going West* (fig. 2-23), convey quite a different feeling, a unidirectional sense that these great beasts are just raring to go and, at the obvious risk of reifying or anthropomorphizing them, that they haven't the remotest intention of returning! Benton said it very well in his autobiography: "For the nomadic urges of our western people, the prime symbol of adventurous life has for years been the railroad train. . . . All during my boyhood it was the prime space cutter and therefore the great symbol of change."[51]

If we turn to major authors of the American Renaissance, we will find

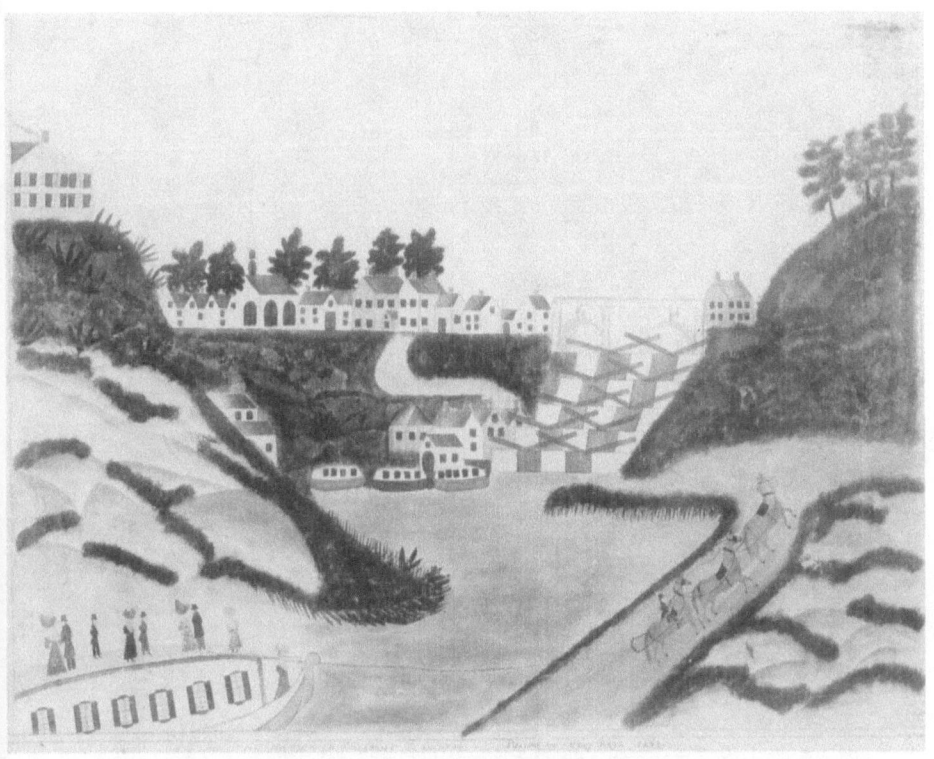

2-19. Mary Keys, *Lockport on the Erie Canal,* 1832. Watercolor on paper, 15 1/4 × 20 1/4 in. Munson-Williams-Proctor Institute Museum of Art, Utica, New York.

literary support for both positions. Writing at mid-century, James Fenimore Cooper contended that "portions of the Erie railroad, and the whole of the Hudson River" possessed "the advantage of sharing in the sublimity and grace through which they pass."[52] The machine and the garden were entirely compatible.

In *The House of the Seven Gables,* however, also written at mid-century, Hepzibah and Clifford Pyncheon, two utterly immobile people, flee the ancestral house in which they have been figuratively self-imprisoned and board a train, destination unknown, moving swiftly through space and time. Although the two eventually return to Salem, Hawthorne titles this critical chapter "The Flight of Two Owls."[53] For fugitives from the Pyncheons' cursed past, the railroad might just as well be unidirectional— a mechanical means of escaping the constraints of time and space.

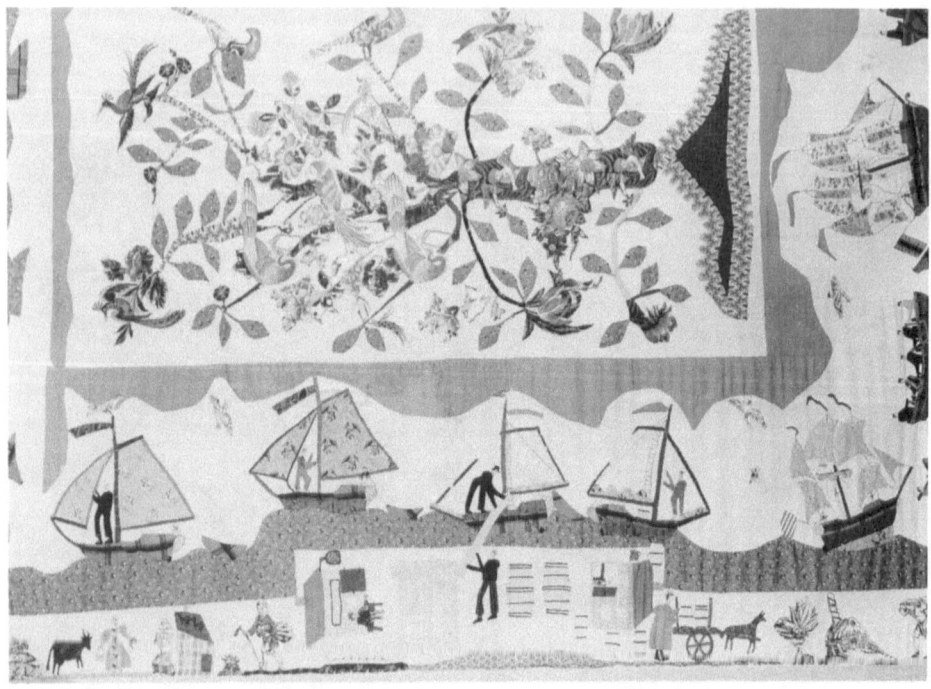

2-20. Attributed to Hannah Stockton Stokes, *Trade and Commerce Quilt* (also called *Land and Sea Quilt*), c. 1830 (detail). Appliqué cotton on muslin, 103 × 91 in. New York State Historical Association, Cooperstown.

When Michel Chevalier visited the United States during the mid-1830s, a few years after Tocqueville, he felt puzzled by what seemed to him sluggish governmental procedures "among a people which, above all things, strives to save time, and which is so much given to haste and despatch that its most suitable emblem would be a locomotive engine or a steamboat. . . ."[54]

What Chevalier and so many other astute critics of American haste had failed to notice, however, was that the sheer vastness of space (and consequently of time), along with the underdeveloped nature of American transportation and communication systems, meant that *waiting* was an inevitable adjunct of haste, unpredictable speed, and networks that did not perfectly connect. American artists understood all too well, however, and they reported the phenomenon from time to time. We can watch it happening in *Waiting for the Stage Coach* by Alvan Fisher (fig. 2-24); or

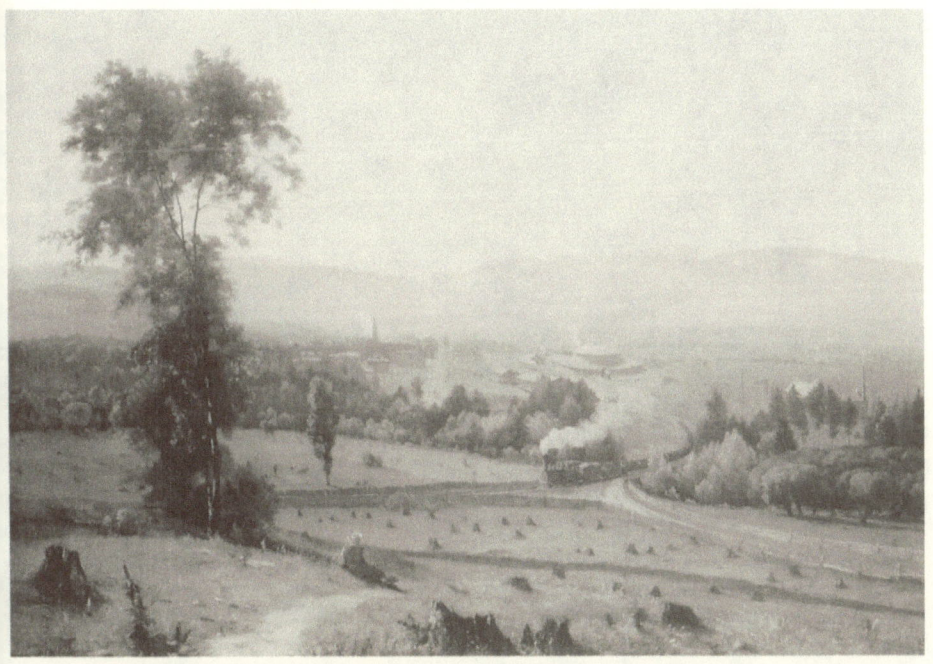

2-21. George Inness, *The Lackawanna Valley,* 1855. Oil on canvas, 33 7/8 × 50 1/4 in. National Gallery of Art, Washington, D.C. Gift of Mrs. Huttleston Rogers.

Waiting for the Stage by Richard Caton Woodville (fig. 2-25); or *In a New Land* by Worthington Whittredge, where a couple awaits the canal boat (fig. 2-26); or, to skip down to modern art, in *Western Motel* by Edward Hopper (fig. 2-27), where a woman sits and waits with her luggage. Even a society that seems perpetually on the move must wait for wind, for repairs, or for people who have been unaccountably delayed. We have little to lose but our patience, though that has been known to wear thin.

We stop and wait in order to continue on our way, and some of the most remarkable American works of art (which combine landscape with narrative, and history with genre) are all about the movement and busyness that go along with waiting for connections. That is precisely the case with *Fairview Inn or Three Mile House on Old Frederick Road* (fig. 2-28). The inn was erected in 1802 on the road that linked Baltimore with Frederick, Maryland, and for 115 years it served as a stopping place for farmers en route to the Baltimore market.[55]

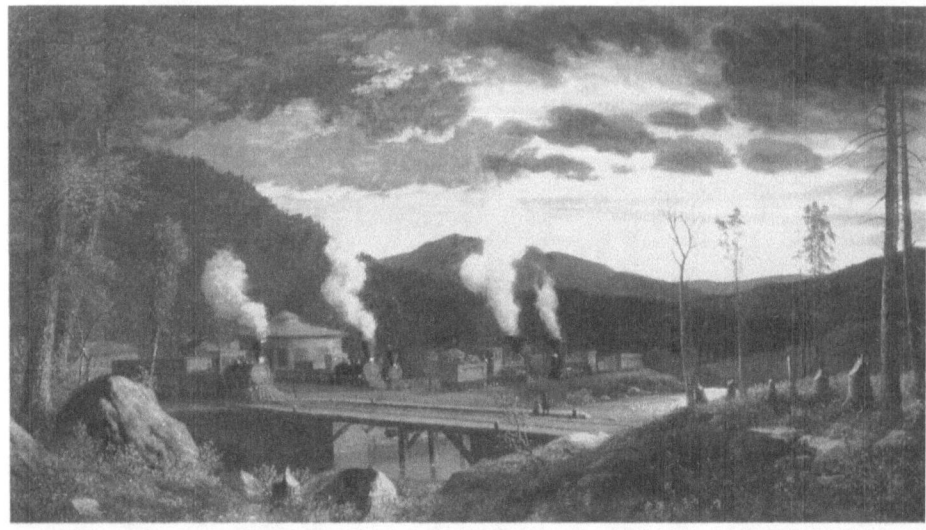

2-22. Thomas P. Rossiter, *Opening of the Wilderness*, c. 1846–1850. Oil on canvas, 17 3/4 × 32 1/2 in. Museum of Fine Arts, Boston. Bequest of Martha C. Karolik for the Karolik Collection of American Paintings, 1815–1868.

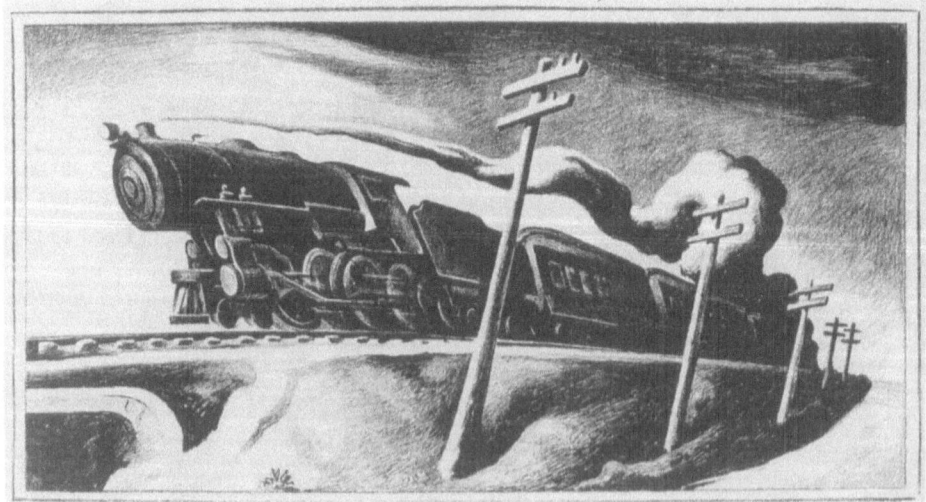

2-23. Thomas Hart Benton, *Going West*, 1934. Lithograph, 12 5/16 × 23 3/8 in. Amon Carter Museum, Fort Worth, Texas.

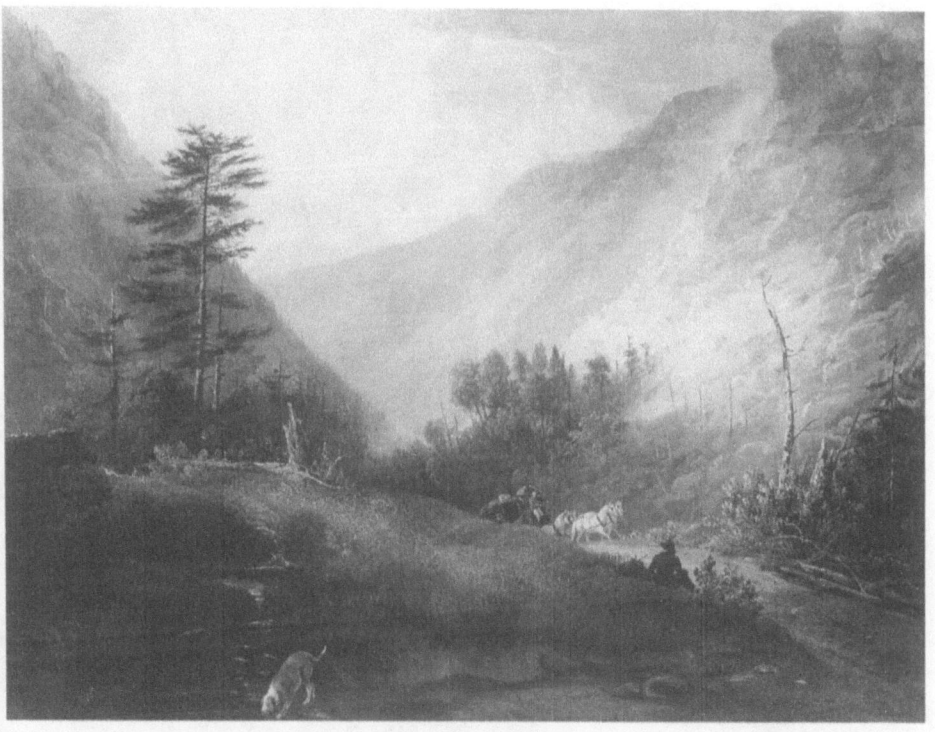

2-24. Alvan Fisher, *Waiting for the Stage Coach*, 1834. Oil on canvas, 24 1/2 × 35 in. The New Britain Museum of American Art, New Britain, Connecticut.

Similarly, *A View in Medford*, made in the early 1830s, shows a small train crossing a stream, a boat moving along a canal, and a manned balloon in flight: earth, water, and air as transportation media amidst a modest New England hamlet.[56] In William Hahn's *Sacramento Railroad Station* (c. 1874), a train is met by a stagecoach and many bustling people.[57] In *The Approaching Train*, a late nineteenth-century painting by Edward Lamson Henry, four coaches or buggies await the arrival; women are crossing the tracks and two children plus a pooch hurry along the tracks. The viewer feels an imminent sense of expectation.[58]

With that variety of pictures in view, I want to return to the extract from Thomas Hart Benton's autobiography, but this time to put back two sentences that I earlier supplanted with ellipses:

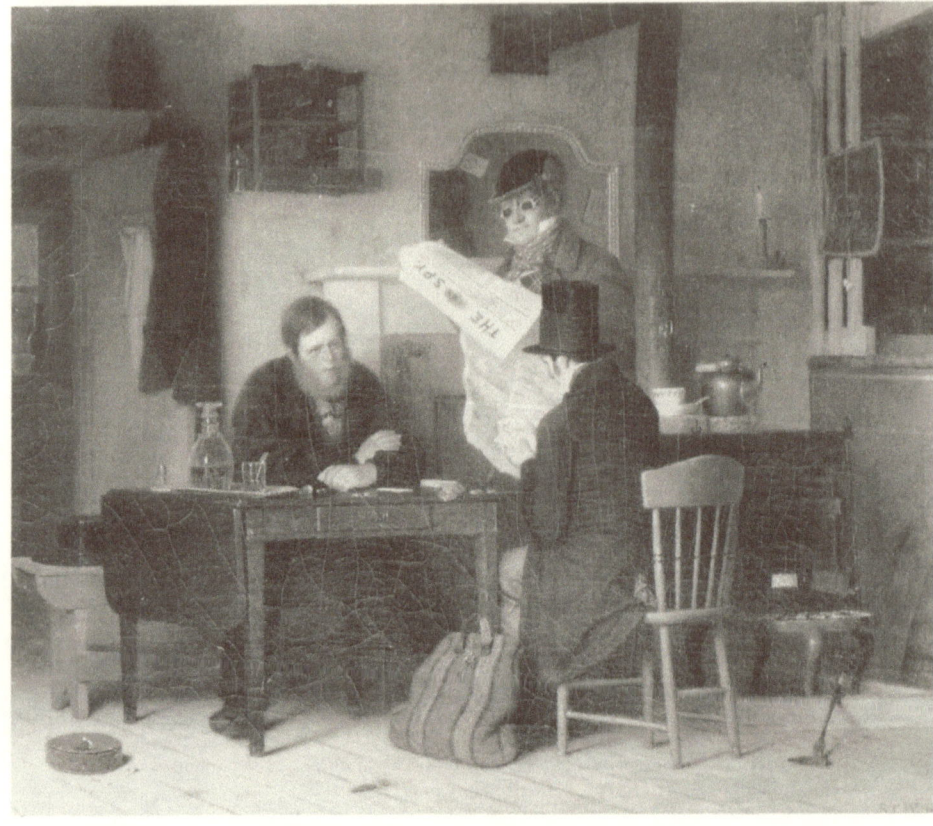

2-25. Richard Caton Woodville, *Waiting for the Stage,* 1851. Oil on canvas, 15 × 18 1/2 in. In the collection of the Corcoran Gallery of Art, Museum Purchase, Gallery Fund, William A. Clark Fund, and gifts of Mr. and Mrs. Lansdell K. Christie and Orme Wilson.

> For the nomadic urges of our western people, the prime symbol of adventurous life has for years been the railroad train. No doubt before its advent, the Conestoga wagon, the six-horse stage, and the river boat held a place equally suggestive. With the coming of the automobile, the railroad train is losing its high place. . . .[59]

With all due respect for Benton's sense of history, and for the contingencies of any author's phrasing, I submit that the works of art just described serve to remind us that diverse modes of movement through American space have been simultaneous as well as sequential. They have overlapped, even interacted, and not simply displaced one another like some ceremonial pageant from the vehicular past.

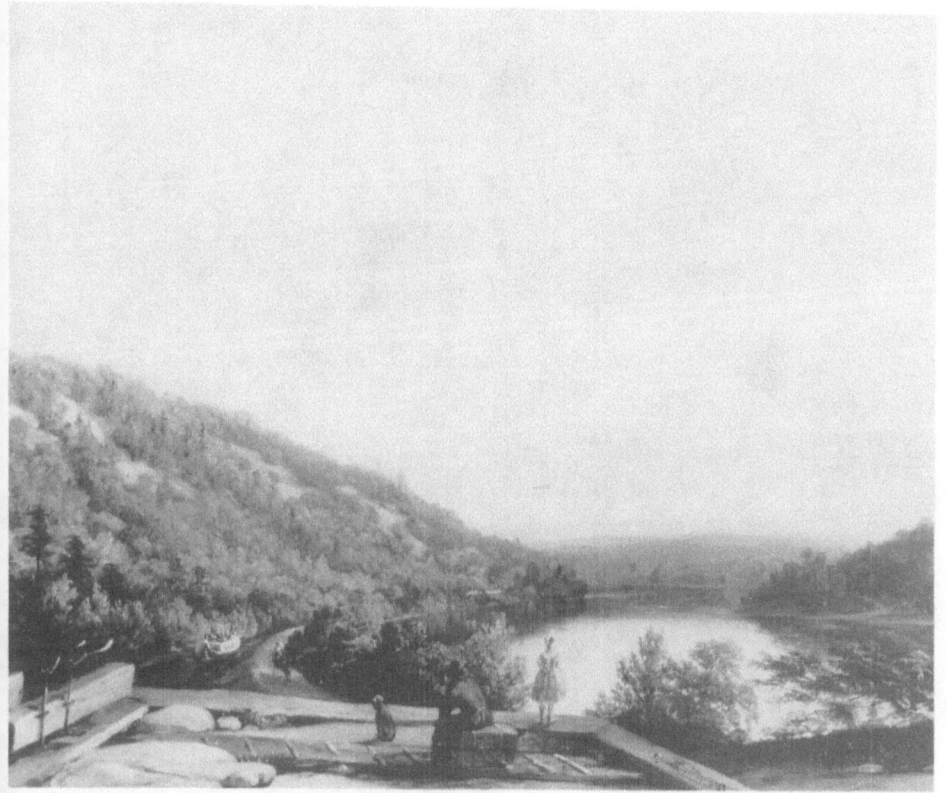

2-26. Thomas Worthington Whittredge, *In a New Land,* c. 1850s. Oil on canvas, 15 × 19 1/2 in. Photo courtesy of Cincinnati Art Galleries. Mr. and Mrs. James H. Allen, Covington, Kentucky.

There is a lovely linkage between transportation and art, then, which was superbly summarized by an observer in 1858: "Latterly, steam and the fine arts have scraped acquaintance. The real and the ideal have smoked pipes together. The iron horse and Pegasus have trotted side by side in double harness, puffing in unison, like a well-trained pair." [60]

In the next section, devoted to history as a process of change, I shall begin with the Cole-Leutze-Benton variations on that well-worn theme, Westward the Course of Empire. Here, in order to complete the present section properly, I want to take as my pictorial text the familiar work by Fanny Palmer—derivative more in its title than in its manner of rendering

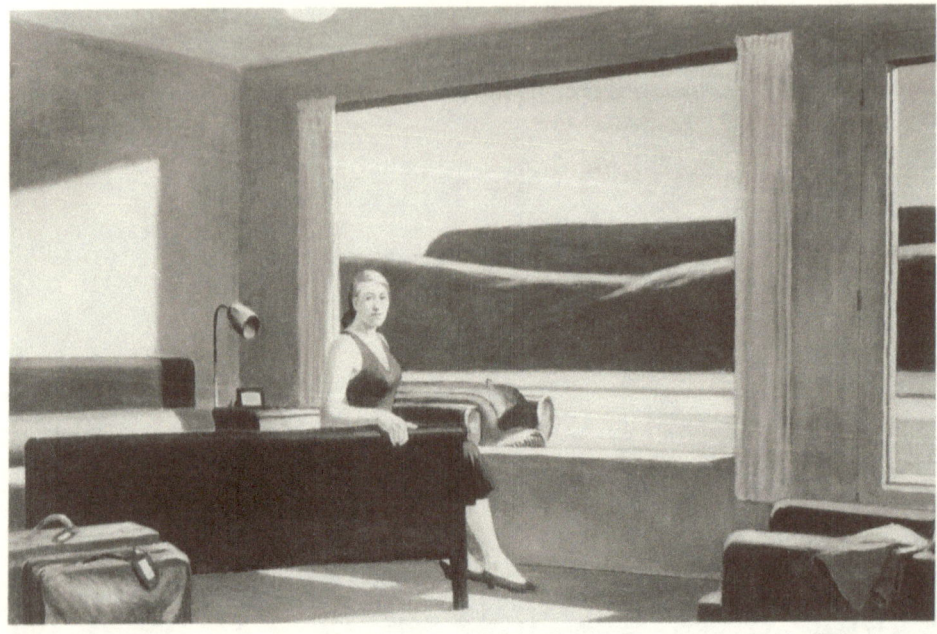

2-27. Edward Hopper, *Western Motel*, 1957. Oil on canvas, 30 1/4 × 50 1/8 in. Yale University Art Gallery. Bequest of Stephen Carlton Clark, B.A. 1903.

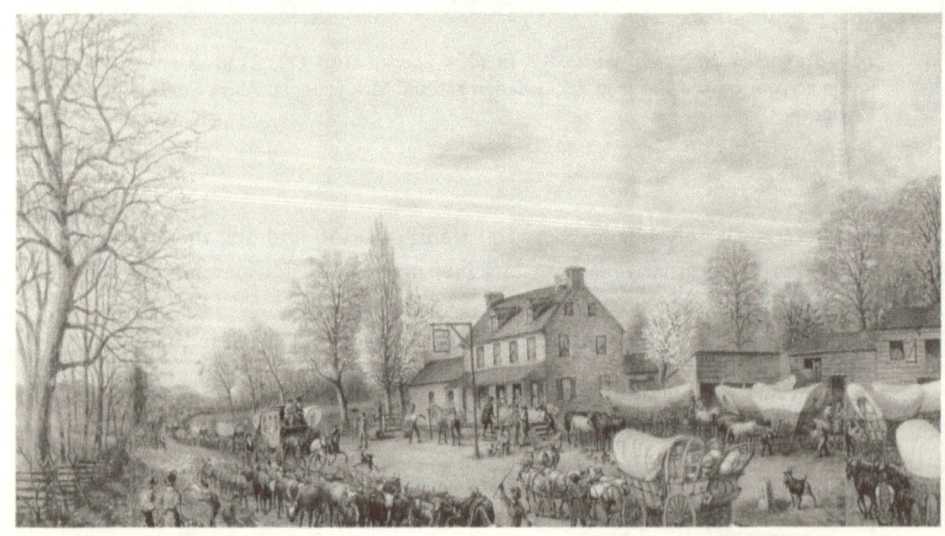

2-28. Thomas Coke Ruckle, *Fairview Inn or Three Mile House on Old Frederick Road* [as it was c. 1829], 1889. Watercolor on paper, 18 × 32 1/4 in. From the Collection of the Maryland Historical Society.

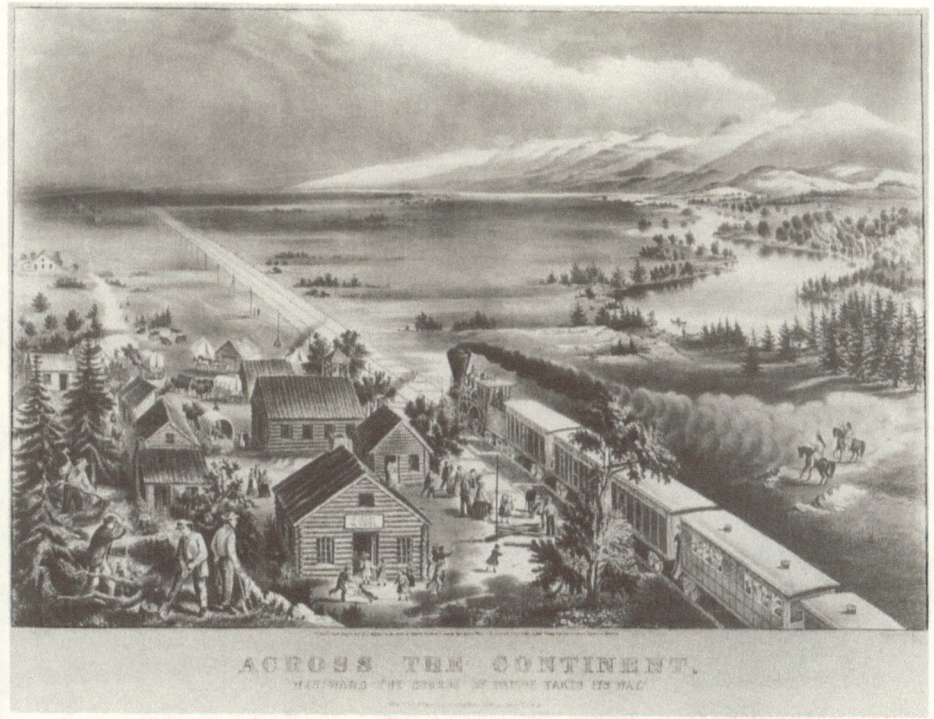

2-29. Fanny F. Palmer, *Across the Continent: "Westward the Course of Empire Takes Its Way,"* 1868. Hand-colored lithograph, 22 3/4 × 31 5/8 in. Courtesy Amon Carter Museum, Fort Worth, Texas.

the subject—called *Across the Continent: "Westward the Course of Empire Takes Its Way,"* a colored lithograph published by Currier and Ives in 1868 (fig. 2-29). There, too, people have met a railroad train which has interconnected with ox-drawn wagons and horse-drawn carts.[61]

The dominant mood and thrust of this extremely popular icon, however, is unidirectional. On the first three cars behind the locomotive we read the words "Through Line. New York to San Francisco"; and off to the left, already in the distance, a wagon train accompanied by men on horseback has begun its irrevocable trek. We simply cannot ignore the fact that a pervasive angle of vision in American culture from the 1840s through the 1870s looked westward as though the continent sloped downward from the Appalachians to the Pacific—as though geographic tilt had foredestined the descendants of Europeans to file their way across the Great

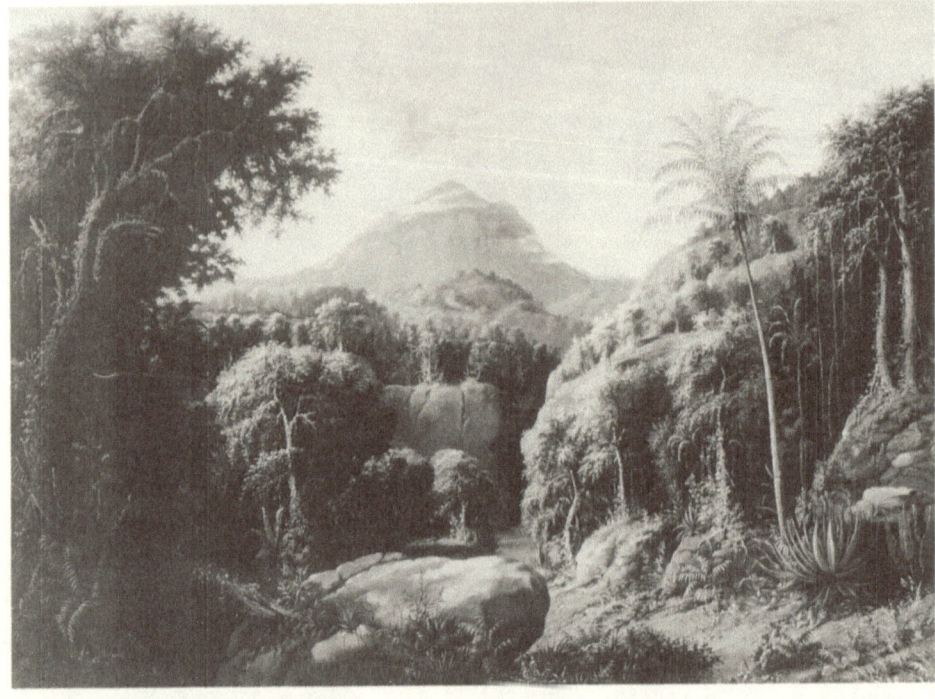

2-30. Alburtis De Orient Browere, *The Trail of the 49'ers*, c. 1852–1858. Oil on canvas, 33 × 48 in. Collection of The Newark Museum. Purchase 1956 Edward F. Weston Bequest Fund.

Plains, over the Bighorns, the Rockies, and the Sierras until permanent settlers should catch up with the 80,000 people who had raced to California in 1849—around Cape Horn or across the Central American jungles if necessary—in order to get rich quick (figs. 2-30 and 2-31).

My point here is that the third quarter of the nineteenth century witnessed not only a psychological transformation from boundlessness to consolidation, as John Higham has so astutely suggested,[62] but for large numbers of Americans a broadened vision of boundlessness. Prospects for personal travel, migration, and the transport of goods seemed infinite.[63] Artists contributed mightily to the creation and communication of that vision.[64]

I do not share William H. Truettner's view that American artists of this period painted the age of discovery several centuries earlier *primarily* as a symbolic means of legitimizing the imperatives of Manifest Destiny at mid-century.[65] They painted and then photographed "the plains across" with as much unabashed gusto as they depicted the activities of Columbus,

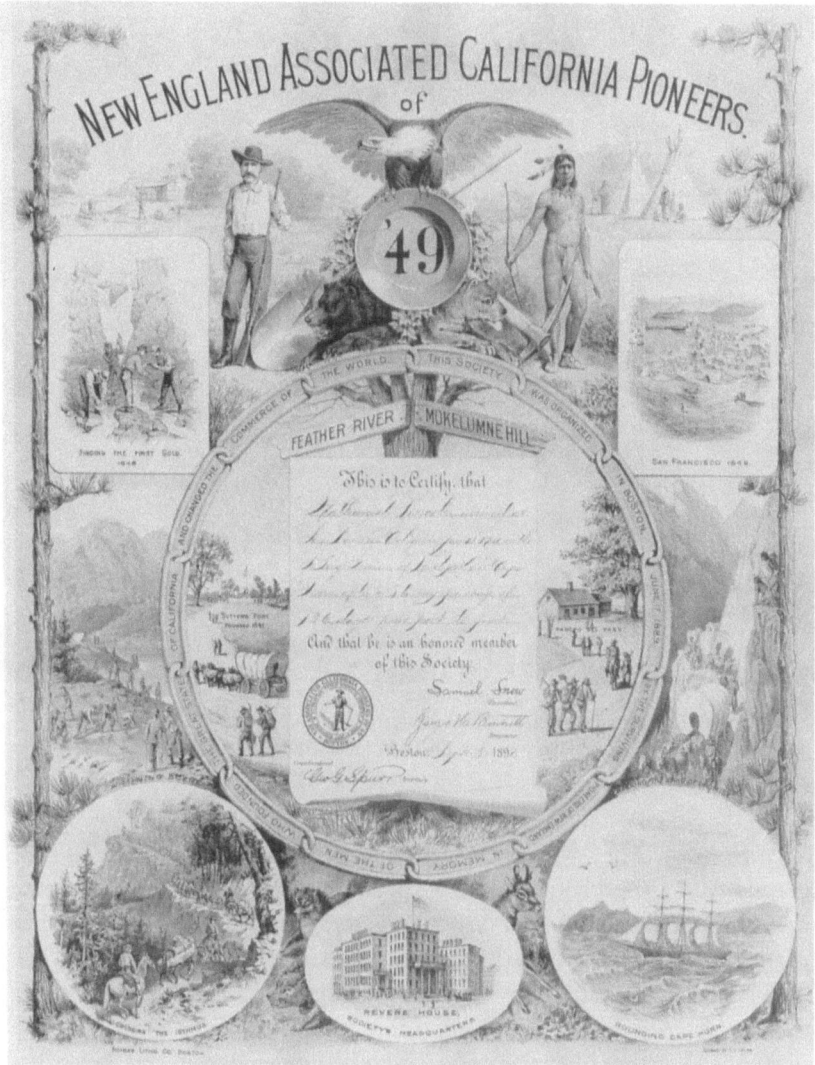

2-31. Unknown artist, *New England Associated California Pioneers of '49*, c. 1890. Color lithograph, 25 7/8 × 19 3/4 in. Amon Carter Museum, Fort Worth, Texas.

DeSoto, and LaSalle.[66] Representative examples from a vast range of possibilities include *Crossing the Rocky Mountains* (fig. 2-32), in which a very long wagon train, extending to the left in the middle distance, approaches the seemingly insurmountable mountains, and *The Covered Wagon* (fig. 2-33), which depicts a much lonelier and apparently more vulnerable party.[67]

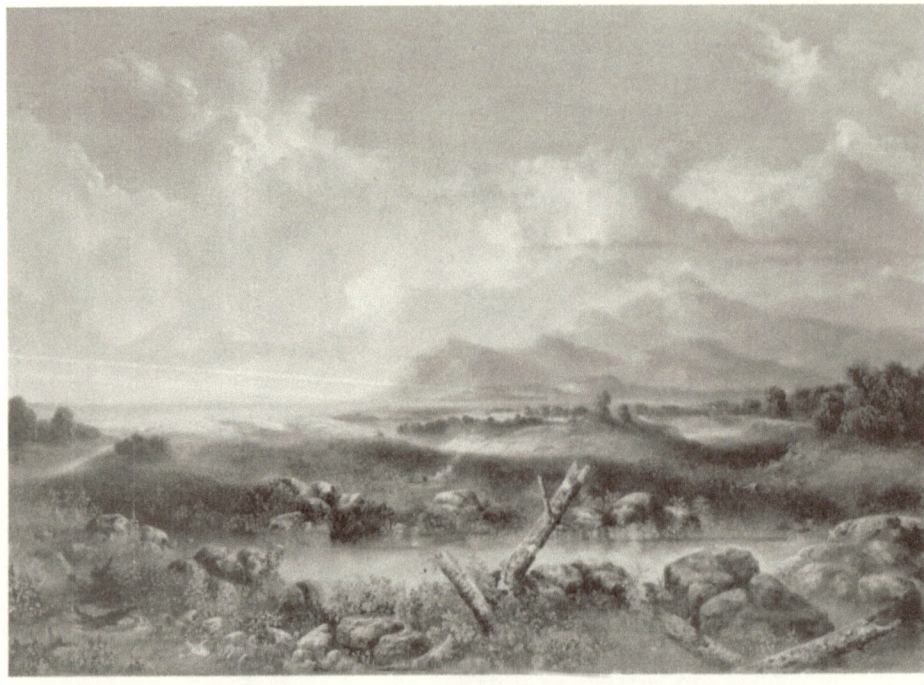

2-32. George Douglass Brewerton, *Crossing the Rocky Mountains*, 1854. Oil on canvas, 30 × 44 1/4 in. Corcoran Gallery of Art. Gift of William Wilson Corcoran.

Various sorts of art remind the viewer that this entire process was dangerous—indeed potentially deadly. Indians also crossed and recrossed the prairie in the course of their seasonal migrations (fig. 2-34), and scouting parties were well advised to keep wary eyes alert.[68] Occasional pictorial commentaries visualized unsuccessful westering without actually showing the hostile natives: in the colored wood engraving titled *Bust*, the only signs of Indians are their arrows in the bodies of dying oxen and the corpse of a white man who did not make it to Pike's Peak (fig. 2-35).

Whether or not to go, under what circumstances, when, and with whom: those determinations may properly be designated as historical because they permeated American life throughout the nineteenth century. They constitute important aspects of what Leutze called "migratory emotions," about which I will say more on pp. 102–117. As likely as not, such determinations were made on the basis of desperation or intuition, which brings to mind a line written by William Whewell of Cambridge Univer-

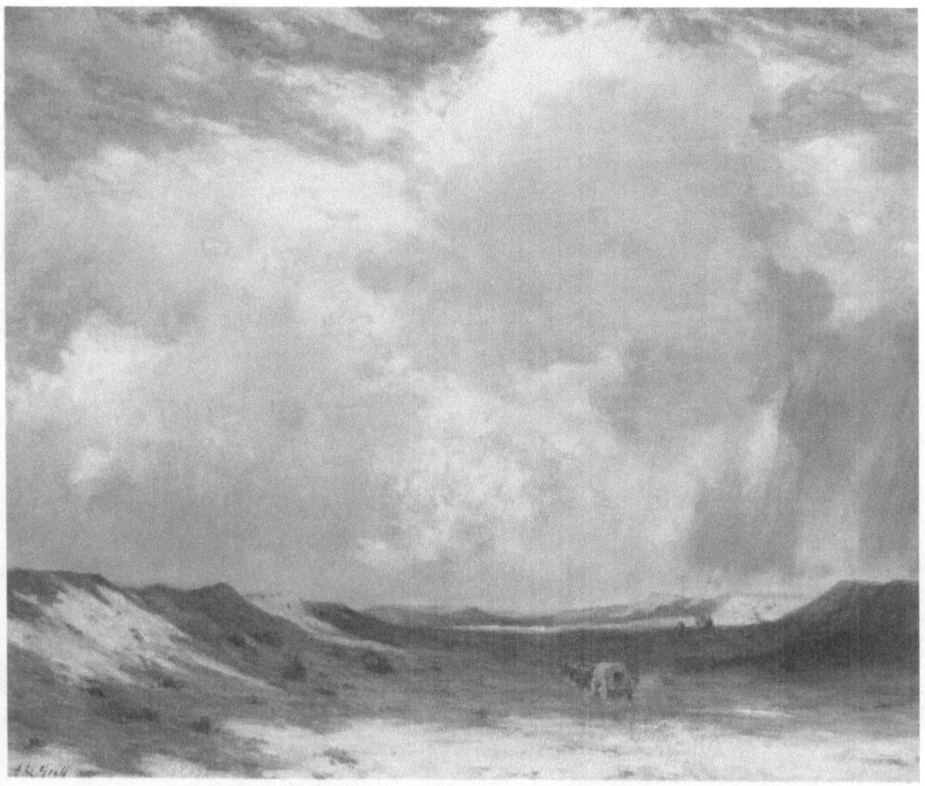

2-33. Albert L. Groll, *The Covered Wagon*, n.d. Oil on canvas, 28 × 36 in. The Thomas Gilcrease Institute of American History and Art, Tulsa, Oklahoma.

sity in 1858: "Time, like space, is not only a form of perception, but of *intuition*."[69]

Implied Narrative: History as Change over Time

Turning our attention to history as change over time (or history as process), and more particularly to artistic perceptions of such change, we find a wonderfully apposite entry that Tocqueville recorded in his diary on June 7, 1831:

> Born often under another sky, placed in the middle of an always moving scene, himself driven by the irresistible torrent which draws all about him, the

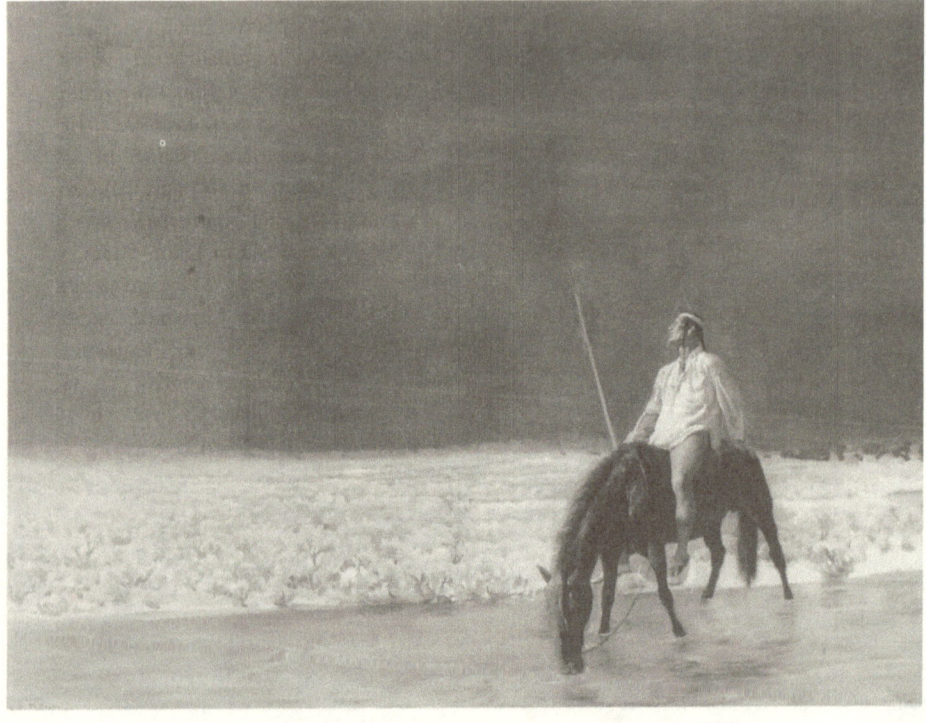

2-34. George De Forest Brush, *Crossing the Prairie,* 1886. Oil on panel, 16 × 22 in. The Thomas Gilcrease Institute of American History and Art, Tulsa, Oklahoma.

American has not time to tie himself to anything, he grows accustomed only to change, and ends by regarding it as the natural state of man.[70]

Specific applications of that sweeping assertion were frequently made by American observers throughout the subsequent century, and often those observers pleaded with artists to record what was, before "it" disappeared altogether.[71] When Washington Irving wrote *Astoria* in 1836, he explained the value of literary accounts of unknown regions in terms of the visibly accelerating pace of change: "It is the object of our task to present scenes of the rough life of the wilderness, and we are tempted to fix these few memorials of a transient state of things fast passing into oblivion."[72]

In a very real sense the phrase "narrative art" is appropriated from the writer's craft. Although we all find the notion of "narrative painting" a useful one, we tend to employ it rather casually.[73] More often than not, however, when artists undertake descriptive series or incorporate narrative

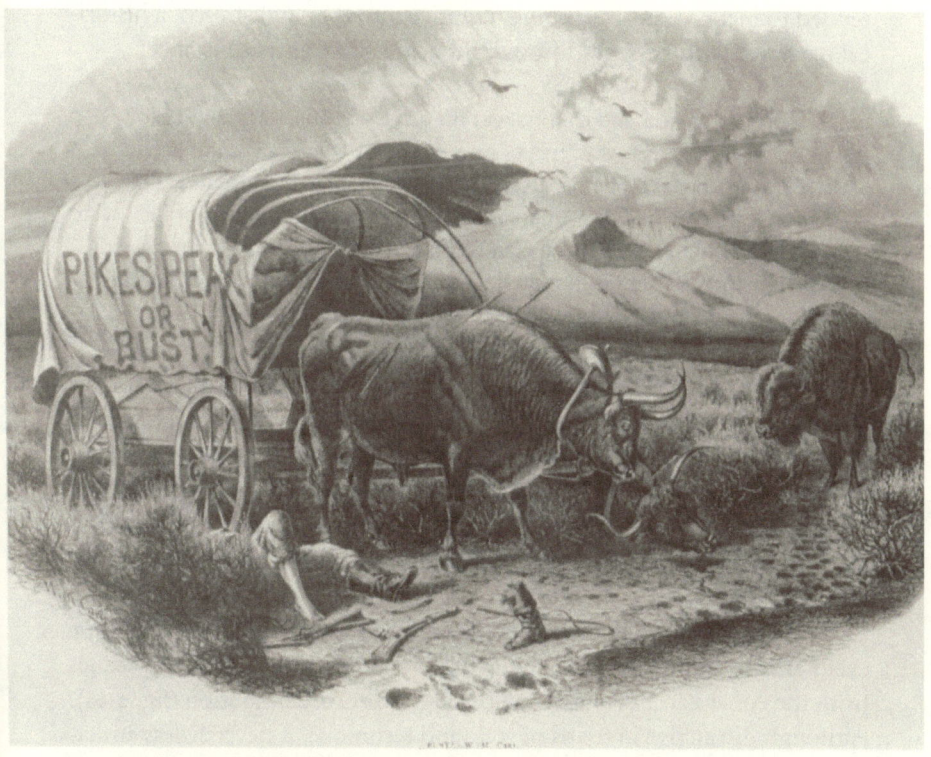

2-35. William M. Cary, *Bust,* c. 1860. Colored wood engraving, 10 1/4 × 16 in. Courtesy Amon Carter Museum, Fort Worth, Texas.

into an epic painting, criticism is likely to rain down from contemporary critics as well as from posterity. That is precisely what happened to Emanuel Leutze's massive mural for the United States Capitol, called *Westward the Course of Empire Takes Its Way* (1861). Because this painting has not been neglected by scholars, I intend to concentrate narrowly upon the aspect of it that is pertinent to this section.[74]

Happily, Leutze has left us rather full notes for his conception of the work, and I find them fascinating. His description in "Design" is highly detailed, so I quote only from the opening sentence: "A party of Emigrants have arrived near sunset on the *divide* (watershed) from whence they have the first view of the pacific slope, their 'promised land' Eldorado, having passed the troubles of the plains. . . ." Eventually, when he makes a summary statement of his entire scheme, it becomes clear that Leutze in-

tended to incorporate a sweeping narrative into the single fresco, a historical narrative with passages through time and space as its substance:

> To represent as near and truthfully as the artist was able the grand peaceful
> conquest of the great west. [paper torn off] . . . without a wish to date or
> localize, or to represent a particular event, it is intended to give in a con-
> densed form a picture of western emigration, [and] the conquest of the Pacific
> slope, while if ever the general plan be carried out the side walls will have the
> earlier history of Western Emigration, in illustrations from Boone's adven-
> tures[,] the discovery of the valleys of the Ohio, Mississippi—[75]

Whether or not Leutze deserves the torment that he has taken for his
attempt at epic narrative, it should be noticed that *Westward* is the second
in a sequence of at least four such thematic efforts. The one that is best
known—Thomas Cole's five-part series *The Course of Empire* (1833–
1836)[76]—interests us not at all here because it is altogether allegorical
rather than historical. The other two, although much less familiar, are far
more germane.

In about 1855 an unknown American "naive" artist prepared a unique
cyclorama, combining wood engraving with watercolor, depicting scenes
from the American Revolution on through westward migration (fig. 2-36).
Although distinctive in terms of style and technique, it nevertheless anticipated the rendering of history as process in Leutze as well as the pano-
ramic mural that Thomas Hart Benton completed for the Harry S. Truman Library and Museum in 1961 (fig. 2-37).

Benton has written an enchanting account of his relationship with
Truman when he was planning the mural. "I knew he was a very good
historian," Benton observed, "but I was pretty sure he would not take into
account the technical limitations that would have to be faced in a *pictorial*
representation of history." After describing "our many discussions,"
Benton gets down to the nitty-gritty:

> Independence, in the early part of the nineteenth century, had been one of
> the greatest of the "jumping off" places for exploration and settlement of the
> West. It had outfitted for both the Oregon and Santa Fe trails and for the
> river, plains, and mountain fur traders. It was the pivot from which radiated
> some of the most consequential lines of America's western development. The
> town's history encompassed enough subject matter for ten murals.
> However, our continued speculations began leading us beyond Indepen-
> dence to that earlier history of the Missouri and Mississippi valleys which

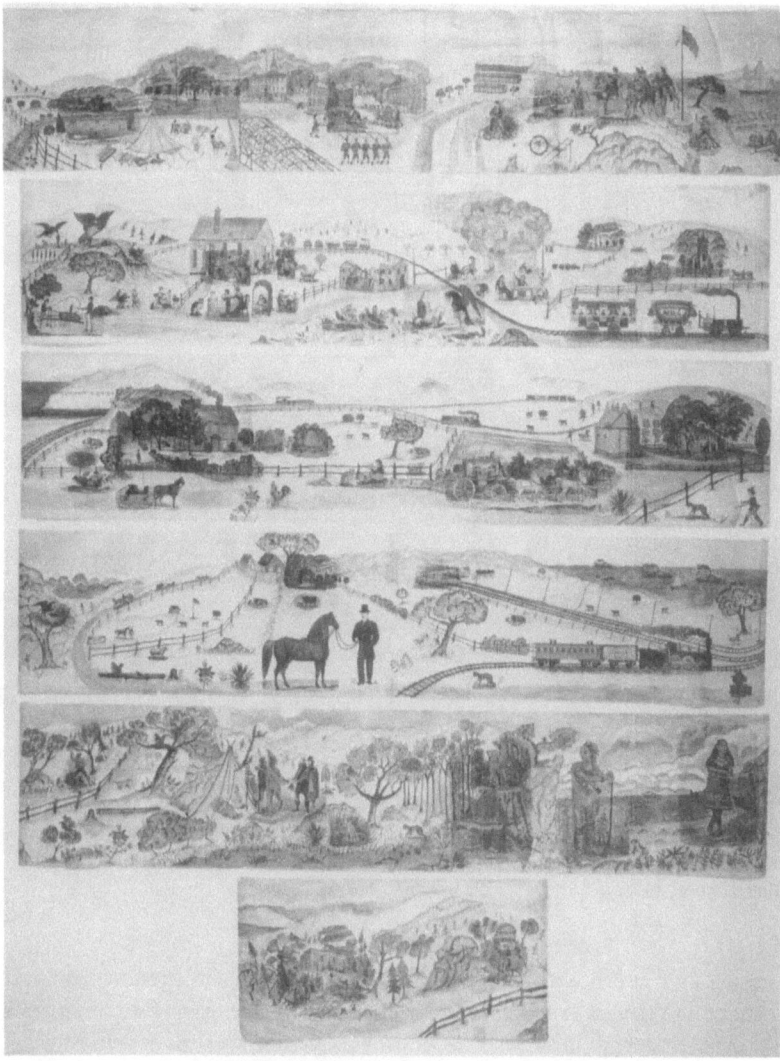

2-36. Anon. American, Cyclorama showing scenes from the Revolution through westward migration, c. 1855. Wood engraving with watercolors, 8 in. × 17 ft. 3 in. The Old Print Shop, Inc., New York.

preceded and led to the foundation of the town. Eventually we were back to the Louisiana Purchase and, of course, to one of the President's most revered predecessors, Thomas Jefferson. Before long Jefferson began occupying too much of the President's thoughts for my comfort. I could see our theme

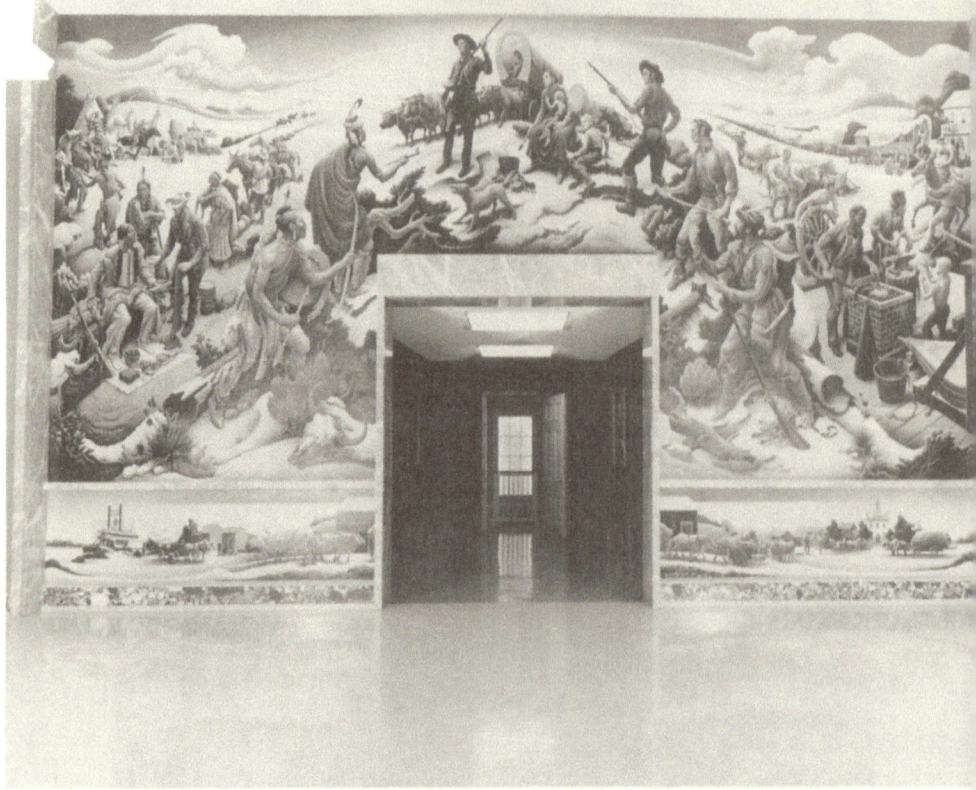

2-37. Thomas Hart Benton, *Independence and the Opening of the West,* 1961. Acrylic polymer latex paint applied to a Belgian linen surface, 19 × 32 ft. The Harry S. Truman Library, Independence, Missouri.

taking on vast proportions. I had fears of its running from Jefferson's administration to that of Truman, a pictorially unmanageable mass of subject matter.

The President's ideas were all perfectly reasonable in terms of verbal history. The sequence of events he envisioned from the Louisiana Purchase to the foundation of Independence and onwards were historically logical, but they could not be combined successfully in a single painting, no matter how extensive. So I began to fence off one line of thought after another, trying to narrow our subject to a practicable size. I made the point at one interview that, if the logic of history led from Independence to the Louisiana Purchase and Thomas Jefferson, it also led from the Purchase to the whole Napoleonic era and *that* I said was just too much to handle. The President agreed that it might be difficult.

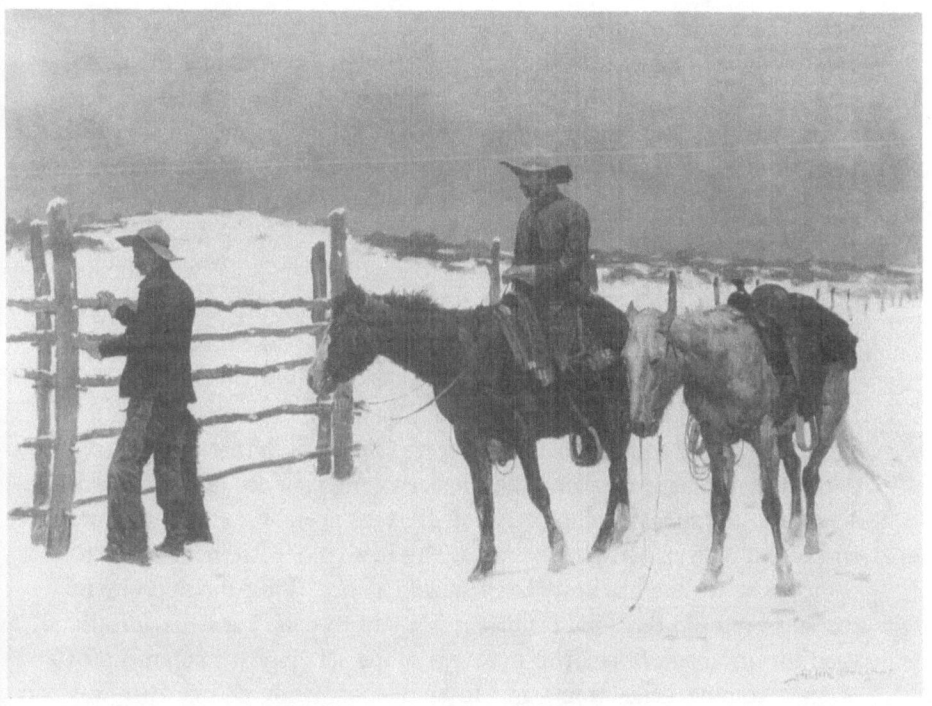

2-38. Frederic Remington, *The Fall of the Cowboy,* 1895. Oil on canvas, 25 × 35 1/8 in. Courtesy Amon Carter Museum, Fort Worth, Texas.

One day, maybe tired of my dodging around with, "You can't paint this," and "You can't paint that," the President said laughingly, "Well, what the hell is it you *can* paint?" I grabbed the opportunity. "Mr. President," I said, "I'll write out my plan for this mural and bring it over for you to read."[77]

There are assorted other examples of what I have called the history as process panorama, such as Philip Evergood's incredibly comprehensive *Cotton From Field to Mill* (1938), a marvelous mural in the Jackson, Georgia, post office which shows how so many modes of transportation and labor interconnect.[78]

A painting need not be explicitly comprehensive, however, in order to convey a sense of inexorable change over time. *The Fall of the Cowboy* by Remington (fig. 2-38) does so with remarkable economy and symmetry in the shrewdly managed symbol of passage through a gate that must be carefully opened and closed. Barbed wire had been invented in 1874, and as the range was rapidly fenced in, the cowboy's role and significance diminished. His heyday occurred in the quarter-century following 1866, when he drove longhorn cattle great distances to market. Constraining the range meant trivializing the cowboy and the lifestyle associated with him. A year before Remington painted *The Fall,* Owen Wister wrote to his mother from Arizona: "The frontier has yielded to a merely commonplace society. . . . The survivors of Tombstone sit there and dwell on how things used to be."[79]

The same sort of craft and cerebral economy occur when we shift our gaze from the American West to the old maritime frontier. One of my favorite marine paintings, for example, is Fitz Hugh Lane's *Boston Harbor* (fig. 2-39), which differs from almost all the rest of his harbor scenes because it is such a deliberate visualization of a historic transition: from the age of sail to the age of steam. The larger schooners in that picture have dark hulls and light sails, and the smaller sailing craft are dimly colored. The large steamboat making its way swiftly into port, by contrast, is white and bright with jet black smokestacks. This new color pattern, designed to compensate for the black smoke of steam engines, is just the opposite of the anchored old three-master that it is about to pass. Lane has adroitly used this inversion of color to make his subtle yet emphatic commentary upon a coming generation—and to speak poignantly of one that was passing.[80]

The Amon Carter Museum's *Boston Harbor* is an unusual work by Lane, but not a unique one. Around 1863 he painted *Merchantmen off Boston Harbor,* in which he mingled a few steamships among the sailers.[81] In 1880 Francis Silva placed a steam-powered tug among the sailing ships in *New York Harbor.*[82] In 1856 Charles Christian Nahl painted *Fire in San Francisco Bay,* a frightful scene in which the anonymous ship blazing beyond control is considerably older than the large and handsome clipper moored at the dock. Here, too, we have a vivid commentary on the transformation of American maritime history.[83]

I do not claim, by the way, that Fitz Hugh Lane "invented" this type of history-as-process statement, only that he did it particularly well. At the Kelvingrove Art Gallery and Museum in Glasgow, Scotland, we find a lovely landscape titled *First Steamboat on the Clyde* by John Knox (1778–1845). In it are quite a number of traditional boats with their sails well filled, plus one smallish steamboat belching black smoke just to the left of center. This work qualifies quite well as a "machine in the garden," to use Leo Marx's famous phrase,[84] and is more aesthetically attractive and historically persuasive than James Hamilton's *Steamship Coming Up the Delaware* (fig. 2-40), which also intermingles a very new steam vessel with a

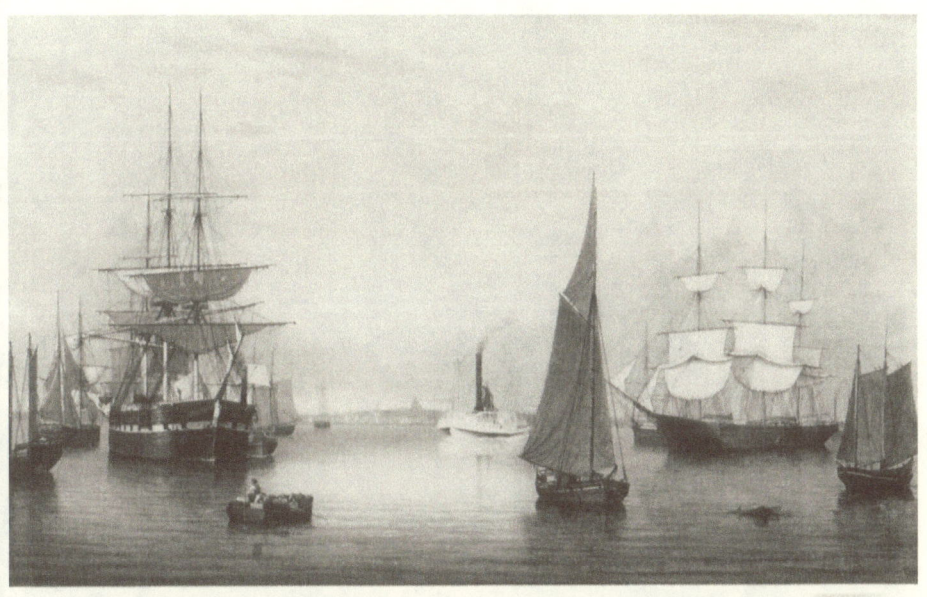

2-39. Fitz Hugh Lane, *Boston Harbor*, 1856. Oil on canvas, 24 1/2 × 41 1/2 in. Courtesy Amon Carter Museum, Fort Worth, Texas.

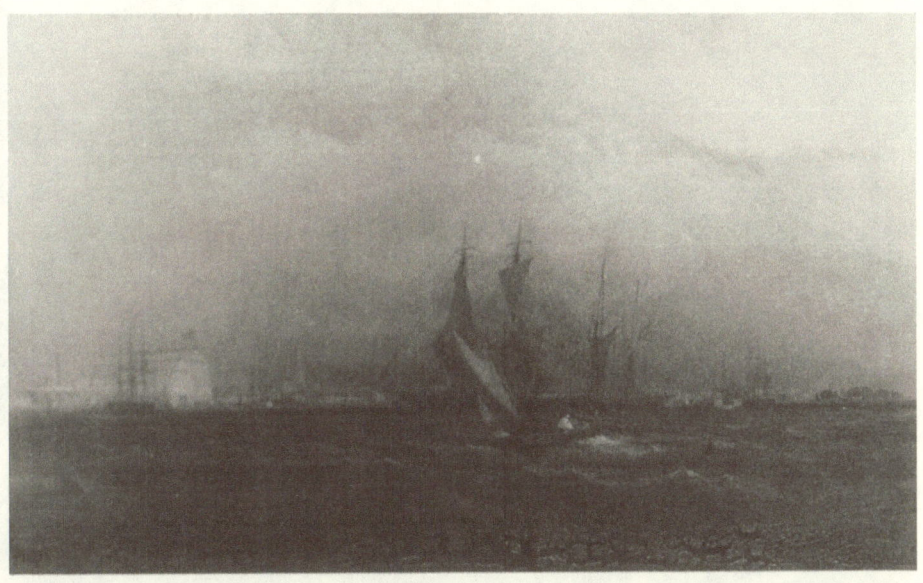

2-40. James Hamilton, *Steamship Coming Up the Delaware*, c. 1850. Oil on canvas, 20 × 34 in. Washington and Lee University, Lexington, Virginia.

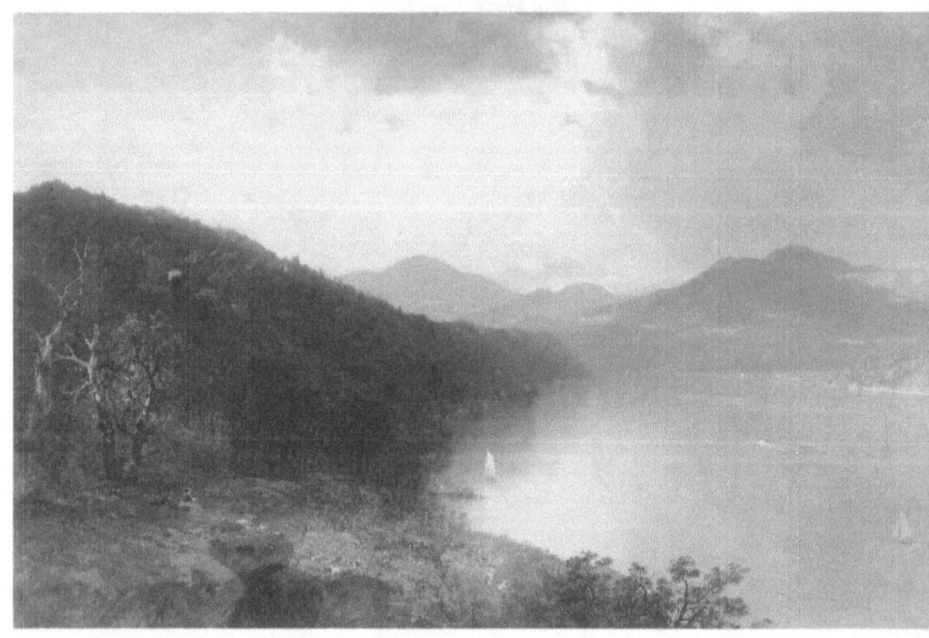

2-41. John Federick Kensett, *View on the Hudson*, 1865. Oil on canvas, 28 × 45 in. The Baltimore Museum of Art. Gift of Mrs. Paul H. Miller, BMA 1942.4.

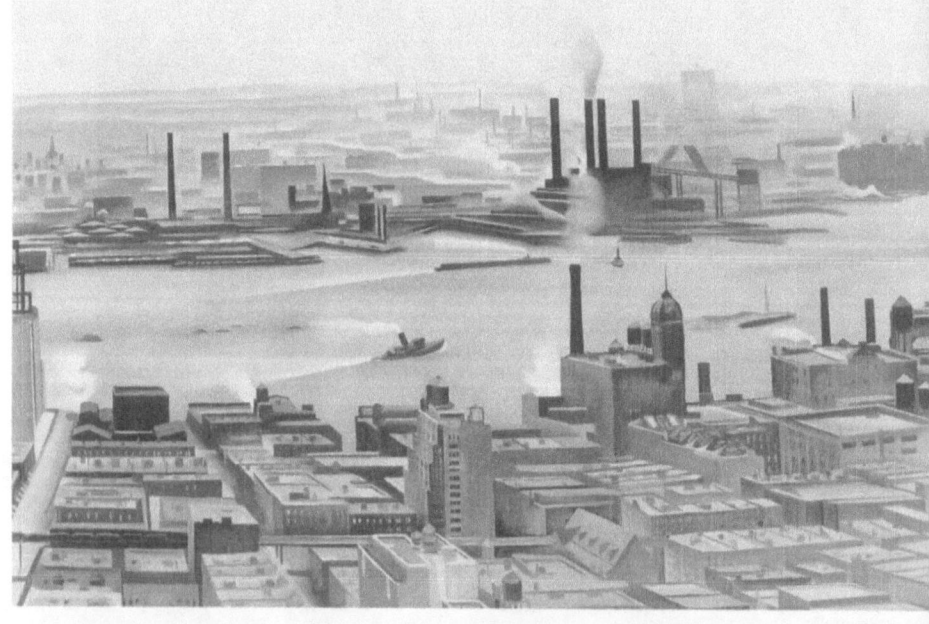

2-42. Georgia O'Keeffe, *East River from the 30th Story of the Shelton Hotel, New York*, 1928. Oil on canvas, 30 × 48 in. The New Britain Museum of American Art, New Britain, Connecticut.

small sailer partially obstructing our view of it and several large schooners at the line where water merges with land.[85]

Rivers have long been immensely attractive as sources of metaphor in American literature and as symbolic subjects for American artists.[86] Synchronic comparisons are feasible and instructive, but diachronic contrasts are more meaningful if our principal concern is with change over time. For synchronic purposes, therefore, we can always compare John F. Kensett's *View on the Hudson* (fig. 2-41), in which a sidewheeler churns among the sailboats and a four-car train crosses a bridge in the distance, with the more rustic and traditional *View of the Hudson River from Near Sing Sing, New York*, by Robert Havell, Jr. (c. 1850).[87]

It is far more striking, however, to compare the unobtrusive presence of "progress" in Kensett's arcadia with Georgia O'Keeffe's radically different perspective revealed in *East River from the 30th Story of the Shelton Hotel, New York* (fig. 2-42), in which tugs and barges leave large wakes that seem entirely in phase with the smoke billowing from assorted industrial chimneys. Despite the solid angularity of O'Keeffe's blue and gray cityscape, she achieves a sense of movement even though the bustle is partially occurring beneath the surface.

Once again synchronic comparisons turn out to be less instructive. *From Brooklyn Heights* by George C. Ault (1925) simply anticipates the volumetric geometry and steam in O'Keeffe's *East River;* and *Prosperity's Increase* by John Kane (1933) provides a charming (because "naive") restatement of *East River,* with its numerous industrial smokestacks, a steaming locomotive in the foreground, river barges passing beneath a modern bridge, and factories lining the far riverbank.[88] Ault and Kane offer variations on a theme, whereas the contrast between O'Keeffe and Kensett reminds us not merely that our waterways have changed, but that our *perception* of them has changed with equal power and drama.[89]

So long ago as 1864, Henry Tuckerman, an acute observer, noted that a three-hour train trip from New York to Albany had once required thirty hours by water. "What has been gained in speed," he mused, "is often lost in rational entertainment." By contrast, Tuckerman reminisced, "In that deliberate progress of the canal enthusiast, not a phase of the landscape, not an historical association . . . was lost to his view."[90]

At the conclusion of Tuckerman's long but engaging volume, this man of letters who devoted a lifetime to travel, art, and literature—primarily American—offered an *aperçu* on history as process that achieved in focus what it lacked in scope: "Two principal agencies have caused the rapid transition in outward aspect and social conditions which make the present and the past offer so great a contrast even within the space of an average American life—immigration, and locomotive facilities."[91] Although Tuckerman did not specify it, locomotion and migration also had a significant emotional impact.

The Historical Power of Migratory Emotions

In the detailed notes that Emanuel Leutze composed while preparing to execute his commission for *Westward the Course of Empire Takes Its Way*, one descriptive phrase stands out with particular force: "migratory emotions."[92] If, indeed, Michel Chevalier saw "a passion for movement" in Americans and found them "always in the mood to move on," then the historian of culture with any interest in mental and spiritual outlooks wants to watch for manifestations and consequences.[93]

War and its ravages, for instance, have been responsible for emotions that we can read in the faces and crippled bodies of those who fought and wandered for years afterwards, as in *The Old Veteran*, which George Inness composed around 1881. The stooped and venerable man ambulates, but slowly and with difficulty. We also encounter migratory emotions (of many sorts) when wayfaring immigrants who are lost or perplexed pause to seek assistance (fig. 2-43). And we witness with sympathy when participants in the westward movement pause for intimate moments to share their feelings.[94]

At one level these emotions look fairly uncomplicated, whatever their degree of intensity may be. Governor Dunmore of Virginia had declared of Americans that "wandering about Seems engrafted in their Nature." And Thomas Hart Benton wrote of the locomotive that "its steam pushed promises, shook up the roots of generations, and moved the hearts of men and women with all the confused mixtures of joy and pain that accompany the thought of separation and departure."[95] Those words bring to mind such pictures as *Leaving Home* by Edward Lamson Henry (1889)[96]—which shows the departure of a newly married couple from a colonial home, with a group of well-wishers waving farewell from the front porch and the bride appearing to blow them a fond kiss from the open back of her carriage—and *The Pemigewasset Coach* by Enoch Wood Perry (fig. 2-44). Above all they resonate with the picture that was voted most popular at the Chicago World's Columbian Exposition in 1893: *Breaking Home Ties* by

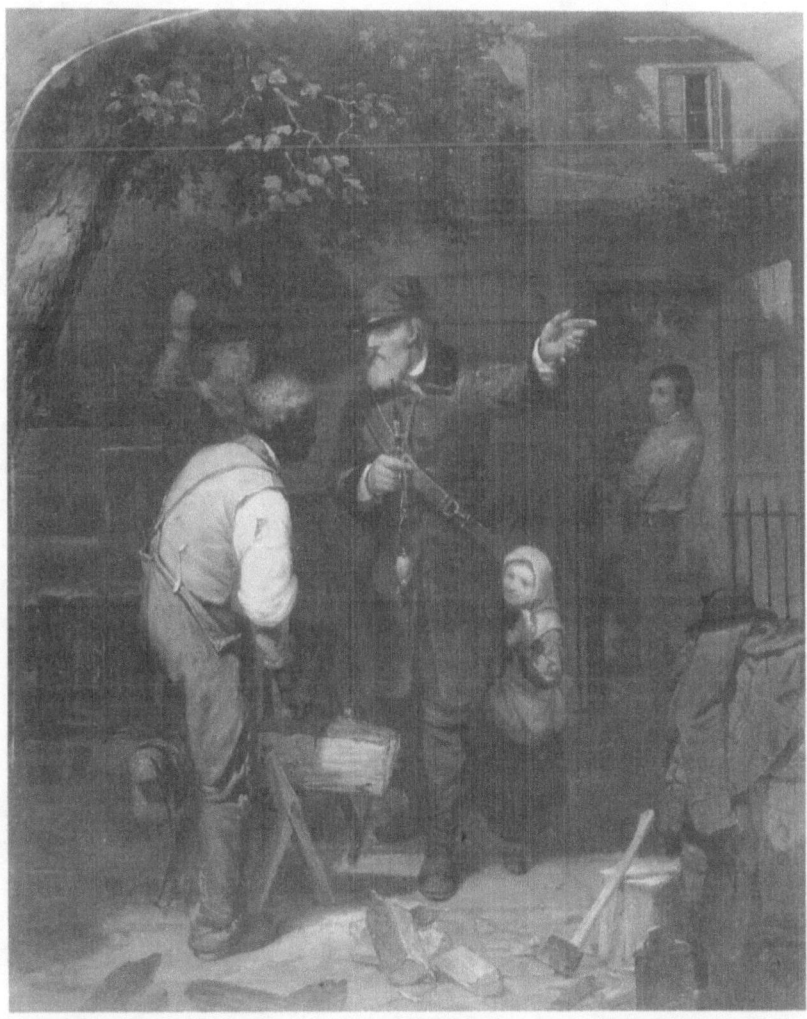

2-43. Charles Blauvelt, *A German Immigrant Inquiring His Way,* 1855. Oil on canvas, 36 × 29 in. North Carolina Museum of Art, purchased with funds from the state of North Carolina.

Thomas Hovenden (fig. 2-45). These expressions of "migratory emotion" are among my favorites because they highlight American attitudes toward social and personal change. They are ultimately historical because they portray some of the deepest feelings that we have experienced—natives and newcomers alike—about the family and distant separations inflicted by space and time.

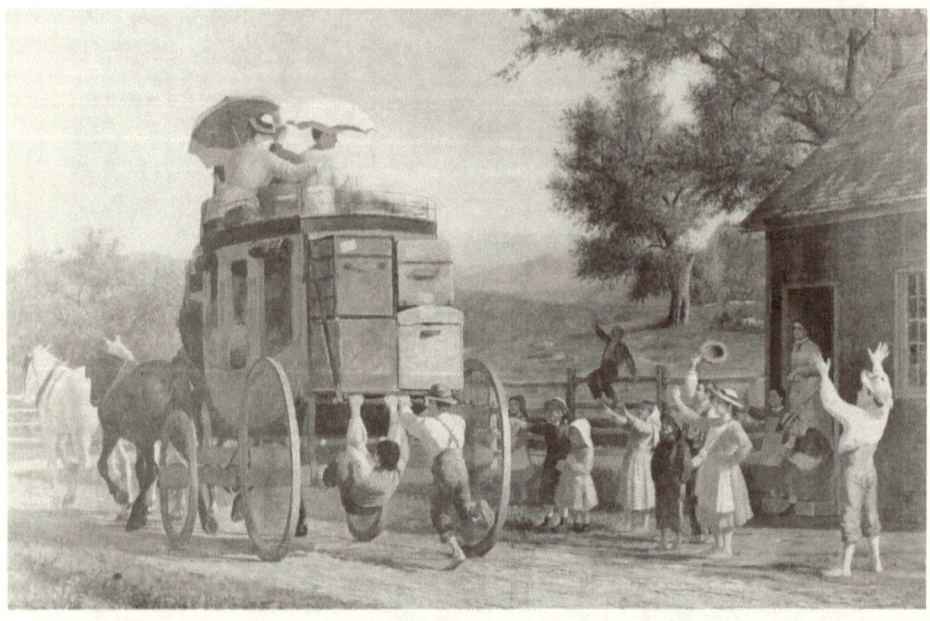

2-44. Enoch Wood Perry, Jr., *The Pemigewasset Coach*, c. 1899. Oil on canvas, 42 1/2 × 66 1/2 in. Shelburne Museum, Shelburne, Vermont.

They also remind us that abundant opportunities for mobility can generate profound ambivalence. Writing in *Walden*, Henry David Thoreau complained that "we have the St. Vitus' dance." Some years later, however, in *Walking*, he conceded that "I must walk toward Oregon, and not toward Europe. And that way the nation is moving, and I may say that mankind progress [*sic*] from east to west." [97]

This tension within the society as a whole is lucidly conveyed in Carl Becker's classic essay called "Kansas" (1910):

> The home-keeping and timid are well content. They sit in accustomed corners, disturbed by no fortuitous circumstance. But there are those others who are forever tugging at the leashes of ordered life, eager to venture into the unknown. Forsaking beaten paths, they plunge into the wilderness. They must be always on the frontier of human endeavor, submitting what is old and accepted to conditions that are new and untried. [98]

Using yet another mode, John Greenleaf Whittier would convey this mood in one of the most memorable of his *Anti-Slavery Poems*, titled "The Kansas Emigrants" (1854):

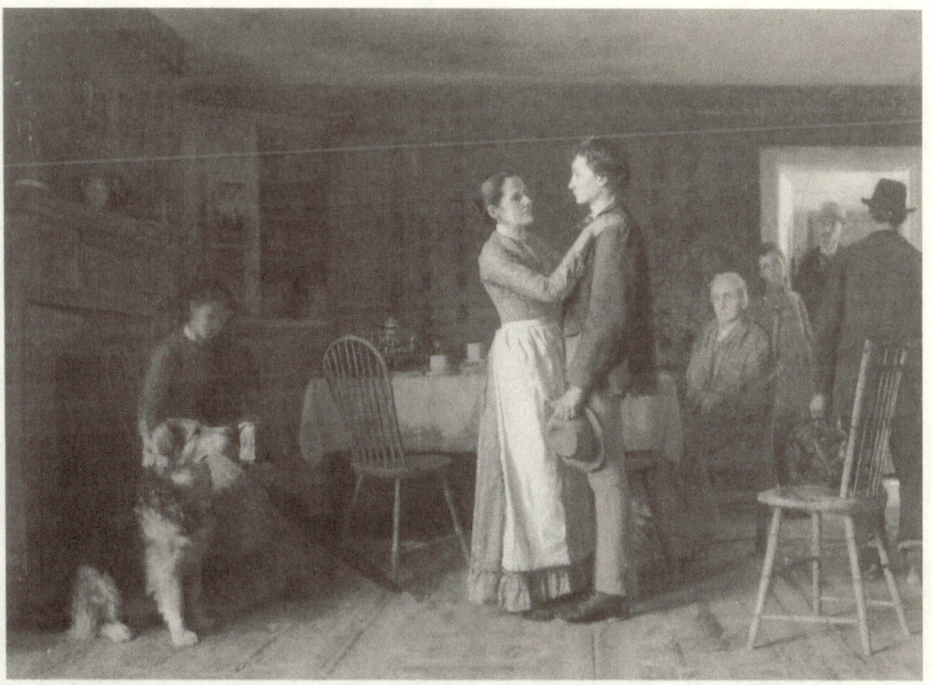

2-45. Thomas Hovenden, *Breaking Home Ties*, 1890. Oil on canvas, 52 1/8 × 72 1/4 in. Philadelphia Museum of Art. Gift of Ellen Harrison McMichael in memory of C. Emory McMichael.

We cross the prairie as of old
   The pilgrims crossed the sea,
To make the West, as they the East,
   The homestead of the free!

We go to rear a wall of men
   On Freedom's southern line,
And plant beside the cotton-tree
   The rugged Northern pine!

We're flowing from our native hills
   As our free rivers flow;
The blessing of our Mother-land
   Is on us as we go.[99]

Abolitionism and the struggle for African-American freedom require us to remember one of the most terrifying types of "migratory emotion." Eastman Johnson depicted the feelings of escaped slaves on several occa-

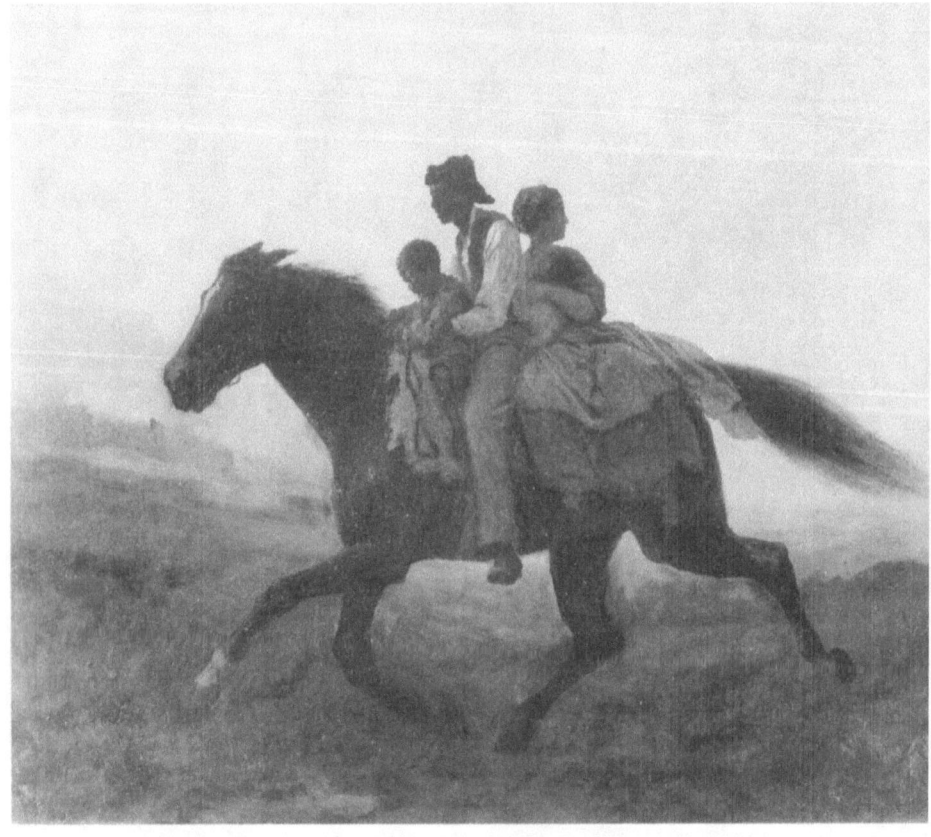

2-46. Eastman Johnson, *A Ride for Liberty—The Fugitive Slaves*, c. 1862. Oil on board, 22 × 26 1/4 in. The Brooklyn Museum. Gift of Miss Gwendolyn O. L. Conkling.

sions; *A Ride for Liberty—The Fugitive Slaves* (fig. 2-46) is a scene that he actually witnessed. Thomas Moran made the situation seem equally desperate in *Slaves Escaping through the Swamp* (fig. 2-47). David Edward Cronin treated the same theme with a very different sort of composition, *Fugitive Slaves in the Dismal Swamp, Virginia* (fig. 2-48); and Charles T. Webber created a scene that may be the most explicitly documentary, *The Underground Railroad* (fig. 2-49).[100]

Also important among the modes of "migratory emotion" that we must consider are those generated by intercultural struggle, primarily between

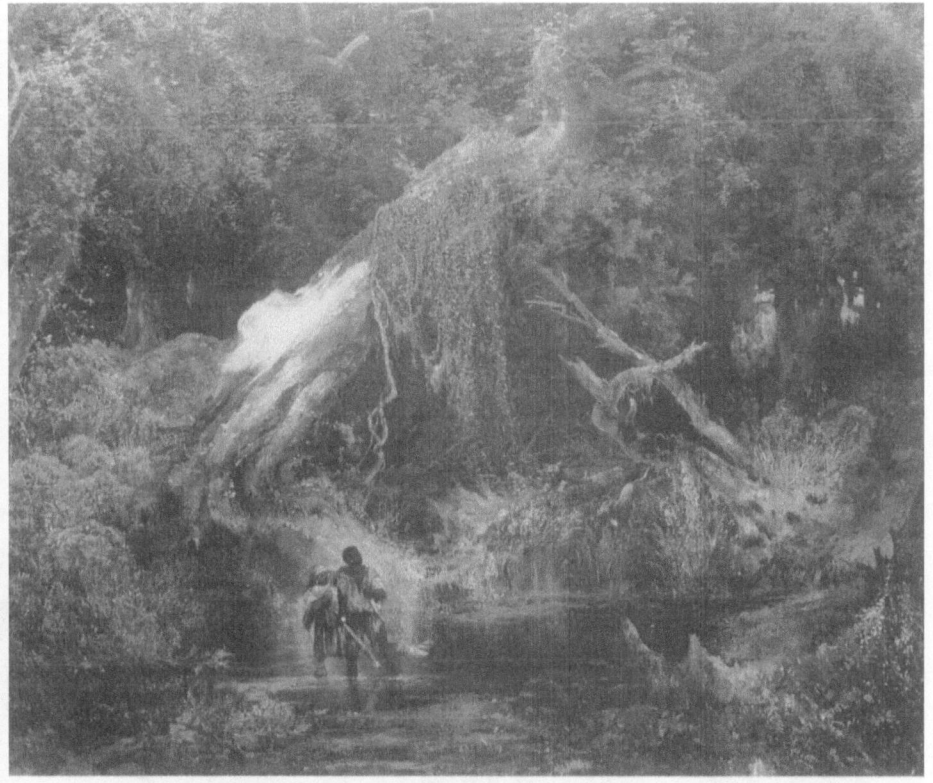

2-47. Thomas Moran, *Slaves Escaping through the Swamp,* 1863. Oil on canvas, 38 × 44 in. The Philbrook Museum of Art, Tulsa, Oklahoma.

Native Americans and persons of European descent. Although this has been a long-established theme in American art—see, for instance, *Escape of General Israel Putnam from the Indians* [101]—it flourished especially during the half-century following 1870 when western American art emerged as a powerful and popular genre.

Artistic approaches to the conflict of wills have varied widely. In *A Disputed Passage* by Jules Tavernier (fig. 2-50), Indians ambush a wagon train struggling through a deep and densely forested canyon. Frederic Remington, needless to say, painted many aspects of this theme, such as *Return of the Blackfoot War Party* (1887) and *The Quest* (c. 1902), which depicts federal troops *en file* accompanied by Indian scouts.[102]

One of the grimmest and most explicit expressions of the genre is *The*

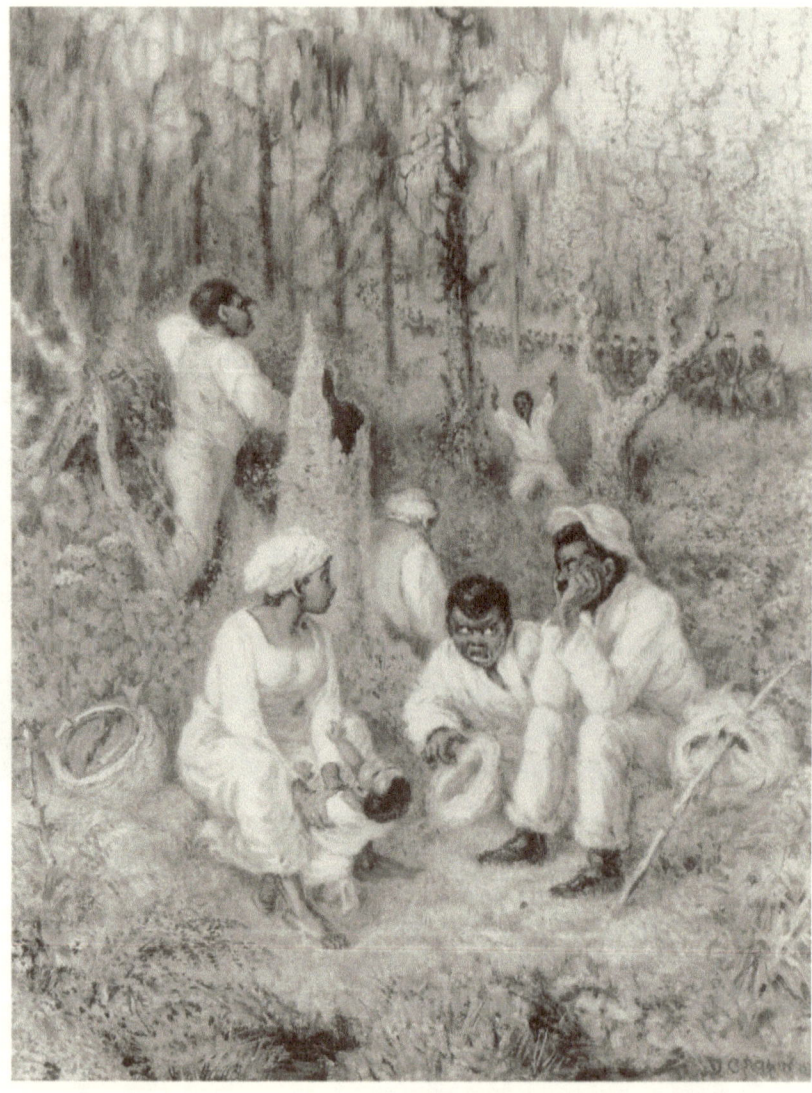

2-48. David Edward Cronin, *Fugitive Slaves in the Dismal Swamp, Virginia*, 1888. Oil on canvas, 14 × 17 in. The New-York Historical Society, New York.

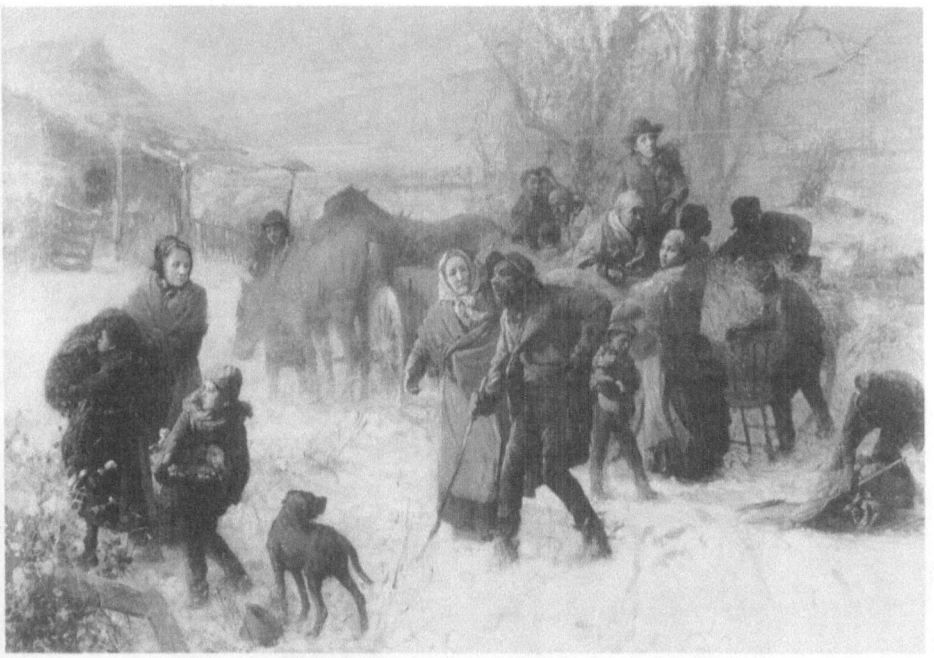

2-49. Charles T. Webber, *The Underground Railroad,* 1893. Oil on canvas, 53 3/16 × 76 1/8 in. Cincinnati Art Museum. Subscription Fund Purchase.

End by Charles Schreyvogel (fig. 2-51), which may have an autobiographical aspect because it was painted in 1912, the artist's last year. Violence— imagined, actual, or potential—recurs constantly in the western experience; and the imminence of an unnatural death became one of the most prominent "migratory emotions" in American art.

When Walt Kuhn undertook his "Imaginary History of the West," a series of twenty-nine paintings completed between 1918 and 1920, representative subjects included *Indian Raid* (fig. 2-52) and *Attack on the Stage Coach* (fig. 2-53). The former is reminiscent of John Vanderlyn's famous massacre scene, *The Murder of Jane McCrea* (1803–1805).[103]

Finally, and ever so fully, migratory emotions have been dominant themes in the life work of Jacob Lawrence, the contemporary African-American artist. His interest in black history has been manifest ever since 1938–1939, when he prepared his *Frederick Douglass* series (fig. 2-54). In 1940–1941 he undertook an even more ambitious series of sixty paintings

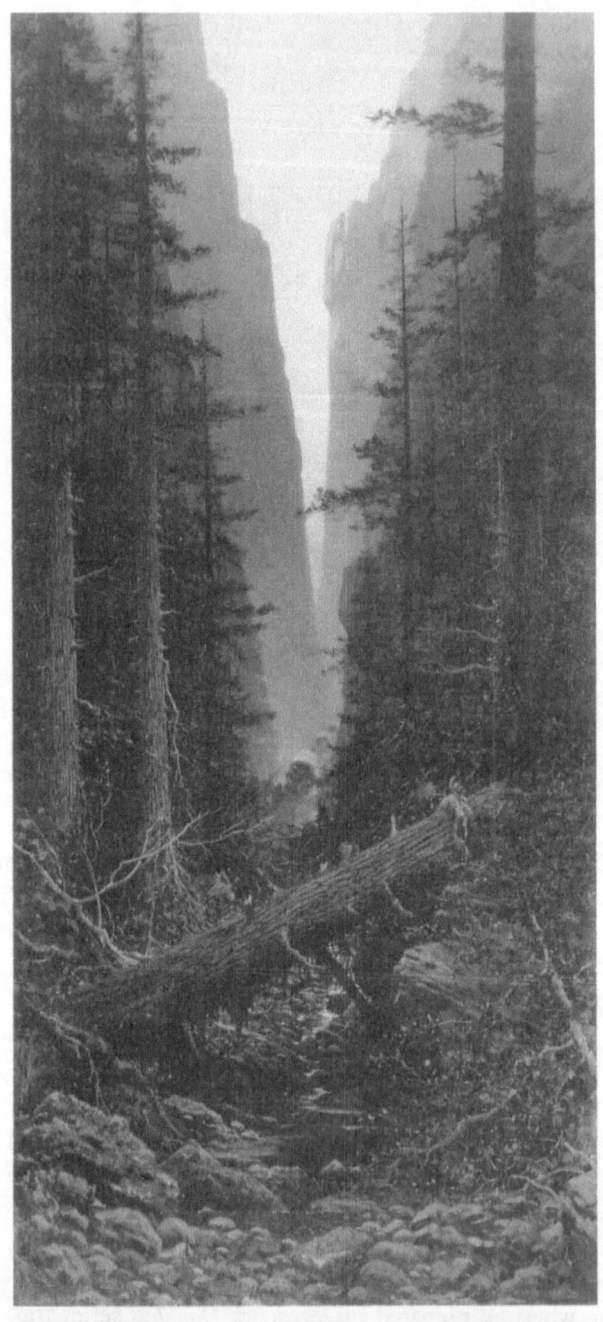

2-50. Jules Tavernier, *A Disputed Passage,* n.d. Oil on canvas, 50 × 24 in. The Thomas Gilcrease Institute of American History and Art, Tulsa, Oklahoma.

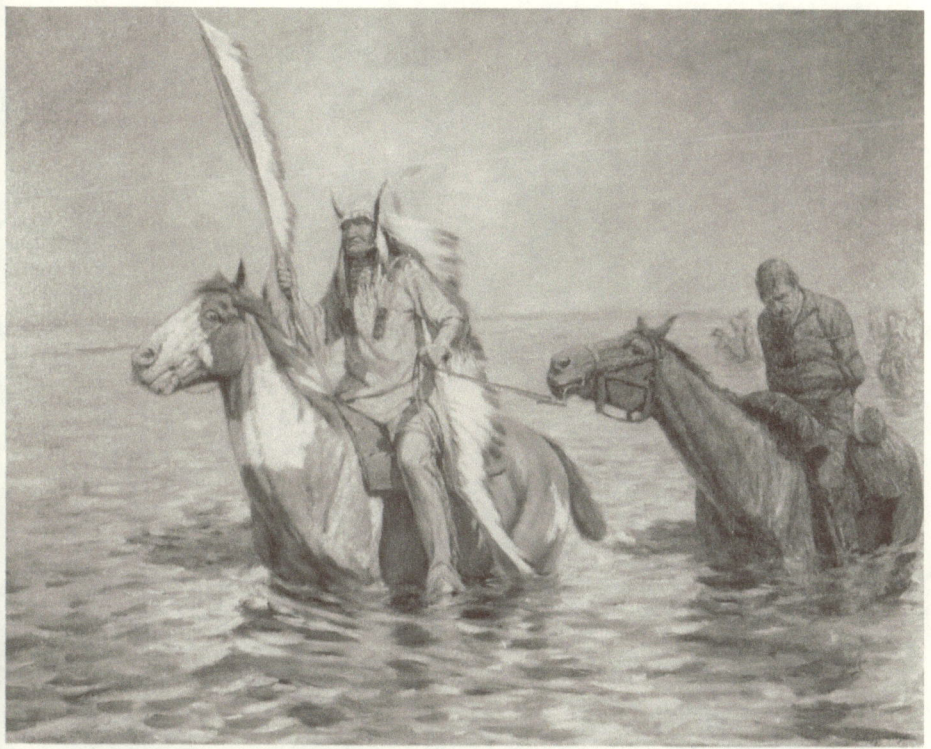

2-51. Charles Schreyvogel, *The End,* 1912. Oil on canvas, 53 × 40 in. The Thomas Gilcrease Institute of American History and Art, Tulsa, Oklahoma.

titled *The Migration of the Negro* (figs. 2-55 and 2-56), in which his intense use of primary colors and a flat, cubist style produce a vigorous sense of movement through space and time and communicate "migratory emotions" in powerful ways.[104]

This *Migration* series received immediate acclaim in November 1941 when it was exhibited at the Downtown Gallery in New York City. As though the twenty-four-year-old had been foredestined for impact, *Fortune* magazine reproduced twenty-four pictures from the series in its November issue that year. Lawrence's comment on his *Toussaint L'Ouverture* series in 1940 is equally applicable to this series and resonates as well with Courbet's famous statement about the contemporaneity of history: "I didn't do it just as a historical thing, but because I believe these things tie up with the Negro today."[105]

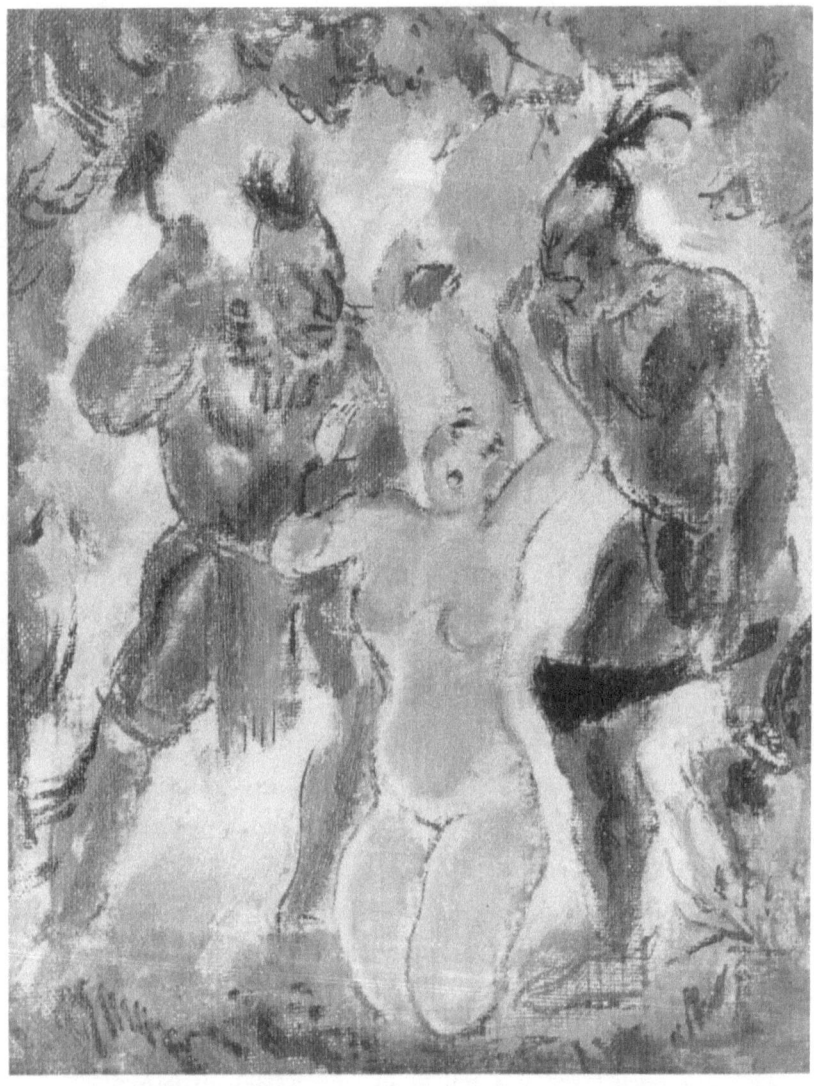

2-52. Walt Kuhn, *Indian Raid,* 1920. Oil on canvas, 11 × 9 in. Colorado Springs Fine Arts Center, Gift of Brenda and Vera Kuhn.

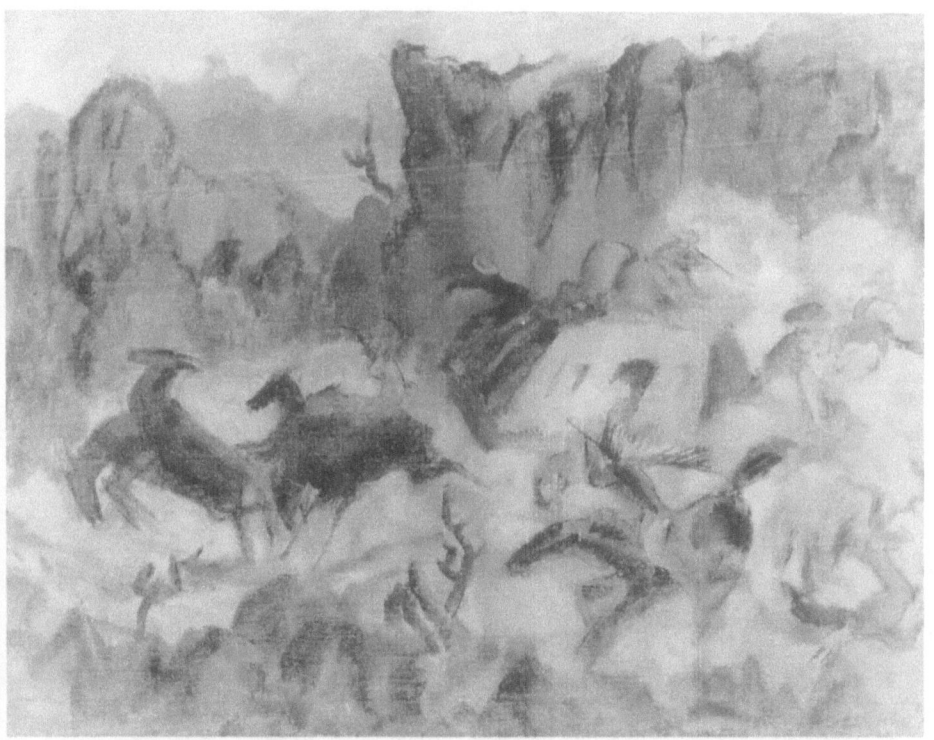

2-53. Walt Kuhn, *Attack on the Stage Coach*, 1918. Oil on canvas, 14 × 19 in. Colorado Springs Fine Arts Center, Gift of Brenda and Vera Kuhn.

Lawrence painted thirty-one panels of his *Harriet Tubman* series in 1939–1940. Subsequently, in 1967, when he was invited to prepare a children's book (his first), Lawrence returned to the Tubman story because, in his words, "it is a dramatic tale of flight and fugitives." The illustrations for *Harriet and the Promised Land* are packed with movement through space and time, as well as emotion.[106] Lawrence encountered publishing barriers, however, that censored certain historical realities. Harriet Tubman had actually carried a gun, for example; but that seemed inappropriate in a childrens' book. Lawrence compromised for the publication but painted several Tubman pictures to satisfy himself. In one of the most powerful, called *Forward* (fig. 2-57), Tubman holds a gun in her right hand.[107]

In 1973 Lawrence returned once again to historical narrative in general and migratory emotions in particular. The State of Washington commis-

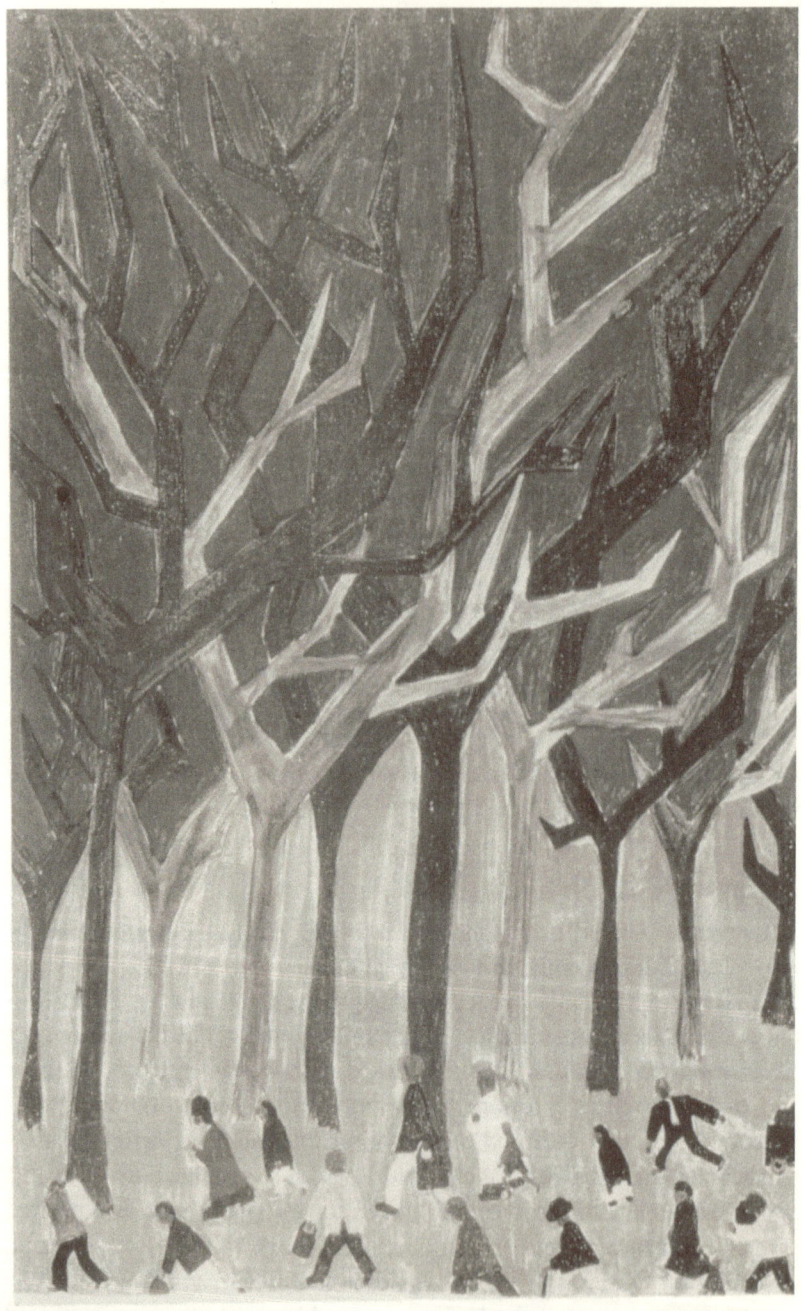

2-54. Jacob Lawrence, *Frederick Douglass* Series, 1938–1939, Panel No. 29, *The War Was Over,* 1938–1939. Casein on gessoed hardboard, 17 7/8 × 12 in. Hampton University Museum, Hampton, Virginia.

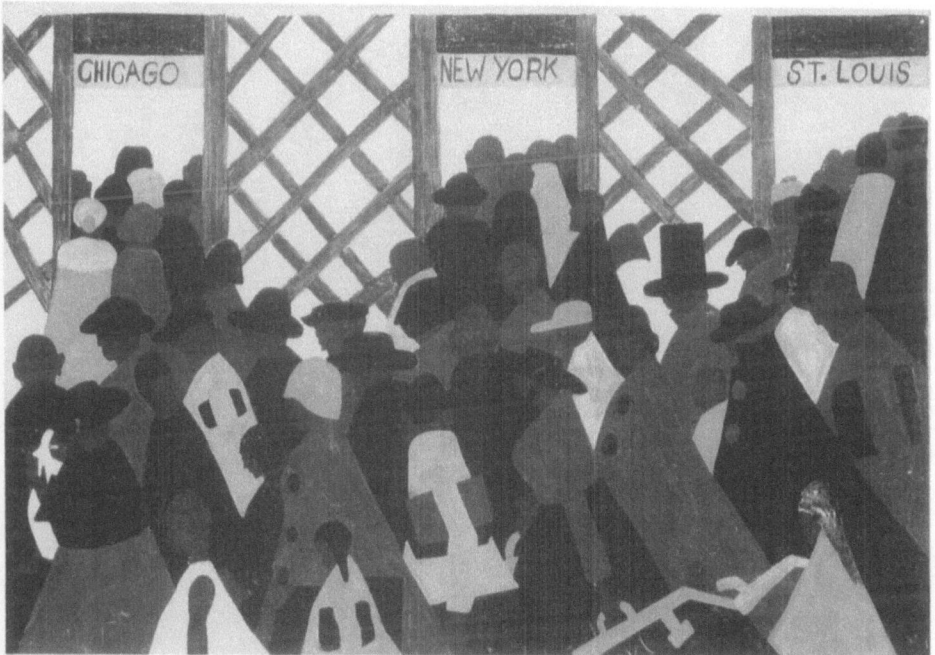

2-55. Jacob Lawrence, *The Migration of the Negro,* Panel No. 1, 1940–1941. Tempera on masonite, 12 × 18 in. © The Phillips Collection, Washington, D.C.

sioned Lawrence (who had permanently relocated from New York to Seattle in 1971) to paint a series for the State Capitol in Olympia. His chosen subject was George Washington Bush, an African-American explorer and pioneer very much in the mold of Daniel Boone. Bush leads his band over the Oregon Trail (and across five panels) with such captions as this one for Panel 2: "In the Iowa Territory, they rendez-voused with a wagon train headed for the Oregon Trail."[108]

In 1940 Lawrence explained that he had "always been interested in history, but they never taught Negro history in the public schools. . . . It was never studied seriously like regular subjects."[109] In that same year, 1940, William H. Johnson painted *Going to Church* (fig. 2-58) in a manner more placid than (yet allied with) Lawrence's. There is thematic continuity, moreover, with the well-established motif of *Going to Worship* in American art (see fig. 2-16).

If we harken back to the nineteenth century, however, we should close

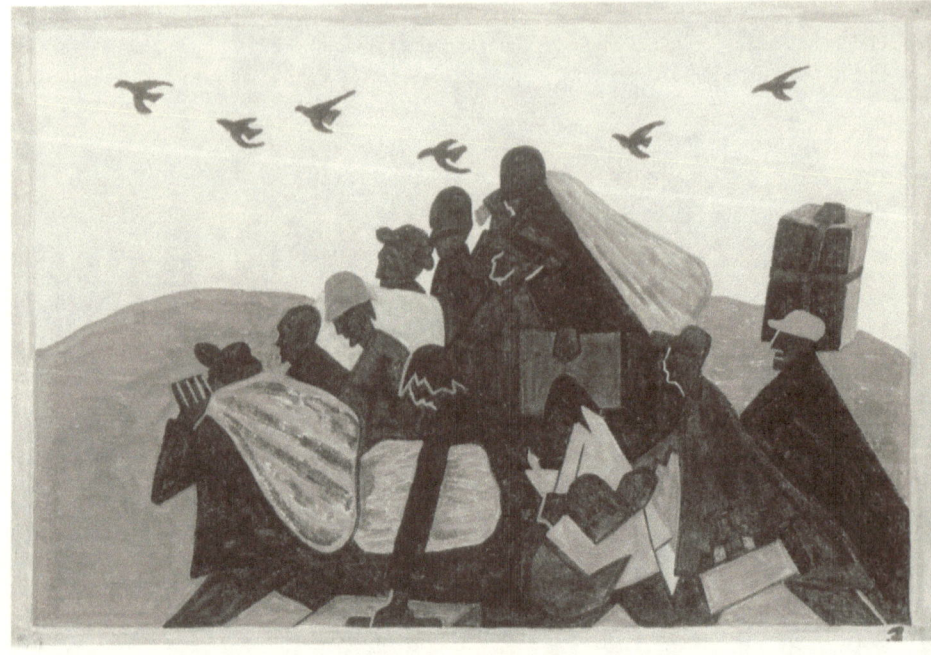

2-56. Jacob Lawrence, *The Migration of the Negro,* Panel No. 3, 1940–1941. Tempera on masonite, 12 × 18 in. © The Phillips Collection, Washington, D.C.

this section with homage to an enigmatic painting that, in my view, has never been adequately understood. *Ellen's Isle* (fig. 2-59) was the work of Robert S. Duncanson, the son of a Scottish-Canadian white father and a mulatto mother. As a landscape painter he is regarded as the earliest African-American to achieve artistic mastery and distinction. Although *Ellen's Isle* has usually been interpreted as an allusion to "The Lady of the Lake" by Sir Walter Scott, I am persuaded that it is very much an American historical landscape with a racial message.[110]

When we look carefully at the composition we find that all of the figures in the foreground boat, which is bathed in light, are white; and they face the viewer. All six figures in the shaded boat in the middle distance have their backs to us, but they appear to be black. The more prominent boat is moving vigorously, whereas the second one seems to be scarcely moving at all. Finally, the bright boat is deliberately putting distance between itself and the shadowy boat. If we recall that by 1870 Reconstruction had begun to fail, that whites (North as well as South) *did* want to distance them-

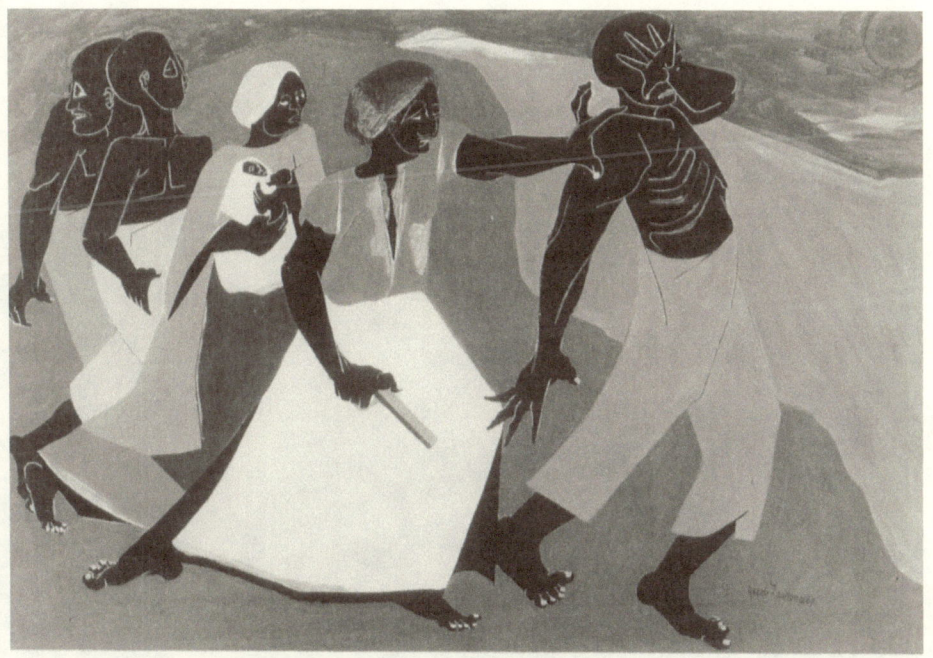

2-57. Jacob Lawrence, *Forward*, 1967. Egg tempera on gesso panel, 24 × 35 3/4 in. North Carolina Museum of Art, purchased with funds from the State of North Carolina.

selves from blacks, and that most freedmen were quite literally going no-where, I am persuaded that this is a painting about a critical moment in the history of American race relations rather than a fantasy embroidered upon the work of Sir Walter Scott.

William Gerdts has made the important observation that American painters tended to blur traditional European distinctions between history and genre painting.[111] I would like to add that we have also done the same with respect to history and landscape art.[112] It is that conflation of time and space into singular artistic statements that has not yet received due notice.

Coda: Modern Artists Moving through Space and Time

In 1940 Stuart Davis asserted that "an artist who has traveled on a steam train, driven an automobile, or flown in an airplane doesn't feel the same

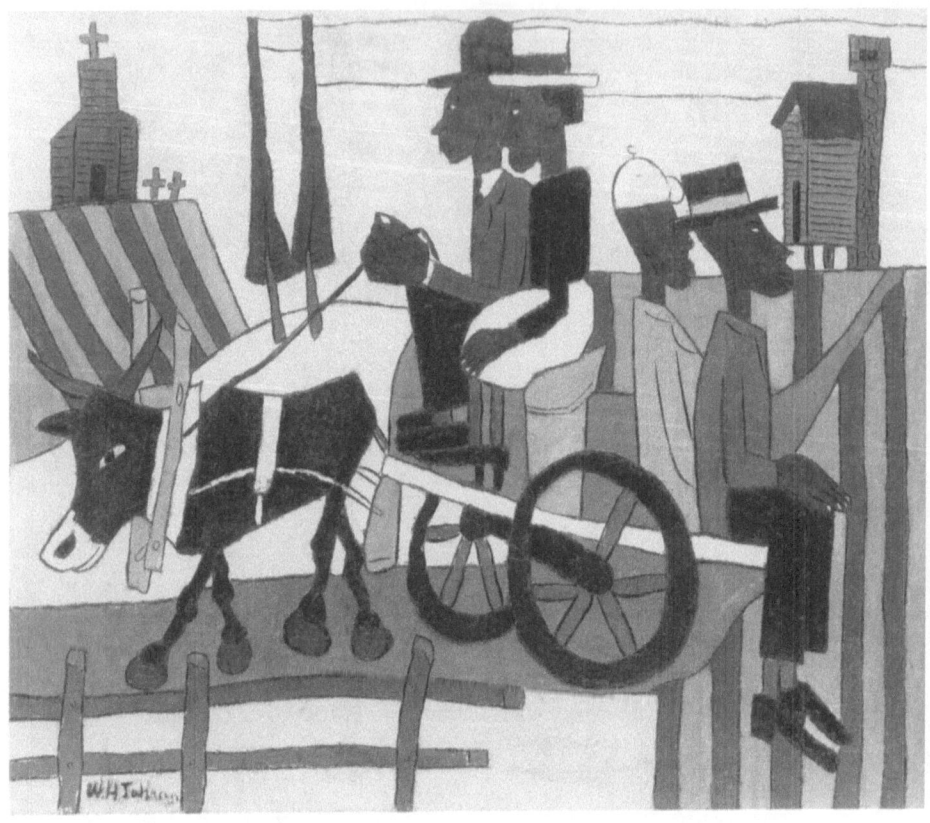

2-58. William H. Johnson, *Going to Church,* c. 1940. Oil on burlap, 38 1/8 × 44 1/8 in. National Museum of American Art, Smithsonian Institution. Gift of the Harmon Foundation.

way about form and space as one who has not." Three years later, describing "things which have made me want to paint," Davis specified "fast travel by train, auto, and aeroplane which brought new and multiple perspectives."[113]

It seems altogether fitting to conclude this essay with a few pages on the more personal meaning of time, space, and migratory emotions for American artists in the twentieth century. It is difficult to imagine, for example, a more peripatetic or emotion-laden existence than Marsden Hartley's: born in Lewiston, Maine, in 1877, he spent his teen years largely in Cleveland, received artistic training in New York City, and made the first of many

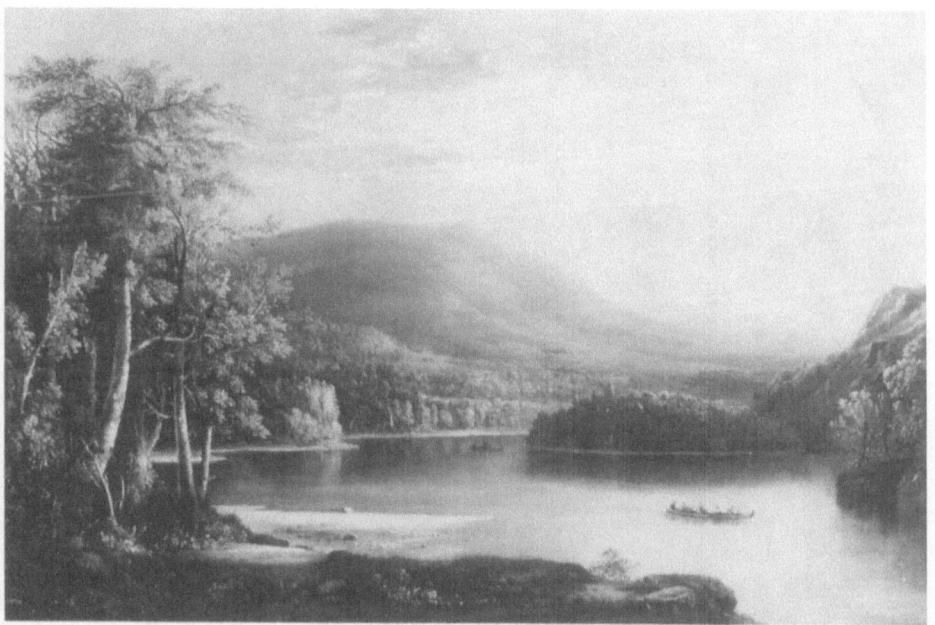

2-59. Robert S. Duncanson, *Ellen's Isle,* c. 1870. Oil on canvas, 28 1/2 × 49 in. © The Detroit Institute of Arts. Gift of the Estate of Razelmond D. Parker.

trips to Europe in 1912, when he was warmly received in Paris by Gertrude and Leo Stein. After moving on to Berlin for a period, he traveled extensively in the United States. This pattern of relentless movement, and his particular ambivalence about the Southwest, is reflected in one of his most attractive paintings, *Last of New England—The Beginning of New Mexico* (fig. 2-60). Interestingly enough, however, his return to Maine in the later years of his life stimulated new creative powers.[114]

We have already discussed Walt Kuhn, who said that his "Imaginary History of the West" series (1918–1920) was "painted from memory from material gathered out of books about the pioneer west." Kuhn, like Hartley, was born in 1877, but in Brooklyn, New York. At the age of twenty-four, after wandering out west for a while, Kuhn also went to study in Europe. Following sojourns in Paris and Munich, he returned to New York City, settled down, and began to reflect upon the significance of his travels. John Quinn's reaction in 1920 to Kuhn's "Imaginary History" paintings is noteworthy: "They give us back a vision of a van-

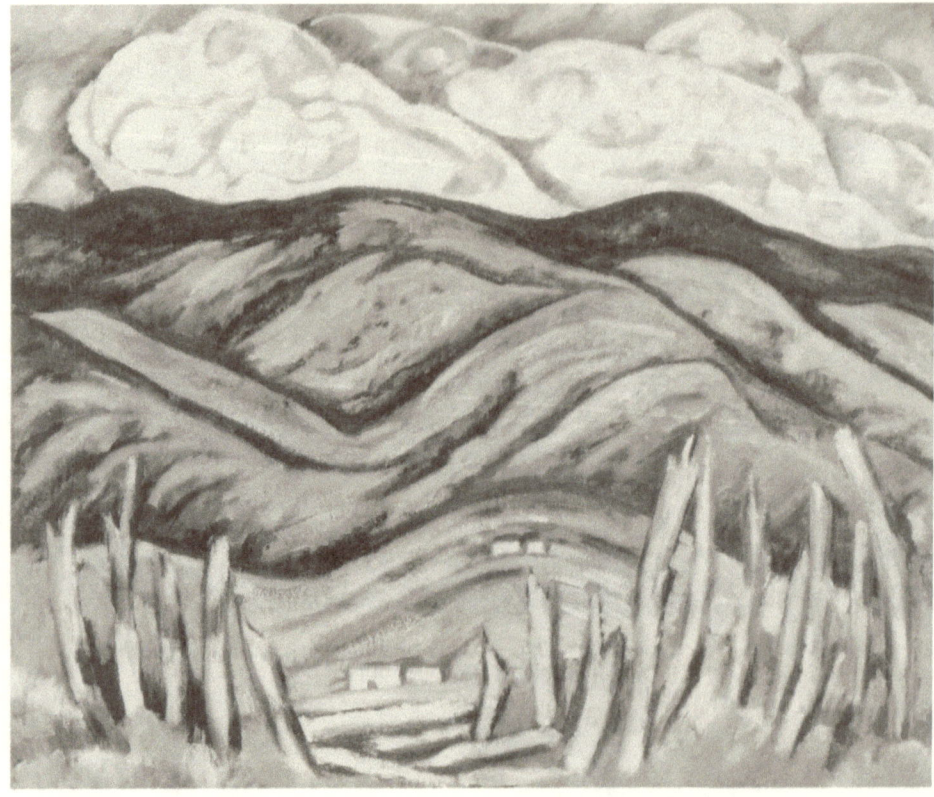

2-60. Marsden Hartley, *Last of New England—The Beginning of New Mexico,* c. 1920. Oil on cardboard, 24 × 30 in. Alfred Stieglitz Collection, 1949.546. Photograph © 1990, The Art Institute of Chicago. All Rights Reserved.

ished life that was not all comedy or all tragedy, but something strangely mixed." [115]

As we have also seen, Thomas Hart Benton was equally intrigued by the American past and devoted much of his time and energy during the 1920s to his "American Historical Epic," a monumental narrative mural, projected for sixty-four panels, for which he never found a permanent site. He referred to groups of panels as "chapters" and conceived of the epic as a people's history enacted by bands of anonymous pioneers who casually committed injustices while subjugating Indians and blacks. In 1924 he finally got the chance to display his first five-part "chapter" at the Architectural League in New York City. The second "chapter," called *Colonial Expansion,* was exhibited three years later at the New Gallery; but then the project began to lose steam as Benton's energies and attention moved in other directions.[116]

Those directions included all points of the compass, from Cape Cod to the Southwest, because Benton was an incredibly restless man: a stereotype, if not the prototype, of Tocqueville's caricature a century earlier. Benton begins chapter three of his autobiography, "On Going Places," with these words: "We Americans are restless. We cannot stay put. Our history is mainly one of migrations."[117] The autobiography is even structured in terms of simultaneous movement through space and time, with successive chapters titled "The Mountains," "The Rivers," "The South," "The West," and "Back to Missouri." The point of Benton's perpetual motion, more often than not, was to seek the meaning of America in its people and to sketch them. Thus his wanderlust had vocational motives along with a kind of uncontrollable personal gyroscope.

Perhaps I can close with one last icon that is symbolic of the American artist's quest for experience, for subjects, and for the diversity of a vast land. Peter Blume was born in Russia in 1906, came to the United States five years later, and eventually settled in Sherman, Connecticut. His *South of Scranton* (fig. 2-61) is more than a marvelous fantasy; it is a synoptic diary of an actual automobile trip. Blume depicts his drive to the coalfields near Scranton, then down to the steel mills at Bethlehem, and eventually south by way of the Shenandoah Valley to Charleston, South Carolina, where he watched sailors on a battleship "doing complicated calisthenic exercises on its enormous deck—making a curious contrast with the atmosphere of the old town."[118]

In 1947 Denis de Rougement utilized a wonderful double entendre in describing us as a people of the road. The American way of life, he observed, is literally *sa route de vie.*[119]

For much too long, history painting in the United States has been defined in conventional terms of tragic, noble, or heroic events set somewhere in a detached past that is clearly discrete from the present. I prefer to think about history painting in terms of a felicitous phrase that Henry James used in *The Golden Bowl:* successions of consciousness. That is what Arthur Bowen Davies's haunting picture *Meadows of Memory* is all about. I also find successions of consciousness apropos for both the artists *and* their subjects where movement through time and space has been an abiding concern.

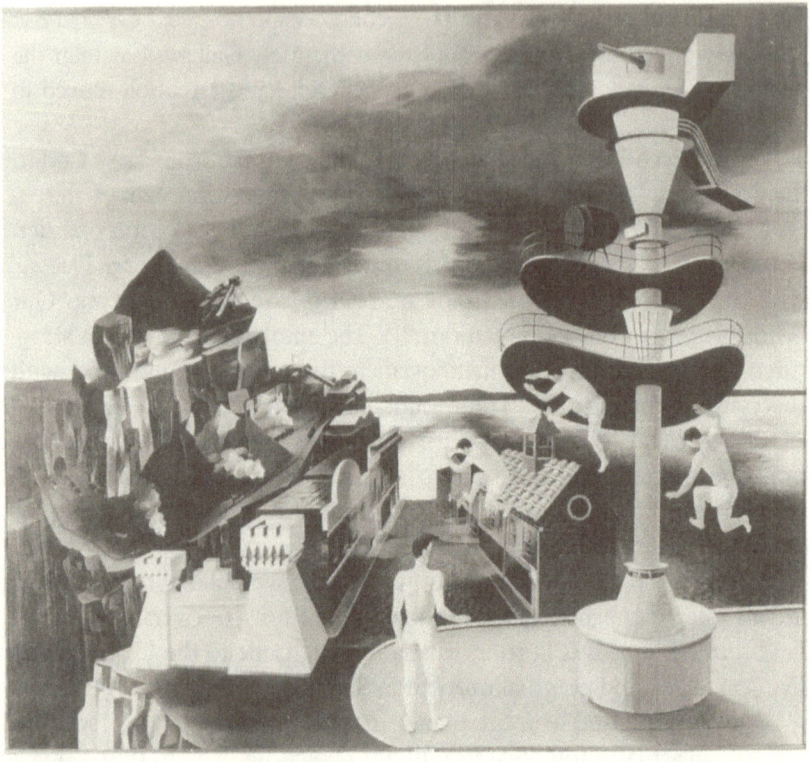

2-61. Peter Blume, *South of Scranton,* 1931. Oil on canvas, 56 × 66 in. The Metropolitan Museum of Art, New York. George A. Hearn Fund, 1942.

Notes

1. Thornton Wilder, "Toward an American Language," *Atlantic Monthly* 190 (July 1952): 31.

2. In addition to the extraordinary number of paintings devoted to the landing of Columbus in 1492, see Emanuel Leutze, *The Landing of the Norsemen* (c. 1845), in Barbara S. Groseclose, *Emanuel Leutze, 1816–1868: Freedom Is the Only King* (Washington, D.C., 1975), p. 75; Robert W. Weir, *The Landing of Henry Hudson* (c. 1838), in William H. Truettner, "The Art of History: American Exploration and Discovery Scenes, 1840–1860," *American Art Journal* 14 (Winter 1982): 5; Michele Felice Corné, *The Landing of the Pilgrims* (c. 1809), in the Diplomatic Reception Rooms, Department of State, Washington, D.C.; Samuel F. B. Morse, *Landing of the Pilgrims at Plymouth* (c. 1810–1811), in the Boston Public Library, Charlestown Branch; the Pilgrim landing rendered on various pieces of transfer-printed earthenware made for export from Staffordshire (c. 1819–1840), various examples of which are

in the Henry Ford Museum, Dearborn, Michigan; Erastus Dow Palmer, *Landing of the Pilgrims* (1857), pediment group in clay, Albany Institute of Art, Albany, New York; Emanuel Leutze, *The Founding of Maryland* (1860), in Groseclose, *Emanuel Leutze*, pp. 58, 93–94.

3. Quoted in Jerome Hamilton Buckley, *The Triumph of Time: A Study of the Victorian Concepts of Time, History, Progress, and Decadence* (Cambridge, Mass., 1966), p. 54. See also Ralph Waldo Emerson's observation in 1844 that the railroad and the steamship had "given a new celerity to *time*"; "The Young American" in Emerson, *Nature, Addresses, and Lectures*, ed. Robert E. Spiller (Cambridge, Mass., 1979), pp. 223, 226.

4. See, e.g., Peter Paul Rubens, *Return of Peasants from Work*, Pitti Palace, Florence, Italy; Jan Both, *Travellers in an Italian Landscape* (c. 1648–1650), Toledo Museum of Art, Toledo, Ohio.

5. Cole is in the Metropolitan Museum of Art, New York; for Homer see Christie's auction catalogue *Important American Paintings, Drawings and Sculpture of the Nineteenth and Twentieth Centuries*, May 26, 1988, no. 132.

6. Richard J. Boyle et al., *In This Academy: The Pennsylvania Academy of the Fine Arts, 1805–1976. A Special Bicentennial Exhibition* (Philadelphia, 1976), pp. 100, 122.

7. David C. Huntington, *The Landscapes of Frederic Edwin Church: Vision of an American Era* (New York, 1966), pp. 27–28, is rather dismissive of this painting; but if it is an "immature" work by Church (his first ambitious landscape), it nonetheless depicts an important episode in the history of immature New England. It clearly had special significance for the artist as well, because one of Hooker's forebears had been a founder of Hartford.

8. Quoted in Boyle et al., *In This Academy*, p. 100.

9. Jared B. Flagg, *The Life and Letters of Washington Allston* (1892: New York, 1969), p. 72; John W. McCoubrey, ed., *American Art, 1700–1960: Sources and Documents* (Englewood Cliffs, N.J., 1965), pp. 133–134. See also Charles Lanman, "Our National Paintings," *Crayon* 1 (Feb. 28, 1855): 136–137.

10. William Gilmore Simms, *Views and Reviews in American Literature, History, and Fiction*, 1st series, ed. C. Hugh Holman (Cambridge, Mass., 1962), p. 87; "The Conditions of Art in America," *North American Review* 102 (Jan. 1866): 22.

11. George Inness, "A Painter on Painting," *Harper's New Monthly Magazine* 56 (Feb. 1878): 458–461. Frederick Jackson Turner frequently described the American frontier experience as a process of change.

12. Quoted in Boyle et al., *In This Academy*, p. 100.

13. Motley F. Deakin, ed., *The Home Book of the Picturesque: Or American Scenery, Art, and Literature* . . . (1852: Gainesville, Fla., 1967); William H. Gerdts, "American Landscape Painting: Critical Judgments, 1730–1845," *American Art Journal* 17 (Winter 1985): 28–59; William S. Talbot, "American Visions of Wilderness," *Bulletin of the Cleveland Museum of Art* 56 (Apr. 1969): 151–166.

14. McCoubrey, ed., *American Art, 1700–1960*, pp. 43, 102, 104–105, 108–109; Durand's "Letters on Landscape Painting" appeared in regular installments in the

Crayon during 1855. The quotation is taken from 1 (May 2, 1855): 275. See also the observation made by F. C. Adams in 1870, quoted in William H. Gerdts and Mark Thistlethwaite, *Grand Illusions: History Painting in America* (Fort Worth, 1988), pp. 34, 51.

15. See Frank H. Goodyear, Jr., "American Landscape Painting, 1795–1875," in Boyle et al., *In This Academy*, pp. 124–141; Barbara Novak, *Nature and Culture: American Landscape and Painting, 1825–1875* (New York, 1980).

16. See Richard J. Koke, comp., *American Landscape and Genre Paintings in the New-York Historical Society* (Boston, 1982), 1:45; Susan Danly Walther, *The Railroad in the American Landscape: 1850–1950* (Wellesley, Mass., 1981), p. 50; John D. Unruh, Jr., *The Plains Across: The Overland Emigrants and the Trans-Mississippi West, 1840–1860* (Urbana, 1979), pp. 49–50.

17. McCoubrey, ed., *American Art, 1700–1960*, pp. 93–95.

18. Quoted in Lee Clark Mitchell, *Witnesses to a Vanishing America: The Nineteenth-Century Response* (Princeton, 1981), p. 72. See also pp. 35–40, "Painters as Historians of the Wilderness."

19. Bingham to J. S. Rollins, June 19, 1871, quoted in Albert Christ-Janer, *George Caleb Bingham of Missouri: The Story of an Artist* (New York, 1940), pp. 109–110.

20. E. Maurice Bloch, *The Paintings of George Caleb Bingham: A Catalogue Raisonné* (Columbia, Mo., 1986), pp. 92, 172, 200.

21. In Deakin, ed., *The Home Book of the Picturesque*, pp. 119, 133–134. See also George W. Bethune, "Art in the United States," in ibid., pp. 186–188; and Georgia Stamm Chamberlain, *Studies on John Gadsby Chapman: American Artist, 1808–1889* (Annandale, Va., 1963), p. 22.

22. Quoted in Gerdts and Thistlethwaite, *Grand Illusions*, p. 45. In April 1869, *Appleton's Journal* rejected the John Trumbull approach to historical art—heroic figures participating in epic events in the receding past—and offered up a paraphrase of Courbet as an original insight: "Historical art is the best *contemporary* art. . . ." Ibid., p. 112.

23. Ann Uhry Abrams, *The Valiant Hero: Benjamin West and Grand-Style History Painting* (Washington, D.C., 1985).

24. Truettner, "The Art of History," pp. 5–6, 10, 31.

25. Quoted in George W. Pierson, *The Moving American* (New York, 1973), pp. 8, 162.

26. Ibid., p. x. See also George Heard Hamilton, "Cézanne, Bergson, and the Image of Time," *College Art Journal* 16 (Fall 1956): 2–12; John Golding, *Cubism: A History and an Analysis, 1907–1914* (London, 1959), p. 185.

27. See, especially, Thistlethwaite, "The Most Important Themes: History Painting and Its Place in American Art," chap. 1 in Gerdts and Thistlethwaite, *Grand Illusions;* Truettner, "The Art of History."

28. Michael Kammen, *A Season of Youth: The American Revolution and the His-

torical Imagination (New York, 1978), chap. 3; Kammen, *Spheres of Liberty: Changing Perceptions of Liberty in American Culture* (Madison, Wis., 1986), pp. 54–64, 175–180; Kammen, *Sovereignty and Liberty: Constitutional Discourse in American Culture* (Madison, Wis., 1988), pp. 33–42, 126–136.

29. For historical art inspired by Longfellow's "The Courtship of Miles Standish" (1858), see David C. Huntington et al., *The Quest for Unity: American Art Between World's Fairs, 1876–1893* (Detroit, 1983), pp. 50–51, 89.

30. For additional information concerning the episode and the print, see *Philadelphia, Three Centuries of American Art: Bicentennial Exhibition, April 11– October 10, 1976* (Philadelphia, 1976), pp. 84–86.

31. Alfred Frankenstein, *William Sidney Mount* (New York, 1975), p. 376 and fig. 131 on p. 369. For a delightful "primitive" painting of one of Washington's most historic passages (from Mount Vernon to New York in order to be inaugurated in 1789), see J. Califano, *Washington's Reception at Trenton* (1889), oil on canvas, in Sotheby Parke Bernet sale catalogue, *Fine Americana*, May 3, 1980, no. 234.

32. See *Philadelphia, Three Centuries of American Art*, p. 181. For a historic, two-mile parade of a very different sort, see *The Procession of Victuallers of Philadelphia*, an aquatint and etching by Joseph Yeager (1821) after a lost painting by John Lewis Krimmel. The occasion was the largest exhibition of livestock ever driven to market, "which for number, quality, beauty and variety has never been slaughtered at any one time in this, or probably in any other country." Ibid., pp. 253–254.

33. See Paul Russell Cutright, *A History of the Lewis and Clark Journals* (Norman, Okla., 1976); and John Seelye, "Beyond the Shining Mountains: The Lewis and Clark Expedition as an Enlightenment Epic," *Virginia Quarterly Review* 63 (Winter 1987): 36–53. For an attractive landscape that is sui generis in our imaginative iconography, see Thomas Hart Benton, *Lewis and Clark at Eagle Creek* (1965), in Matthew Baigell, *Thomas Hart Benton* (New York, 1973), plate 135.

34. Jefferson to Congress, Jan. 18, 1803, in *The Works of Thomas Jefferson*, ed. Paul Leicester Ford (New York, 1905), 9:433–434.

35. Jefferson to Lewis, June 20, 1803, in ibid., pp. 423–428.

36. See *Masterpieces of the American West: Selections from the Anschutz Collection* (Denver, 1983), plate 7; Patricia Hills, *The American Frontier: Images and Myths* (New York, 1973), figs. 17–18.

37. Henry Tuckerman, "Over the Mountains," in Deakin, ed., *The Home Book of the Picturesque*, p. 123.

38. See, e.g., James Belton, *U.S. Naval Fleet on Lake Champlain* (c. 1817), and [?] Benson, *Lake Champlain, 1813* (1813), depicting a military encampment along the shore of the lake, in Nancy C. Muller, *Paintings and Drawings at the Shelburne Museum* (Shelburne, Vt., 1976), pp. 28–29.

39. See Theodore E. Stebbins, Jr., and Galina Gorokhoff, comps., *A Checklist of American Paintings at Yale University* (New Haven, 1982), p. 119.

40. See James Jackson Jarves, *The Art-Idea*, ed. Benjamin Rowland, Jr. (Cam-

bridge, Mass., 1960), p. 197; Martha Hutson, "American Narrative Painting. The Painter's America: Rural and Urban Life, 1810–1910," *American Art Review* 1 (Nov. 1974): 95; Gerdts and Thistlethwaite, *Grand Illusions*, pp. 49–50, 110–113.

41. Quoted from A. D. Richardson in James C. Malin, "Mobility and History," *Agricultural History* 17 (Oct. 1943): 180. See also the Metropolitan Museum of Art, *Life in America: A Special Loan Exhibition of Paintings Held During the Period of the New York World's Fair* (New York, 1939), pp. 137–151; and the apt quotation from *Appleton's Journal* (1869) in Gerdts and Thistlethwaite, *Grand Illusions*, p. 112.

42. See Julian Grossman, *Echo of a Distant Drum: Winslow Homer and the Civil War* (New York, 1974); Christopher Kent Wilson, "Winslow Homer's *The Veteran in a New Field:* A Study of the Harvest Metaphor and Popular Culture," *American Art Journal* 17 (Autumn 1985): 2–27, and especially (on pp. 12–14) two works by Thomas Nast that appeared in 1864: "Going to the War" and "Returning from the War."

43. *A Catalogue of the Collection of American Paintings in the Corcoran Gallery of Art* (Washington, D.C., 1966), 1:78, 102; Bloch, *George Caleb Bingham*, p. 223; Franz Stenzel, *James Madison Alden: Yankee Artist of the Pacific Coast, 1854–1860* (Fort Worth, 1975), chap. 4; Gerdts and Thistlethwaite, *Grand Illusions*, pp. 158–159.

44. James G. Randall, *The Civil War and Reconstruction* (Boston, 1953), p. 570. Edward Hopper loved military history, and between 1934 and 1940 painted several scenes concerning the Battle of Gettysburg. See Gail Levin, *Edward Hopper: The Art and the Artist* (New York, 1980), pp. 262–263.

45. See William S. McFeely, *Grant: A Biography* (New York, 1981), chap. 26, "Around the World."

46. See also George H. Durrie, *Going to Church* (1853), oil on canvas, White House Collection, Washington, D.C. Worshipers are arriving on sleighs, in the snow, at a yellow clapboard church in rural New England.

47. For a fine yet unknown example, see Mrs. Ayers Butterfield, *Old Ferryboat on the Merrimack River* (nineteenth century), Littlefield Public Library, Tyngsborough, Massachusetts. And see Joseph Pennell, *The Trains That Come and the Trains That Go* (1919), Philadelphia Museum of Art. The etching depicts the interior of the Pennsylvania Railroad Station in Philadelphia.

48. Some examples would include James McDougal Hart, *Sunday After the Meeting* (n.d.), Detroit Institute of Arts; Winslow Homer, *Crossing the Pasture* (c. 1872), Amon Carter Museum, Fort Worth, Texas; John George Brown, *The Country Gallants* (1876), Toledo Museum of Art, Toledo, Ohio, in which adolescents cross a shallow country stream by walking on a long dead log; and Edward Lamson Henry, *The Itinerant Peddler Displaying His Wares* (1887), in *The Magazine Antiques* 134 (Sept. 1988): 471.

49. See Patrick Campbell, *Travels in the Interior Inhabited Parts of North America in the Years 1791 and 1792 . . .* (Edinburgh, 1793), which includes a fold-out engraving, "Plan of an American New Cleared Farm," in which two boats pass in opposite directions in front of newly cleared fields; Patricia Anderson, *The Course*

of Empire: The Erie Canal and the New York Landscape, 1825–1875 (Rochester, N.Y., 1984).

50. See Nicolai Cikovsky, Jr., "George Inness and the Hudson River School: *The Lackawanna Valley*," *American Art Journal* 2 (Fall 1970): 56; Walther, *Railroad in the American Landscape*, pp. 68–71; Frederic Remington, *A Fur Train from the Far North* (1888), in Mitchell, *Witnesses to a Vanishing America*, p. 81; Colin C. Cooper, *Old Grand Central Station* (1906), in *The American Painting Collection of the Montclair Art Museum* (Montclair, N.J., 1977), p. 90.

51. Benton, *An Artist in America*, 4th ed. (Columbia, Mo., 1983), pp. 70–71. At the close of the nineteenth century Worthington Whittredge remarked that "great railroads were opened through the most magnificent *scenery* the world ever saw, and the brush of the landscape painter was needed immediately." McCoubrey, ed., *American Art, 1700–1960*, p. 120.

52. Cooper, "American and European Scenery Compared," in Deakin, ed., *Home Book of the Picturesque*, p. 65. See also Brantz Mayer, "A June Jaunt," *Harper's New Monthly Magazine* 14 (Apr. 1857): 592–612. Sigmund Freud remarked during the later 1890s that "Moods change like the landscapes before the traveler on a train." Quoted in Peter Gay, *Freud: A Life for Our Time* (New York, 1988), p. 99.

53. Nathaniel Hawthorne, *The House of the Seven Gables: A Romance* (1851: Boston, 1900), chap. 17.

54. Michel Chevalier, *Society, Manners, and Politics in the United States: Letters on North America*, ed. John William Ward (Ithaca, N.Y., 1961), p. 60.

55. See also Hugh Bolton Jones, *Maryland Tavern* (1876), oil on canvas, in Joseph S. Czestochowski, *The American Landscape Tradition: A Study and Gallery of Paintings* (New York, 1982), p. 105.

56. Lyman Allyn Art Museum, New London, Connecticut. For a similar New England scene half a century later, see Charles Lewis Heyde, *Adirondack Mountains, Burlington Bay Over Willard Street* (1884), Shelburne Museum, Shelburne, Vermont.

57. Donelson F. Hoopes, *American Narrative Painting* (Los Angeles, 1974), pp. 156–157.

58. Toledo Museum of Art, Toledo, Ohio. See also John Steuart Curry, *To the Train* (1932), in Joseph S. Czestochowski, *John Steuart Curry and Grant Wood: A Portrait of Rural America* (Columbia, Mo., 1981), fig. 63.

59. Benton, *An Artist in America*, p. 70. See also Robert Salmon's *Dismal Swamp Canal* (1830), oil on wood panel, Virginia Museum of Fine Arts, Richmond. Two sailboats and a steam-powered excursion vessel are shown passing near a lodging house along the Virginia–North Carolina border. Salmon's ulterior subject was the American ideal of progress. This twenty-two-mile waterway linking the Chesapeake to Albemarle Sound had opened just two years earlier in 1828, the year that Salmon arrived in Boston from England.

60. Quoted in Novak, *Nature and Culture*, p. 175.

61. Daniel Webster highlighted this theme on July 4, 1851, in his final Indepen-

dence Day address. He invoked Bishop Berkeley's "Verses on the Prospect of Planting Arts and Learning in America": "Westward the course of empire takes its way; / The four first acts already past. . . ." See Paul D. Erickson, *The Poetry of Events: Daniel Webster's Rhetoric of the Constitution and the Union* (New York, 1986), pp. 108–109.

62. John Higham, *From Boundlessness to Consolidation: The Transformation of American Culture, 1848–1860* (Ann Arbor, 1969).

63. See Laurence M. Hauptman, "Westward the Course of Empire: Geography Schoolbooks and Manifest Destiny, 1783–1893," *Historian* 40 (May 1978): 423–440; Unruh, *The Plains Across*; Peter D. McClelland and Richard J. Zeckhauser, *Demographic Dimensions of the New Republic: American Interregional Migration, Vital Statistics, and Manumissions, 1800–1860* (Cambridge, Eng., 1982); Morton Owen Schapiro, *Filling Up America: An Economic-Demographic Model of Population Growth and Distribution in the Nineteenth-Century United States* (Greenwich, Conn., 1986).

64. See William Sidney Mount, *California News* (1850), in Frankenstein, *William Sidney Mount*, p. 45.

65. Truettner, "The Art of History: American Exploration and Discovery Scenes, 1840–1860," pp. 19, 31. I wrote those observations quite some time before seeing the controversial exhibition at the National Museum of American Art (March to July 1991) titled "The West as America: Reinterpreting Images of the Frontier, 1820–1920," a show curated by Mr. Truettner. I concur in almost none of the criticisms that have been directed at this fascinating and extremely worthwhile exhibition.

66. See Kent Ladd Steckmesser, *The Western Hero in History and Legend* (Norman, Okla., 1965), pp. 18, 29; Marvin C. Ross, *The West of Alfred Jacob Miller*, 2d ed. (Norman, Okla., 1968), esp. plates 51, 142, and 147; Robert V. Hine, *Bartlett's West: Drawing the Mexican Boundary* (New Haven, 1968), esp. plates 2, 8, and 13; Weston J. Naef et al., *Era of Exploration: The Rise of Landscape Photography in the American West, 1860–1885* (Boston, 1975), esp. pp. 44, 54, 56.

67. See also Peter Rindisbacher, *Red River Carts* (n.d.), pen and ink on paper, Thomas Gilcrease Institute of American History and Art, Tulsa, Oklahoma; Thomas P. Otter, *On the Road* (1860), in Hills, *American Frontier*, fig. 33; Otto Sommer, *Westward Ho!* (1867–1868), in ibid., fig. 54; Albert Bierstadt, *Overland Trail* (1871), in *Masterpieces of the American West: Selections from the Anschutz Collection*, plate 19; Metropolitan Museum of Art, *Life in America*, pp. 101–104; and N. C. Wyeth, *Seeking the New Home* (n.d.), owned by Judy Goffman of New York in 1988.

68. See William T. Ranney, *The Scouting Party* (1851), in *Maestri americani della Collezione Thyssen-Bornemisza* (Lugano, Italy, 1983), p. 71;.and "On the Plains in '48," *New York Times*, Jan. 27, 1889, p. 6; John C. Ewers, "Fact and Fiction in the Documentary Art of the American West," in *The Frontier Re-examined*, ed. John Francis McDermott (Urbana, 1967), pp. 86–87.

69. Quoted in Buckley, *Triumph of Time*, p. 7.

70. Quoted in Pierson, *The Moving American*, p. 162.

71. See, e.g., Daniel Drake (1834), quoted in Mitchell, *Witnesses to a Vanishing America*, p. 33; Henry T. Tuckerman, *America and Her Commentators. With a Critical Sketch of Travel in the United States* (New York, 1864), p. 401; Walther, *Railroad in the American Landscape*, p. 39.

72. Irving, *Astoria, or Anecdotes of an Enterprise Beyond the Rocky Mountains* (1836: Norman, Okla., 1964), p. 14. For a similar declaration in 1837, see Clark, *Witnesses to a Vanishing America*, pp. 27–28.

73. See, e.g., Hoopes, *American Narrative Painting*.

74. See Groseclose, *Emanuel Leutze*, p. 60, and figs. 99, 100, and 101 (preliminary versions of this painting are located in the Thomas Gilcrease Institute of American History and Art, Tulsa, Oklahoma, and in the National Museum of American Art, Smithsonian Institution, Washington, D.C.); Gerdts and Thistlethwaite, *Grand Illusions*, pp. 113–114.

75. Justin G. Turner, "Emanuel Leutze's *Westward the Course of Empire Takes Its Way*," *Manuscripts* 18 (Spring 1966): 15.

76. See Koke, comp., *American Landscape and Genre Paintings in the New-York Historical Society*, 1:192–204. The series was exhibited at the Pennsylvania Academy of the Fine Arts in 1852. See Boyle et al., *In This Academy*, p. 123.

77. Benton, *An Artist in America*, pp. 350–351. For Benton's account of the artistic and technical problems presented by the wide passageway, see pp. 356–357. Benton's "Indiana" murals (1933), which also treat the pioneering experience, are located in the lobby of the auditorium at Indiana University in Bloomington.

78. John I. H. Baur, *Philip Evergood* (New York, 1975), fig. 56. For a fascinating study of profound social conflict aroused by art and directed at history as process, see M. Sue Kendall, *Rethinking Regionalism: John Steuart Curry and the Kansas Mural Controversy* (Washington, D.C., 1986). Kendall also does an admirable job of broadening the customary cultural meaning and context of "historical art."

79. Quoted in Fanny Kemble Wister, ed., *Owen Wister Out West: His Journals and Letters* (Chicago, 1958), p. 210. See also Robert G. Athearn, *The Mythic West in Twentieth-Century America* (Lawrence, Kans., 1986), pp. 23–28; Philip Durham, "The Cowboy and the Myth Makers," *Journal of Popular Culture* 1 (Summer 1967): 58–62; Frederic Remington, "A Few Words from Mr. Remington," *Collier's Weekly* 34 (Mar. 18, 1905): 16.

80. Lane also painted harbor scenes of New York, Salem, Gloucester, and Boston in which only schooners appear. See John Wilmerding, *Fitz Hugh Lane* (New York, 1971), plates 3, 6, and 8; figs. 54, 64, 75, and 76.

81. Shelburne Museum, Shelburne, Vermont.

82. New-York Historical Society, New York. For an interesting celebration of the age of sail giving way to the age of steam, see "To Honor Historic Ship," *New York Times*, May 21, 1939, sec. 11, p. 5, when the 120th anniversary of the first transatlantic steamboat trip was observed.

83. Hoopes, *American Narrative Painting*, pp. 108–109.

84. Marx, *The Machine in the Garden: Technology and the Pastoral Ideal in America* (New York, 1964). Fitz Hugh Lane's *Three Master on the Gloucester Railway* (1857) creates a unique picture of an invisible machine on the wharf. No train can be seen—only a rather artificial pole that pokes up between two boats and says "Railway." Time as well as motion seem to have been suspended. (See Wilmerding, *Fitz Hugh Lane*, fig. 71.) Quite the opposite occurs in an anonymous pastel titled *Early Steam Locomotive Crossing Truss Bridge at Bellows Falls, Vermont* (n.d.), which conveys the sense of space and time with intensity and conviction. (See Muller, *Paintings and Drawings at the Shelburne Museum*, fig. 437.)

85. See *American Painting at Washington and Lee University: Some Nineteenth-Century Examples* (Lexington, Va., 1976), no. 10.

86. See John Seelye, *Prophetic Waters: The River in Early American Life and Literature* (New York, 1977).

87. See Koke, comp., *American Landscape and Genre Paintings in the New-York Historical Society*, 2 : 114–115.

88. *American Art in the Newark Museum: Paintings, Drawings, and Sculpture* (Newark, N.J., 1981), p. 157; *Survey of American Painting, 1940: Carnegie Institute*, plate 67.

89. For an intermediate phase between Kensett's bucolic boats and O'Keeffe's intensely busy ones, see Gifford Beal, *The Albany Boat* (1915), in the Metropolitan Museum of Art, New York. The trip from New York City to Albany along the Hudson River was an overnight journey. Many sightseers, however, only went as far as Newburgh and then returned to New York on a boat going in the opposite direction. In Beal's painting the passengers have just disembarked from a large steamboat that rides on the river beneath a parklike panorama.

90. Henry Tuckerman, *America and Her Commentators. With a Critical Sketch of Travel in the United States* (New York, 1864), p. 405. For subsequent statements of ambivalence about the railroad, particularly in painting and photography, see Walther, *Railroad in the American Landscape*, pp. 53, 60–63. See also George F. Bottume, *Canal near Salem, Connecticut* (c. 1848–1855), in Joseph S. Czestochowski, *The American Landscape Tradition: A Study and Gallery of Paintings* (New York, 1982), pp. 80–81.

91. Tuckerman, *America and Her Commentators*, p. 438. For some shrewd observations on history as process in nineteenth-century landscape painting, see Leo Marx, "The Railroad-in-the-Landscape: An Iconological Reading of a Theme in American Art," *Prospects: An Annual of American Cultural Studies* 10 (1985): 93, 104.

92. In Turner, "Emanuel Leutze's Mural," p. 16.

93. Chevalier, *Society, Manners, and Politics in the United States*, p. 270. See Theodore Zeldin, "Personal History and the History of the Emotions," *Journal of Social History* 15 (Spring 1982): 339–347.

94. For the Inness, see *American Painting Collection of the Montclair Art Museum*, p. 83; William Hahn, *California Immigrants* (1879), was owned in 1988 by the Hansen/Yeakel Gallery, New York.

95. Dunmore is quoted in Pierson, *The Moving American*, p. 5; Benton, *An Artist in America*, p. 71. For a fine example provided by an associate of John D. Rockefeller, see the autobiographical reminiscence by Henry Flagler, in which he thinks back to 1844 when he left Medina for Sandusky, Ohio, and refers to "my gloomy journey over canals and lakes." David Leon Chandler, *Henry Flagler: The Astonishing Life and Times of the Visionary Robber Baron Who Founded Florida* (New York, 1986), p. 7.

96. See Steven A. Nash, *Dallas Collects American Paintings: Colonial to Early Modern. An Exhibition of Paintings from Private Collections in Dallas* (Dallas, 1982), pp. 68–69. This historical painting is set in the 1820s. See also the painting by Eugene Vail (1857–1934), *Returning Home* (n.d.), advertised in *The Magazine Antiques* 134 (Oct. 1988): n.p.

97. Henry David Thoreau, *Walden* (1854: Princeton, 1971), p. 93; *Excursions*, vol. 9 of *The Writings of Henry David Thoreau* (Boston, 1893), p. 267.

98. Carl Becker, *Everyman His Own Historian: Essays on History and Politics* (1935: Chicago, 1966), p. 4. See also pp. 12, 17. And see John Steuart Curry, *The Oklahoma Land Rush* (1938), in Czestochowski, *John Steuart Curry and Grant Wood*, plate 7. Curry depicts a historical event that occurred in April 1889.

99. John Greenleaf Whittier, *Anti-Slavery Poems: Songs of Labor and Reform* (Boston, 1888), pp. 176–177.

100. See also Theodor Kaufmann, *On to Liberty* (1867), in Hills, *The Painter's America*, p. 71 and no. 86; and John Steuart Curry, *The Fugitive* (1933–1940), in Czestochowski, *John Steuart Curry and Grant Wood*, fig. 40.

101. Anon, n.d., New York State Historical Association, Cooperstown, New York. See also Marvin C. Ross, *The West of Alfred Jacob Miller* . . . (Norman, Okla., 1968), plate 76, "Threatened Attack—approach of a large body of Indians."

102. See *Masterpieces of the American West: Selections from the Anschutz Collection*, plates 40, 42.

103. Fred S. Bartlett, *Walt Kuhn: An Imaginary History of the West* (Fort Worth, 1964). For the Vanderlyn, see Kammen, *A Season of Youth*, fig. 2.

104. Lawrence's subtitle for Panel No. 1 is "During the World War there was a great migration North by Southern Negroes." For a related poem by Langston Hughes, see Ellen Harkins Wheat, *Jacob Lawrence: American Painter* (Seattle, 1986), p. 75.

105. Ibid., pp. 16, 23–24, 40, 102–109. See also Spencer R. Crew, *Field to Factory: Afro-American Migration, 1915–1940* (Washington, D.C., 1987).

106. See Wheat, *Jacob Lawrence*, p. 137.

107. Ibid., pp. 115–116.

108. Ibid., pp. 145–146, 168–169, 218.

109. Ibid., p. 39.

110. See Joseph D. Ketner II, "Robert S. Duncanson (1821–1872): The Late Literary Landscape Paintings," *American Art Journal* 15 (Winter 1983): 35–47.

111. Gerdts and Thistlethwaite, *Grand Illusions*, pp. 34–35, 38–39, 143.

112. For a delightful example pertaining to the Acadians in the bayou region, see Joseph Rusling Meeker, *The Land of Evangeline* (1874), St. Louis Art Museum.

113. McCoubrey, ed., *American Art, 1700–1960*, pp. 207–208. Ben Shahn observed that Alexander Calder was "the only one of the modern people who has actually and physically introduced a time dimension into his work. . . . Here is sculpture that creates endless patterns in space-time rhythms." Shahn, *The Shape of Content* (Cambridge, Mass., 1957), pp. 66–67.

114. Barbara Haskell, *Marsden Hartley* (New York, 1980), esp. pp. 57–60.

115. See Bartlett, *Walt Kuhn*, pp. 3, 6–7.

116. Matthew Baigell, *Thomas Hart Benton* (New York, 1973), pp. 55–56, 62–63, 68–79; Karal Ann Marling, *Tom Benton and His Drawings: A Biographical Essay and a Collection of His Sketches, Studies, and Mural Cartoons* (Columbia, Mo., 1985), pp. 114–115. Reviewing the "American Historical Epic" in 1927, Lewis Mumford wrote that "life as Mr. Benton depicts it would be a chaos of change and passage, were it not for his orchestral arrangements of the figures. . . . It is not, perhaps, by accident that he has gone to history for the themes of his major mural designs; for history suggests movement through time. . . ." Mumford, "An American Epic in Paint," *New Republic* 50 (Apr. 6, 1927): 197.

117. Benton, *An Artist in America*, p. 65. Edward Hopper remained a restless wanderer, too, and he became fascinated by the psychology of travelers in hotels, motels, trains, highways, and at filling stations. For expressions of migratory emotion in his art, see Levin, *Edward Hopper*, p. 198 and plate 209.

118. Descriptive material provided by the Wallace Gallery of the Metropolitan Museum of Art, New York. In 1935 this painting received first prize from the Carnegie International Jury. See *New York Times*, May 26, 1935, sec. 10, p. 7.

119. Quoted in Pierson, *Moving American*, p. 157. See also Hopper's oil painting titled *Rooms for Tourists* (1945) in Levin, *Edward Hopper*, plate 290.

3.
The Old House and Elm Trees

People who try to explain pictures are usually barking up the wrong tree.
—PABLO PICASSO (1935)

The title of this chapter is taken from a watercolor of the same name painted by Charles E. Burchfield during the later 1930s (fig. 3-20). I have featured it because the old house and the elm—seen singly, or taken together, or else in combination with certain other objects—have been perpetuated in American art as well as literature as powerful symbols of time, memory, and the role of tradition, especially since the mid- and later nineteenth century.

Although authorities have asserted that history painting began to decline in the later nineteenth century,[1] I would like to suggest that this view may only be valid if we define "history painting" according to the most orthodox criteria. When we peruse *Talks about Art* by William Morris Hunt, a prominent Victorian artist who painted neither famous heroes nor historic events, we nevertheless find him observing in 1875 that "there are so many people looking back into the past that they would not see great things that might happen today. If Homer were to come here and sing, they would say 'Hold on! You're in our way! *We're looking back into the past!*'"[2] Hunt was not referring to Winslow Homer.

The extent to which Hunt was correct, and the reasons why, involve a process that is quite the reverse of the pattern we observed in chapter 1. There, a set of European icons that had served as specific symbols of time and history came to be conflated and diluted in the United States. Chronos and Clio gave way to Father Time and the Maiden, who were supplanted in turn by the more generalized concept of Memory.

The set of symbols that I will examine in this chapter, by contrast, appealed to artistic imaginations somewhat later in time, enjoyed distinctive modes of use in American culture, and over the past century has been perpetuated rather than watered down or eroded.

Despite the apparent clarity of such a contrast, however, the cultural meanings of old houses and elm trees have been more variable than one might suppose from simply looking, let us say, at popular ceramic plates commemorating William Penn's treaty (beneath a great elm) in 1682[3] or *The House of the Seven Gables* accompanied by its great Pyncheon Elm.[4] At certain times, old houses and elms have been employed as symbols of enduring tradition, memory, and continuity; yet at others they have called attention to change and deterioration—of families, of communities, or of social values generally.

Either way, though, the pertinent images left to us by artists and writers have indeed been statements about history and time. "Snapshots" might be a better phrase than statements because they bring to mind those perceptively eloquent lines by T. S. Eliot:

> A people without a history
> Is not redeemed from time, for history is a pattern
> Of timeless moments.[5]

The focus of this chapter is the presentation of history as a pattern of "timeless moments," achieved by means of highly particular symbols that form an American configuration despite the persistence of counterparts in Great Britain.

Historic American Elms in Fact, Fiction, and Art

One historic moment of "landing" and intercultural contact that I did not mention in the preceding chapter concerns William Penn's arrival at Pennsylvania in 1682 and his supposed signing of a treaty of peace with the Lenape Indians then living along the Delaware River. That "event" would be immortalized in 1771–1772 by a painting that Benjamin West called *William Penn's Treaty with the Indians, when he founded the province of Pennsylvania in North America* (fig. 3-1). I use the word "supposed" because there exist various discrepancies between historical reality and the legend that began, oddly enough, with Voltaire's *Letters Concerning the English Nation* (London, 1733) about a grand treaty signed beneath an immense elm.

Historical sources do not document a single "Great Treaty," but suggest instead a series of meetings—some with William Penn and others with his

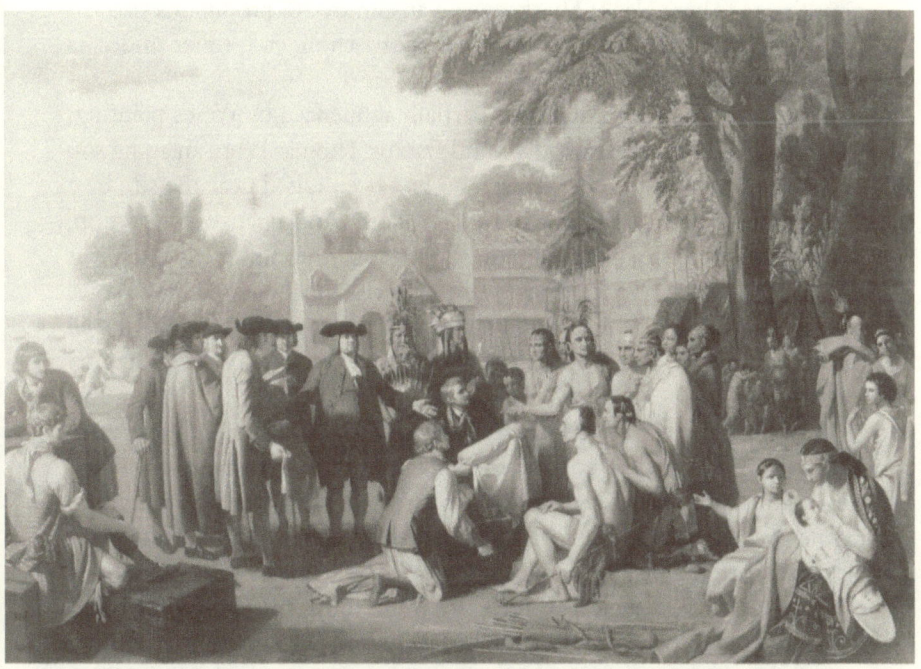

3-1. Benjamin West, *Penn's Treaty with the Indians*, 1771–1772. Oil on canvas, 75 1/2 × 107 3/4 in. Courtesy of the Pennsylvania Academy of the Fine Arts, Philadelphia. Gift of Mrs. Sarah Harrison (The Joseph Harrison, Jr., Collection).

agents. We do, however, have this record written by Caleb Pusey, one of the earliest settlers: "Soon after our proprietor's first arrival here [in 1682] he had an amicable and friendly conference with the native Indians of whom he purchased land and he also concluded a firm peace with them that we might [live] together as brethren without doing the least wrong to each other."[6]

Within three-quarters of a century, however, an American myth came into being with rich implications for art, folklore, and literature. Subsequent Pennsylvanians responded quite positively to Voltaire's pro-Quaker embroidery of the bare facts; they accepted the notion of a single Great Treaty and even fixed upon a specific site at which the determinative event had taken place. An ancient elm located at Shackamaxon (later called Kensington) along the Delaware River henceforth became a sacred place. By 1813, when an abolitionist named Thomas Clarkson published his biography of William Penn, all aspects of the legendary episode had taken luminous form: "There was at Shackamaxon an elm tree of prodigious size. To this the leaders on both sides repaired, approaching each other under its widely-spreading branches."[7]

Clarkson's fanciful account was partially influenced by West's painting, which had been commissioned around 1770 by Thomas Penn, an aging son of the founding proprietor. West, who had been raised near the site by a Quaker family, was also affected by Voltaire's imaginative concoction. Some time after 1810 West referred in a letter to the elm tree "which was held in the highest veneration by the original inhabitants of my native country, by the first settlers, and by their descendants, and to which I well remember, about the year 1755, when a boy, often resorting with my school-fellows."[8]

West later prepared two smaller versions of the same subject, in 1773 and in 1809,[9] but by the time he worked on the second, engravings of the original had already become popular, and assorted other versions on cloth, earthenware, and paper enjoyed a remarkable vogue. Although the great elm was shattered by a fierce gale in the year 1810, "much of the timber was carried away by piece-meal and relics of it carefully preserved, some being manufactured into ink stands, snuff boxes, spools, &c," noted an 1821 biography of Penn. A piece of it went on exhibition in 1893 at the Columbian Exposition held at Chicago.[10] Today the locale can be found northeast of downtown Philadelphia in the modest Penn Treaty Park.

The absence of an actual elm after 1810 did not discourage Edward Hicks, the naive sign painter and artist, from featuring it in several of his own adaptations of West's work (1826–1835). In an 1830 version, for example, the elm has been moved from the right, where West wanted it, to the extreme left (fig. 3-2). It is much easier to move huge trees around, I suppose, when they have ceased to exist.[11] The Quakers and the Indians have also swapped sides in the picture; and a man unrolling a bolt of muslin in West's prototype has been replaced by Penn and a deputy displaying the unfurled, signed treaty.

When Hicks composed his countless renditions of a theme called *The Peaceable Kingdom,* he invariably included in the middle distance a reduced version of *Penn's Treaty* (fig. 3-3). Hicks took diverse liberties, such as eliminating the architectural structures along with quite a few of the negotiating participants and observers. What remained constant, quite literally, was the carefully printed bottom line below the painting:

When the great PENN his famous treaty made
With Indian chiefs beneath the elm-tree's shade.[12]

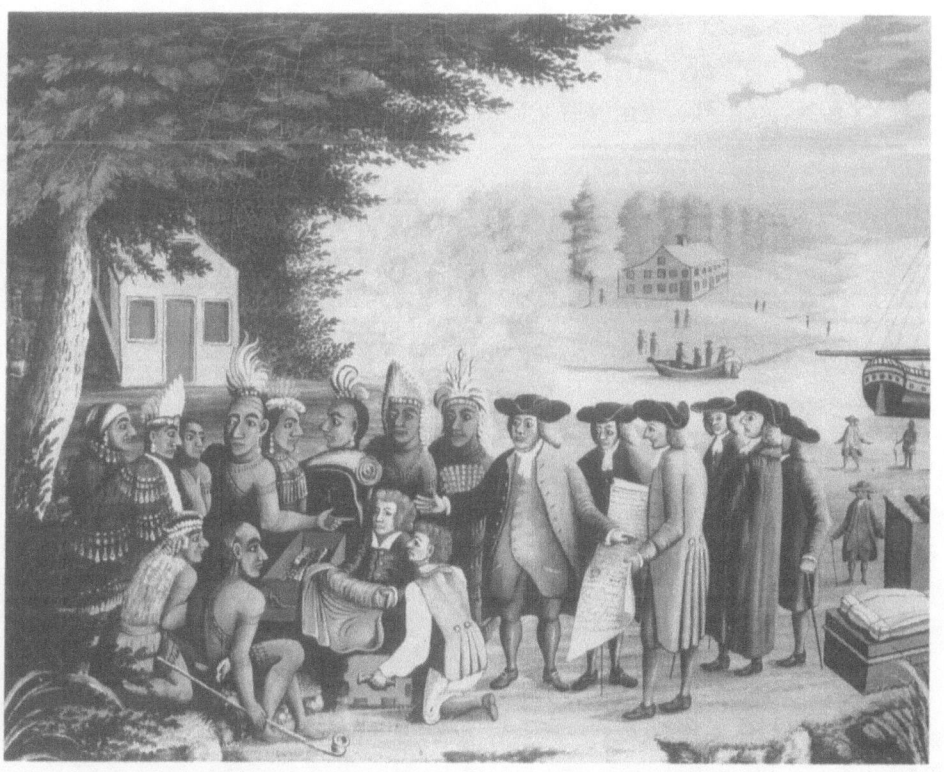

3-2. Edward Hicks, *Penn's Treaty with the Indians*, 1830–1835. Oil on canvas, 17 5/8 × 22 3/4 in. Courtesy of the Abby Aldrich Rockefeller Folk Art Center, Williamsburg, Virginia.

With the passage of time Quakers and Indians largely receded from the artistic imagination, yet the ancient elm still stood, more venerable and visually dominant than ever (fig. 3-4).[13] Over two full generations, from 1796 to 1866, the perspective scarcely changed. The most notable innovation by Xanthus Smith (fig. 3-5) is the improbable placement of a curious goat in an upper crotch of the great elm![14]

In 1861 Nathaniel Currier published a popular lithograph of *Wm. Penn's Treaty with the Indians When He Founded the Province of Pennsa.*, which imitated West. A few years later, however, a painting (and an engraving based upon it) by George Lehman made the elm more dominant than ever (fig. 3-6). The goat is still in the tree, venturing out on a limb, but Penn and company have vanished from the picture. They survive only in the subtitle or legend: "Under which William Penn concluded his Treaty with the Indians in 1682, it fell during a storm in 1810. This block of marble was

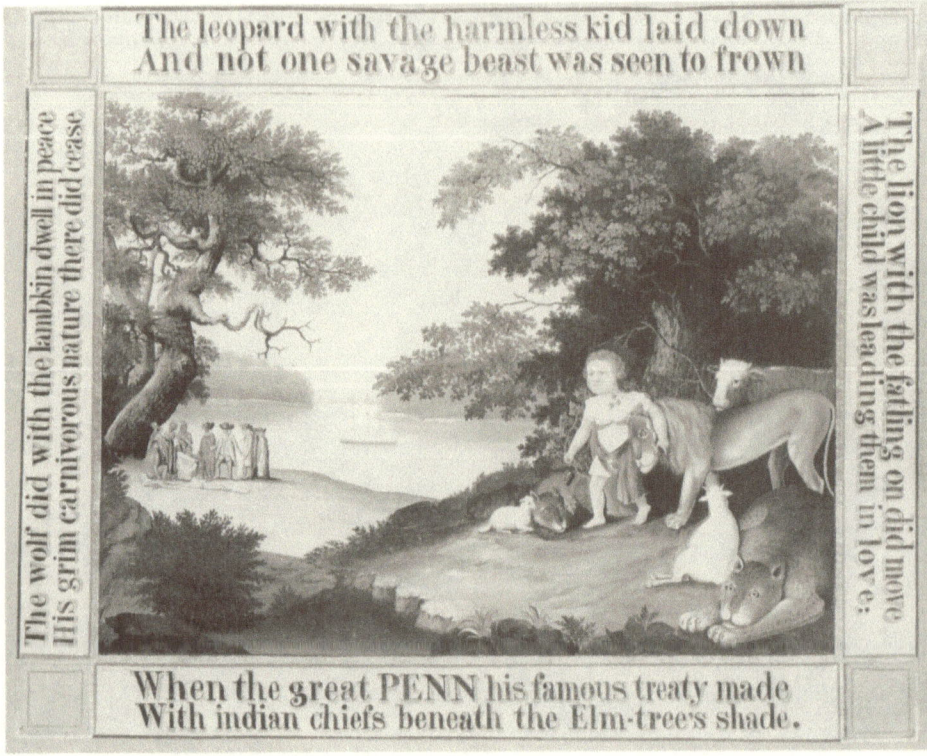

The leopard with the harmless kid laid down
And not one savage beast was seen to frown

The wolf did with the lambkin dwell in peace
His grim carnivorous nature there did cease

The lion with the fatling on did move
A little child was leading them in love:

When the great PENN his famous treaty made
With indian chiefs beneath the Elm-tree's shade.

3-3. Edward Hicks, *Peaceable Kingdom*, 1826. Oil on canvas, 32 1/2 × 41 1/2 in. Philadelphia Museum of Art. Bequest of Charles C. Willis.

placed by the Penn Society A.D. 1827 to mark the site of the Elm Tree and Treaty Ground of William Penn & The Indian Natives in 1682. . . ." A historical legend had now quite literally become lapidary.

The legend lingered on into the twentieth century, though it tended to be noticed at lengthening intervals. Around 1908 Edwin Austin Abbey exhibited paintings intended for the rotunda of the State Capitol in Harrisburg, Pennsylvania, including *Penn's Treaty with the Indians*. In 1967 Red Grooms executed his outlandish spoof, *Penn Shakin' Hands with the Indians* (enamel on plywood). When it was shown at Philadelphia in 1976, Grooms acknowledged that he had chosen the subject "more because of Mr. Benjamin West than Mr. Penn. . . . The atmosphere in his paintings is so thick it looks more like 20 thousand B.C. than just a few hundred years ago." [15] From the pretentious to the parodic in a period of sixty years.

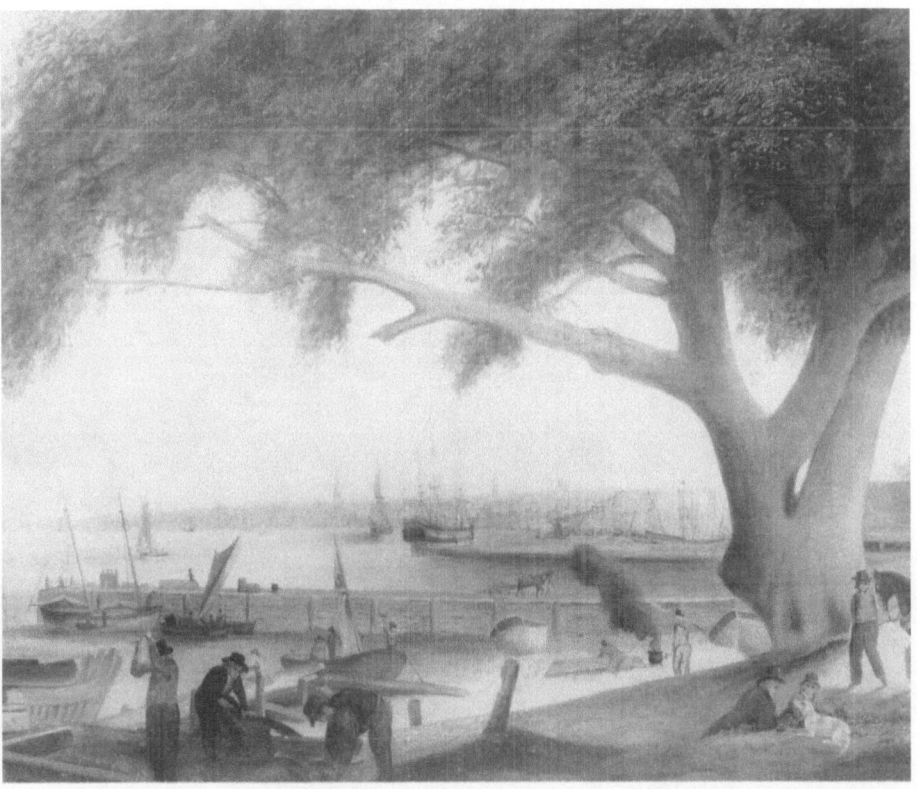

3-4. Thomas Birch, *The City and Port of Philadelphia, on the River Delaware from Kensington (The Treaty Tree)*, c. 1800. Oil on canvas, 39 1/4 × 50 in. The Historical Society of Pennsylvania.

Elms did not disappear as icons in nineteenth- and twentieth-century American art, however, because they remained culturally and aesthetically meaningful in diverse contexts (fig. 3-7). The "glorious old elms of New Haven" brought the Connecticut town renown as Elm City. Mid-nineteenth-century books for children had an almost obligatory "large elm-tree before the door." The Louis Vieux Elm in Louisville, Kansas, was named for a half-French and half-Indian trader who settled close to it in 1857. Now it is more than one hundred feet tall, the height of a ten-story building, and a source of extraordinary local pride.[16]

American homes built in the eighteenth and nineteenth centuries commonly received such names as "The Elms" and "Great Elm."[17] In 1883–1884, when Charles Follen McKim designed a neocolonial house in Lenox,

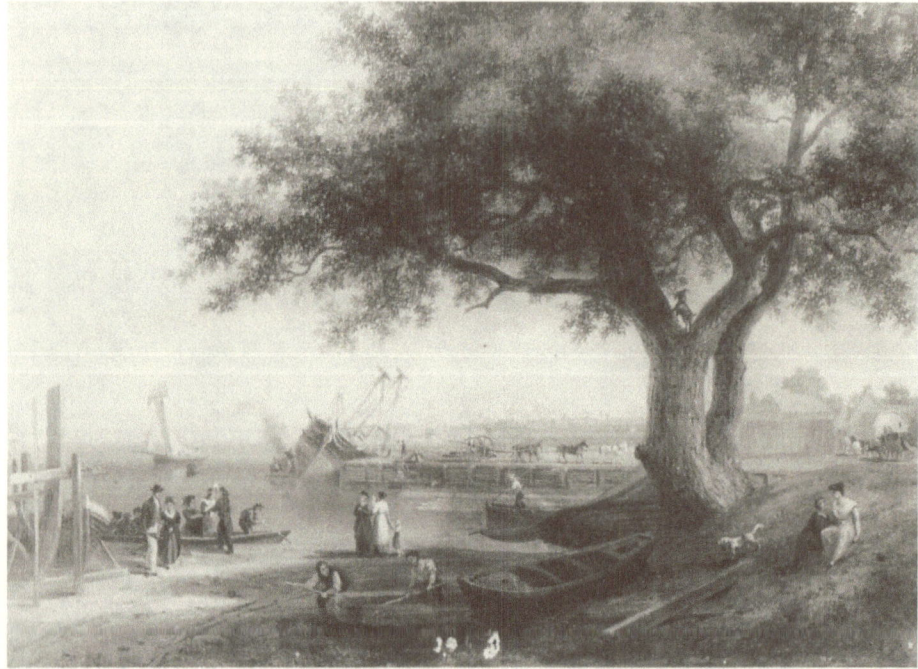

3-5. Xanthus Smith, *Treaty Elm,* 1866. Oil on canvas, 12 1/8 × 18 1/4 in. Historical Society of Pennsylvania.

Massachusetts, for the Appleton sisters, he arranged the entrance court around a large elm tree. During the 1920s some disgruntled urbanites re-settled in rural Connecticut, seeking (according to Van Wyck Brooks) "the charm of old hand-hewn beams and drooping elms." In front of Connie's Inn at the time of the Harlem Renaissance, there was an aging elm, known as the Tree of Hope, that served as a kind of talisman. Residents of Harlem had very superstitious feelings about that tree.[18]

Americans associated the elm with death and rebirth, with mourning and memorials. In 1848, when Daniel Webster lost both a son and a daughter, he planted two weeping elms in front of his home at Marshfield, Massachusetts, to honor their memories. At the time of the Centennial in 1876, Emperor Dom Pedro of Brazil visited the tomb of George Washington at Mount Vernon and planted an elm. In 1937 Delaware celebrated the Sesquicentennial of its ratification of the U.S. Constitution by dedicating thirteen memorial elms around the town green in Dover.[19]

Many New Englanders harbored strong sentiments about native elms.

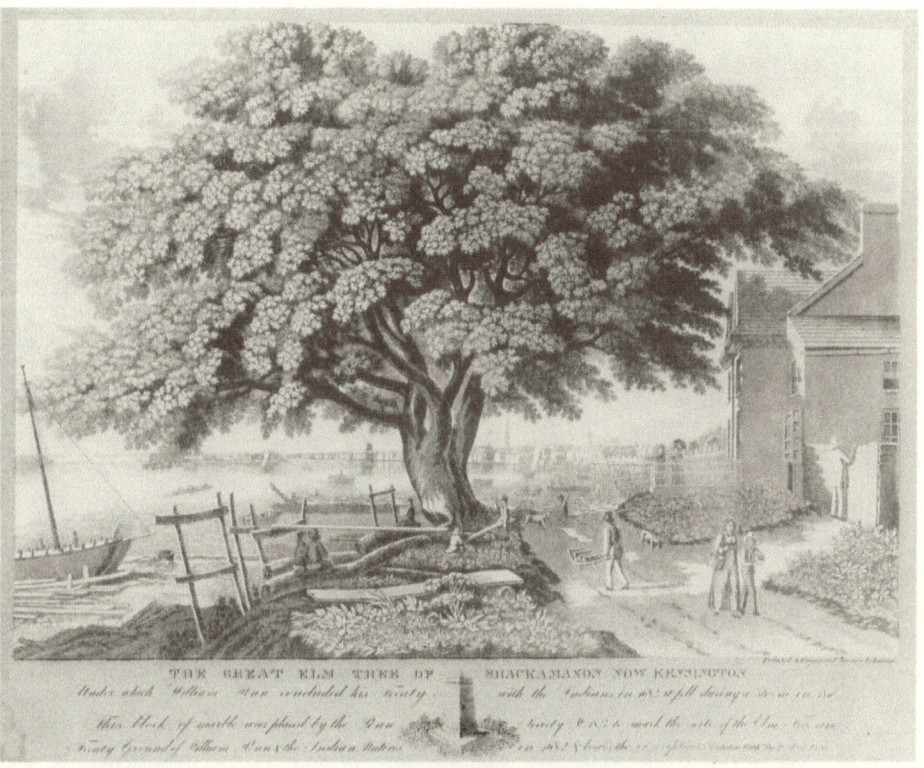

3-6. George Lehman, *The Great Treaty Elm of Shackamaxon (Now Kensington)*, c. 1860s. Engraving, 14 1/2 × 18 1/2 in. American Philosophical Society, Philadelphia.

In 1848, for example, when Reverend George Atkinson and his wife Nancy shipped around Cape Horn to become missionaries in Oregon, they brought an elm tree which they planted in their yard amidst the giant firs—considered to be the first elm tree in Oregon.[20] In 1924, on the other hand, when Eugene O'Neill chose to join the cultural attack upon Puritanism, he set the Gothic tale of Ephraim Cabot and Abbie Putnam in a New England farmhouse around the year 1850. He called that drama *Desire under the Elms*.

Perhaps the best-known elm in all of American fiction is the Pyncheon Elm, which provides such a prominent emblem in *The House of the Seven Gables*. An explicit witness to "the Past," it is wide and sheltering even though it is "a great melancholy elm," like the older Pyncheons who are permanent residents and psychological prisoners of the house. Precisely be-

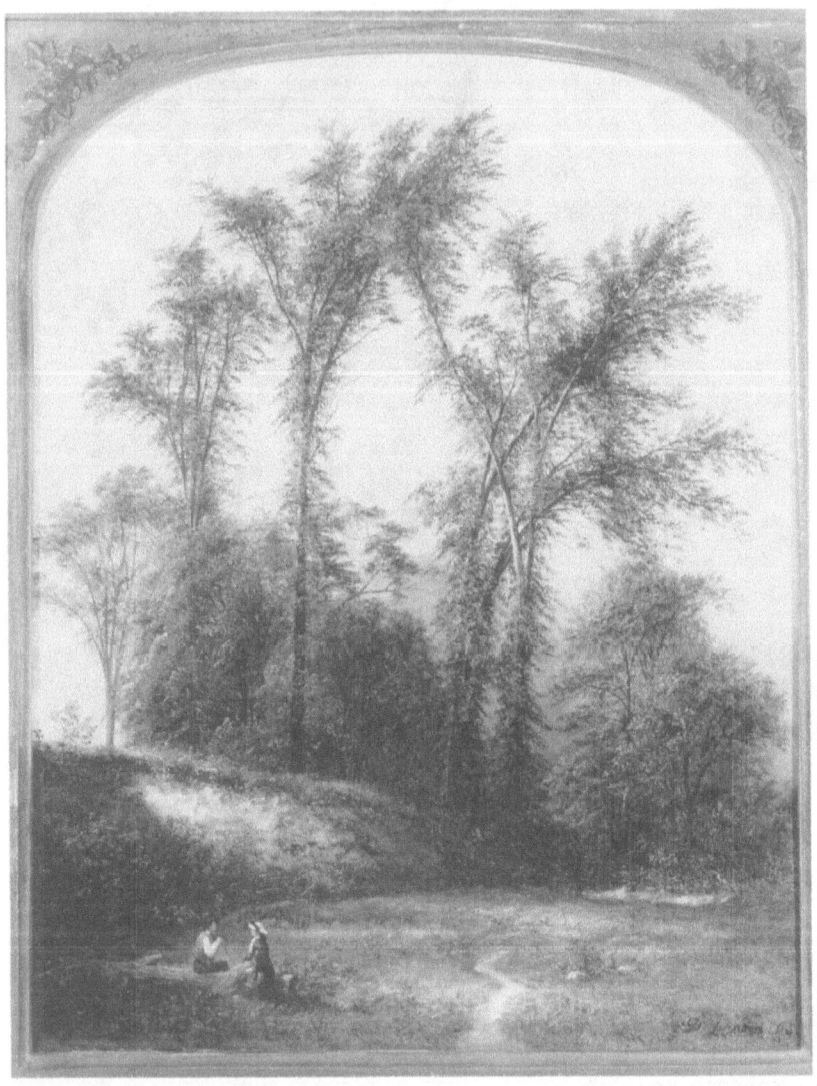

3-7. David Johnson, *Young Elms,* 1863. Oil on canvas, 17 1/2 × 14 1/2 in. Private collection.

cause it is a part of the novel's dramatis personae, it must be accounted for and heard from on the final page: The Pyncheon Elm, "with what foliage the September gale had spared to it, whispered unintelligible prophecies."[21]

Edith Wharton's novella, *Ethan Frome* (1911), the grim story of a *ménage à trois* in the New England village of Starkfield, culminates when Ethan and Mattie Silver, whose love affair seems destined for separation by

Ethan's domineering wife, try to commit a double suicide by smashing their sled into "the big elm" at the bottom of the farm hill, where the aged tree "thrust out a deadly elbow."

> As they took wing for this it seemed to him that they were flying indeed, flying far up into the cloudy night, with Starkfield immeasurably below them, falling away like a speck in space. . . . Then the big elm shot up ahead, lying in wait for them at the bend of the road, and he said between his teeth: "We can fetch it; I know we can fetch it—"[22]

Their brave but futile attempt fails because the elm will not kill them. Ethan is left lame and Mattie crippled for life. They live on at the farm, grimly dominated by Ethan's wife Zenobia.

In Ellen Glasgow's finest novel, *The Sheltered Life* (1932), elms stand as emblems of what still endures when a cultural heritage seems to be disintegrating. Writing of Richmond, Virginia, Glasgow remarks that on Washington Street, "where elegance had once flourished and fallen, only the disfigured elms still struggled to preserve the delusion of grandeur."[23]

In poetry the connection has been even more historically explicit. In 1875, for instance, James Russell Lowell composed "Under the Old Elm: Poem Read at Cambridge on the Hundredth Anniversary of Washington's Taking Command of the American Army, 3d July, 1775."

> Historic town, thou holdest sacred dust,
> Once known to men as pious, learnëd, just,
> And one memorial pile that dares to last;
> But Memory greets with reverential kiss
> No spot in all thy circuit sweet as this,
> Touched by that modest glory as it past,
> O'er which yon elm hath piously displayed
> These hundred years its monumental shade.[24]

For the Centennial, celebrated in 1876, one chair was crafted of wood from that sacred elm under which Washington stood while accepting his command of the Continental army (fig. 3-8).[25]

In 1917 Stephen Vincent Benét composed a poem to the memory of a friend killed in the war—a poem in which an elm is invoked as a tree of remembrance.[26] In many respects, however, the most "poetic" and poignant response to an elm that I have encountered occurred in New Hampshire in 1853, when five hundred men and women petitioned the proprietors of the Amoskeag Manufacturing Company not to cut down a particular elm in order to make room for an additional mill. "It was a beau-

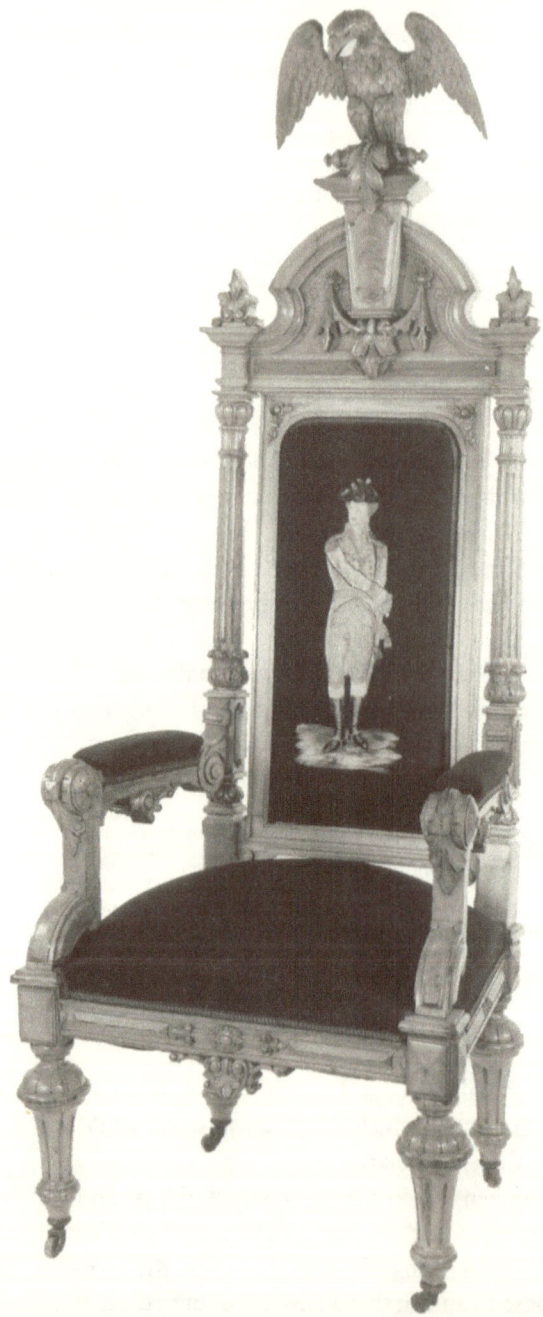

3-8. Armchair made from the "Washington Elm." Smithsonian Institution. Gift of Dr. Leonard Carmichael (photo courtesy of *The Magazine Antiques*).

tiful and goodly tree" and belonged to a time "when the yell of the red man and the scream of the eagle were alone heard on the banks of the Merrimack, instead of two giant edifices filled with the buzz of busy and well-remunerated industry." Each day, the workers said, they viewed that tree as "a connecting link between the past and the present," and "each autumn [it] remind[s] us of our own mortality."[27]

By now some readers surely must be wondering whether the elm has really been, at least historically, the preeminent American tree. What about great oaks, for example, such as the Charter Oak of Connecticut, where seventeenth-century Puritans concealed their legitimizing charter for safekeeping? There is an imaginative painting entitled *The Charter Oak* (1857) by Charles De Wolf Brownell,[28] and maples and cypresses have enjoyed symbolic significance on occasion.[29] Nevertheless, I am prepared to contend for the elm's preeminence, at least in nineteenth- and early twentieth-century American culture. When Frances Wright visited the United States in 1819 she found the elm "a tree of singular grace and beauty." Charlotte Coues of Portsmouth, New Hampshire, writing in 1853, insisted that the elm ranked at the top:

> Every tree has a character of its own, but our native American Elm seems to unite in itself, either in the different stages of its growth, or in some single noble specimen, all the distinguishing beauties of other trees, while it has some peculiar to itself. It combines the grandeur of the Oak, the stateliness of the Linden, the symmetry of the Maple with the delicate grace of a young Weeping Willow.[30]

Although American artists seem to have shared Coues' sentiments, the elm has not been a static, unchanging sort of symbol. In George Inness's irenic landscape, *Peace and Plenty* (1865), the trees (which are almost certainly elms) provide part of the nurturing ambience.[31] They also represent endurance and a sense of national thanksgiving for the termination of four years of Union-shattering conflict. The same sort of tranquil mood is established, though less grandly, in Sanford R. Gifford's *Landscape with Figures* (fig. 3-9).

In the twentieth century, however, aging elms have undergone a shift in emphasis from statements of endurance, as in *Watkins Farm, North Caldwell* by Ernest Lawson (1906),[32] to sheer survival, as in *Old Elm* by John

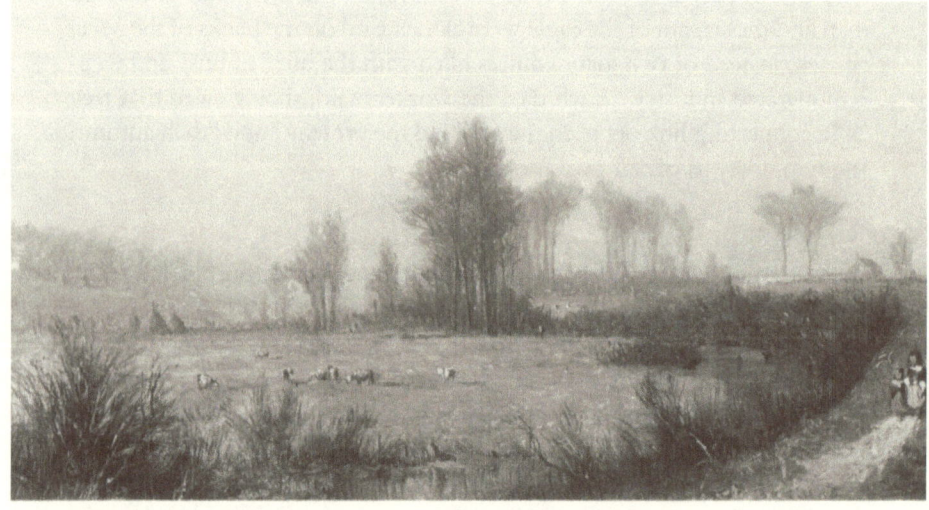

3-9. Sanford R. Gifford, *Landscape with Figures,* c. 1870. Oil on canvas, 6 1/2 × 12 in. Alexander Gallery, 996 Madison Avenue, New York 10021.

Kane (c. 1927). In the latter (fig. 3-10), the tree is accompanied by powerful associations if not memories. Because it is the most important feature of the composition, its size is far out of scale in relation to the Victorian house behind it. "Innocent" artists have their advantages.

Subsequently the elm as an American icon would lack the élan it had displayed from West to Inness, and perhaps even to Kane, because Dutch elm disease was first detected in the United States during the early 1930s. We notice the change in Rockwell Kent's *Ancient Elm* (1961) and Fairfield Porter's *Under the Elms* (1971–1972), one of his final works,[33] but above all in pictures by Charles Burchfield (fig. 3-14). Burchfield wrote the following in his journal entry associated with *The Great Elm* (1939–1941): "I wish it were possible to do significant work without getting so 'wrought up'—In doing a subject like this in which memory and emotion play equal parts, nothing seems to go right, and I must start again and again."[34]

Of Castles and Culture: American Responses to Ruins

In 1819 Frances Wright overheard (or else imagined) a comment from a European to an American farmer: "This is all well. You have all the vulgar

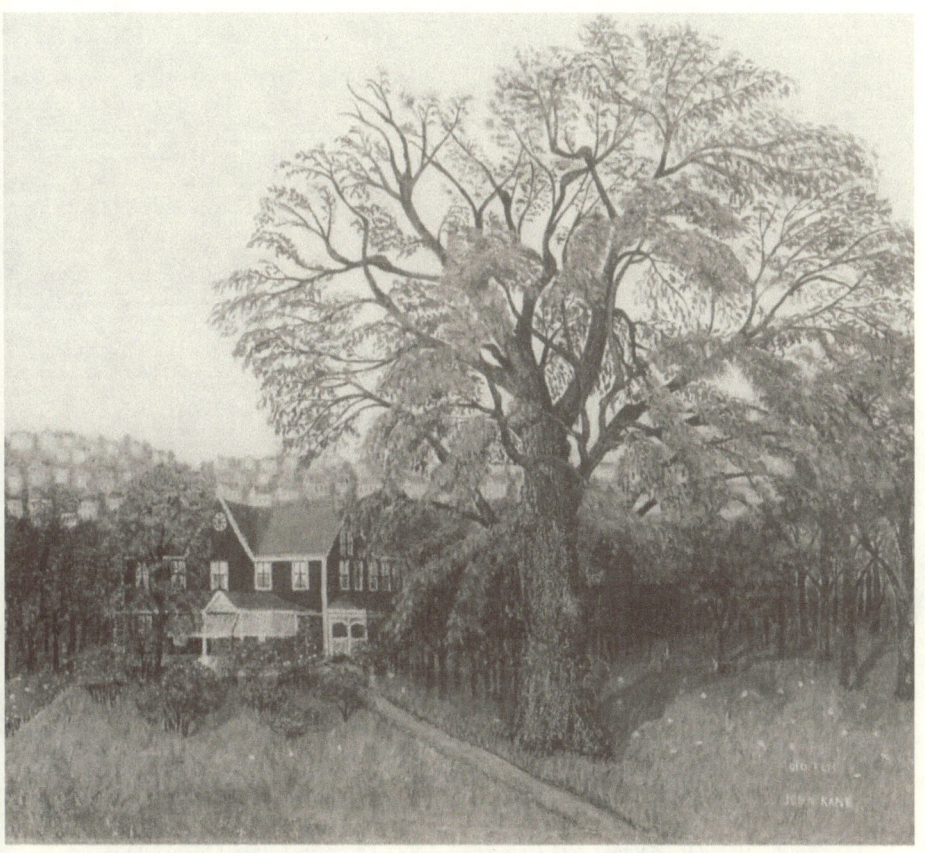

3-10. John Kane, *Old Elm,* c. 1927. Oil on canvas, 21 1/8 × 25 in. The Metropolitan Museum of Art. Bequest of Miss Adelaide Milton de Groot, 1967.

and the substantial, but I look in vain for the *ornamental*. Where are your ruins and your poetry?" Three decades later James Fenimore Cooper flatly asserted that "one does not expect to meet with a ruined castle or abbey, or even fortress, in America." Instead, Cooper added, one watched in America for "the half-hidden church, nestling among the leaves of its elms and pines, the neat and secluded hamlet, [and] the farm-house." [35]

The question raised by the Old World visitor was not at all uncommon, and American responses were not consistently so self-assured as Cooper's. Many of his fellow countrymen flatly felt no need for either ruins or poetry,[36] yet ruins had been an immensely popular motif in European art and poetry during the later eighteenth century and among the Romantics of the early nineteenth. Jerome H. Buckley noted a major reason: "For many

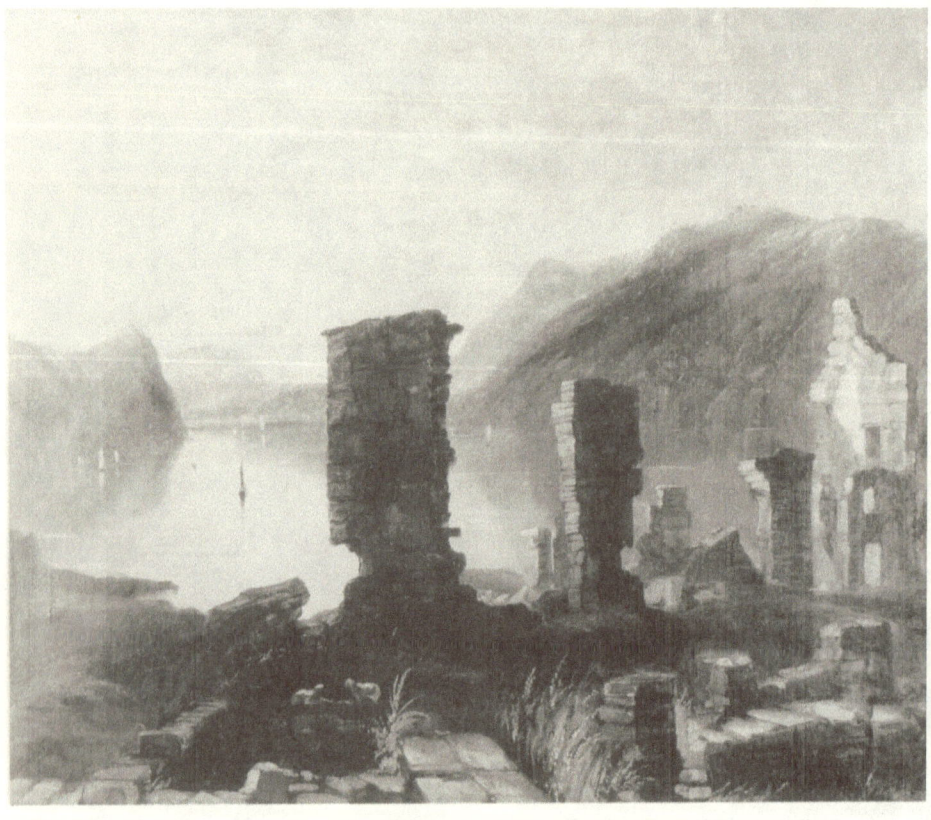

3-11. Anon. American, *Ruins of Fort Ticonderoga, Lake Champlain,* c. 1845. Oil on canvas, 25 1/4 × 30 1/4 in. Courtesy The Margaret Woodbury Strong Museum, Rochester, New York.

years architects had been preserving or creating actual ruins as sentimental adjuncts of an ordered landscape, reminders of life's brevity and time's cruel ravages, a means of titillating the poetic sensibilities of men otherwise devoted to practical prose and reason."[37]

So Giovanni Paolo Pannini in Italy, Georg Forster in Germany, and Hubert Robert in France popularized a rather substantial genre that one scholar has called "Melancholy Among the Ruins."[38] Ruins had for centuries been placed in the distance of pictures because of their scenic qualities, but during the eighteenth century they moved to the foreground and became primary themes. Frequently they symbolized obstinate resistance to the ravages of time.[39] *Tintern Abbey* by J. M. W. Turner (Victoria and

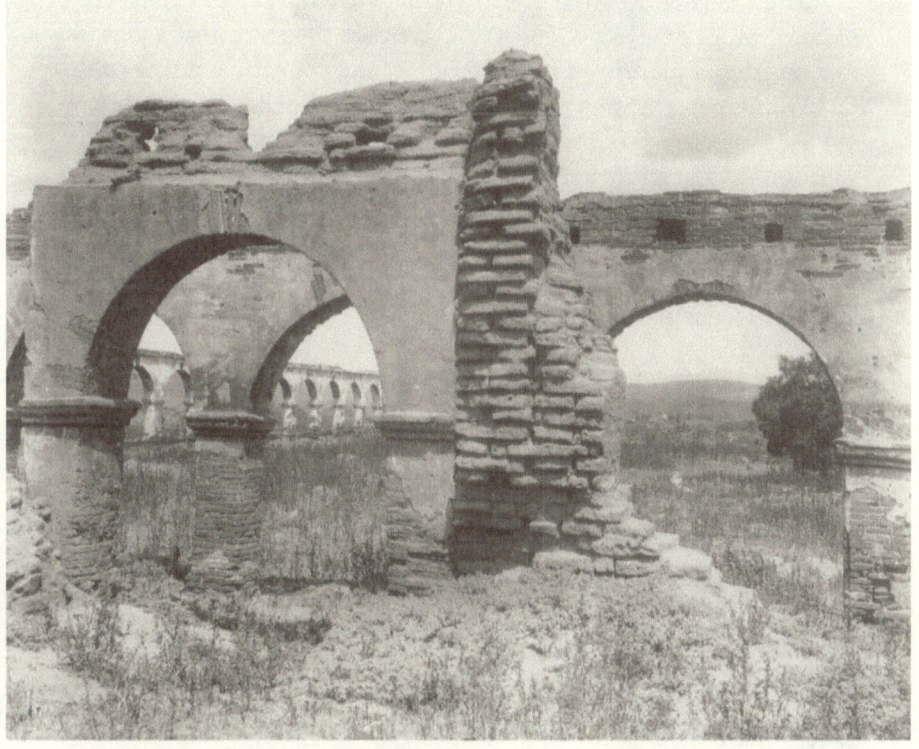

3-12. Adam Clark Vroman, *San Luis Rey Mission, Entrance to the Inner Court,* 1897. Photograph. Seaver Center for Western History Research, Los Angeles County Museum of Natural History.

Albert Museum, London) supplies a superb example of this tendency extending well into the nineteenth century.

American artists were not oblivious to the European fascination with ruins and they responded in varied ways. Some, like Thomas Cole, Frederic E. Church, and Jasper F. Cropsey, shared that interest and painted Old World ruins in certain phases of their careers.[40] Others did, on occasion, visit American ruins from the colonial period[41] and at intervals, especially in the 1840s (fig. 3-11) and 1890s (fig. 3-12), stopped to paint or photograph them. Late in the nineteenth century it was not uncommon to encounter passages of this sort in American magazines and newspapers: "Go to Jamestown, the sacredest spot on this continent, with its crumbling or long crumbled walls, its very ground perishing under the advancing tides of our great river. . . . What will you find? Desolation and ruin; cow-pastures and sheep walks."[42] Wayne Craven has suggested that a gigantic tree was the iconic answer of nineteenth-century American artists to the Old World representation of ruins.[43] I believe, as I indicated in the previous section, that he is partially correct; but the missing variable in the equation—and a rather large variable at that—is the old house.

The Old House as an American Icon

Although some notice has been given to the symbolic importance of old homes in American literature,[44] little has been devoted to the old house in American art. Perhaps that is so partially because of the diverse ways in which old homes have been depicted—sometimes with positive value, but at other times with negative associations. Yet it may also be a consequence of the development of genre painting, which so often describes events taking place *inside* houses, barns, inns, and other structures.[45] As Fernand Braudel once observed, "houses viewed from the outside are one thing, from within another."[46]

Because imaginative writers can move from the outside in, and vice versa, with much greater ease than artists can, I shall begin with a few pertinent novelists and poets before turning to painters. I do so not because I mean to make systematic comparisons between internal and external perceptions of old homes, but rather because each medium lends itself to particular sorts of techniques and statements about the symbols being invoked.[47]

In the opening paragraph of *The House of the Seven Gables,* Hawthorne introduces his readers to "the great elm-tree and the weather-beaten edifice" built in 1691. He reminds us repeatedly that the house and its elderly inhabitants are repositories of memory and custodians of tradition. He coins a quaint phrase for family lore, "chimney corner traditions," and conveys a very balanced view of the virtues and distinctive disadvantages of tradition: it "sometimes brings down truth that history has let slip, but is oftener the wild babble of the time."[48]

Hawthorne uses the interior as well as the exterior to express varied attitudes toward the value and potential tyranny of tradition. He even derives implications for his personae from the nature and extent of their relationship to the seven-gabled house. Phoebe Pyncheon, for example, who is undoubtedly the most cheerful and even-tempered character in the entire tale, grew up in the countryside with no connection to the Salem house. Consequently, for better but also conceivably for worse, she was "ignorant of most of the family traditions." [49]

As we approach the end of this long "romance," Hawthorne seems to tip the balance of his ambivalence—maintained judiciously throughout—concerning the relative merits of past- versus present-mindedness. Even the old, frail, and hitherto hushed Clifford Pyncheon concludes that "there is no such unwholesome atmosphere as that of an old home, rendered poisonous by one's defunct forefathers and relatives." When the historic curse is fulfilled, "the gloomy and desolate old house . . . sitting sternly in its solitude, was the emblem of many a human heart, which, nevertheless, is compelled to hear the thrill and echo of the world's gayety around it." [50]

We do not require an elaborate discourse concerning Henry James and country houses because a fine study is already available.[51] Let it suffice to say that in James's last novel, *The Sense of the Past* (1917), a house in London serves as the metaphor for history itself. Edith Wharton's *Valley of Decision* (1902) engages the question of how to preserve or recover the best of the past while remaining venturesome and open to new prospects. We know from Wharton's notebook that she relied upon the metaphor of a house and garden: "A certain piety for the past, and catholicity of taste, make Odo preserve the rooms and gardens of Pianura unchanged, while adding new galleries, mss., coins." [52]

American poets have also regarded old homes with a curious mix of tentative acceptance or apprehension. Here is Walt Whitman in his opening lines of the Preface to *Leaves of Grass:* "America does not repel the past . . . accepts the lesson with calmness . . . is not so impatient as has been supposed . . . perceives that the corpse is slowly borne from the eating and sleeping rooms of the house . . ." (the ellipses are Whitman's).[53]

More fragile souls feeling burdened by personal pasts have been drawn to the shabby house as a metaphor for melancholy. A poem by Delmore Schwartz begins: "Tired and unhappy you think of houses." John Berryman, an equally self-destructive poet, opened one of his verses with: "Exasperated, worn, you conjure up a mansion." [54]

It is precisely that ironic use of "mansion" that Edward Hopper intended when he called his picture of a shabby red frame house *Gloucester Mansion* (fig. 3-13). Hopper frequently painted old houses: some seem grimly deserted,[55] others do not send any sort of clear symbolic signal,[56]

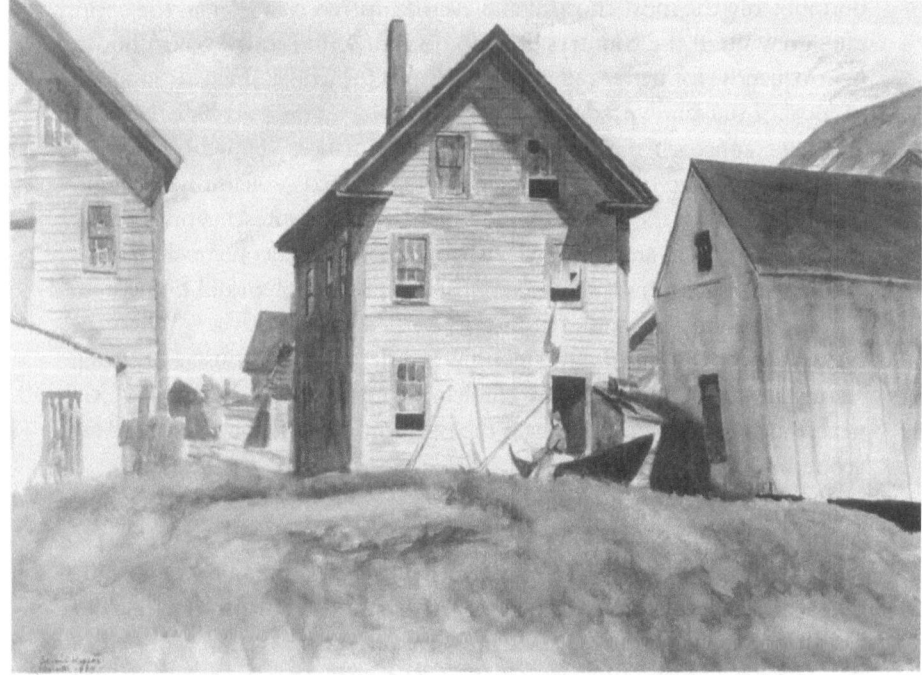

3-13. Edward Hopper, *Gloucester Mansion*, 1924. Watercolor, 13 1/2 × 19 1/2 in. Museum of Fine Arts, Boston. Bequest of John T. Spaulding.

and a few are fairly cheerful.[57] His houses range across the spectrum of emotions from melancholy through acceptance to affirmation.

The same applies to a large number of artists, most of them less famous than Hopper. Many, needless to say, did *not* choose to paint houses as icons of the American past. But a goodly number *did*, and in order to bolster the central theme of this chapter, it might be useful to enumerate some representative titles by categories.

NEW ENGLAND: Samuel L. Gerry, *New England Homestead* (1839); John Twachtman, *Old Holly House at Cos Cob* (c. 1890); Niles Spencer, *New England Houses* (1924); Lyonel Feininger, *Old Gables V* (1943); Sanford Law, *Vineyard Homestead* (1956).

NEW YORK CITY AND ITS ENVIRONS: Henry Farrer, *Old Houses in Five Points* (1871); Henry Metzner, a collection of one hundred sketches depicting old houses in New York City and nearby areas (1850–1905);[58] Jerome Myers, *The Old House* (c. 1910).

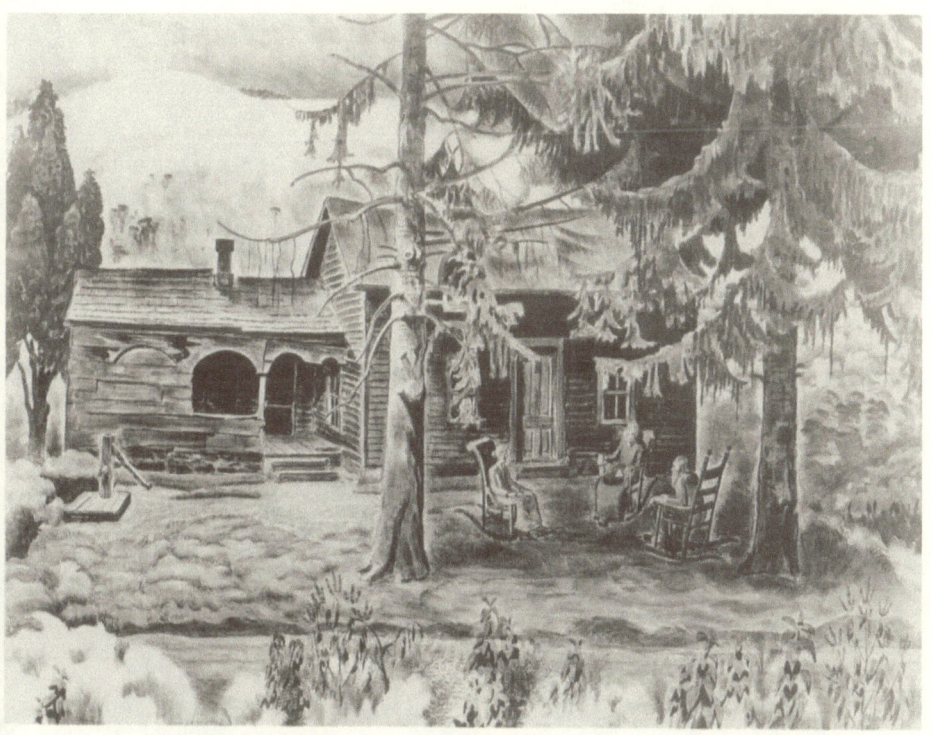

3-14. Charles Burchfield, *Evening,* 1932. Watercolor, 33 1/2 × 45 1/2 in. Collection of The Newark Museum. Purchase 1944.

HISTORIC HOUSES (associated with public events and personages): John Henry Hill, *Sunnyside* (1860); Edward Lamson Henry, *The John Hancock House* (1865); Richard K. Sneden, *Philipse Castle, Tarrytown, New York* (1865); Abram Hosier, Frederick Weller Kost, and Theodore Oscar Fraenkel—views of the Billopp House on Staten Island and others, including the Abigail Adams Smith House, the Morris-Jumel Mansion, and "Old Beekman."

OLD FARMHOUSES: William Sidney Mount, *Long Island Farmhouse Piazza with Imaginary Landscape Vista* (c. 1846); J. Francis Murphy, *Tints of a Vanished Past* (1885); Marjorie Phillips, *The Old Farm House* (1929); John Marin, *Old Dutch Farm House, Tappan, New York* (1932); Rainey Bennett, *Memories of a Farm* (1936).

HOUSES OF SOLITUDE AND LONELINESS: Henry Pember Smith, *Old Homestead* (1880s ?); Oscar Bluemner, *The Last House* (c. 1927); Stow

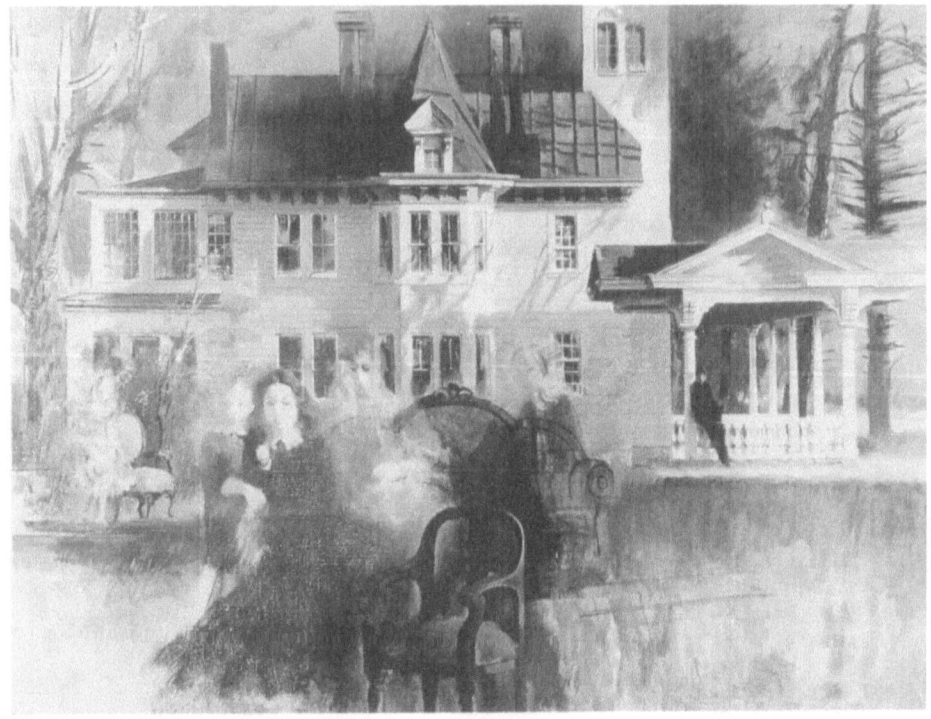

3-15. Adolf Konrad, *The Secret Garden,* 1963–1965. Oil on canvas, 30 × 40 in. Collection of The Montclair Art Museum, Montclair, New Jersey. Museum Purchase.

Wengenroth, *Solitude* (1931); Ogden M. Pleissner, *North of Rawlins* (1941).

The desolate site and decrepit condition of Pleissner's ramshackle house bring to mind Charles Burchfield's obsession with that motif from the 1920s through the 1940s. A particularly striking and explicit example is *Evening* (fig. 3-14), in which three very elderly people rest in rocking chairs with an old and modest farm home behind them. What matters is not so much the time of day, because this trio is sharing memories in the twilight of their lives. We are fortunate to have a letter in which Burchfield indicates that he intended *Evening* to convey no less than four levels of meaning: the end of a day, the end of the year, the closing of the three lives, and also the "Evening of a certain phase of farm life in America. The old farms are going and a new conception is coming in."[59] History as process, sedentary rather than migratory emotions, the passage of time measured in multiple ways: this painting is truly a tour de force.

As we can see, then, pictures of old American homes that are meant to be meaningful or even mysterious have not inevitably had elm trees as companions. Burchfield occasionally chose half-dead or pendulous pines instead, as in *Evening,* and Adolf Konrad did likewise in *The Secret Garden* (fig. 3-15). When the old house and the elm are joined, however, I believe that artists have made their most deliberately stimulating statements about time and memory in American culture—which brings to mind the linkage of Father Time and Clio that we encountered in chapter 1. Their connection may be likened to the confluence of magnetic field lines that flow from one pole to another.

Old American Houses and Elms Juxtaposed

The combination of old houses and elm trees as an American mode of imagery that joins genre and landscape into a nostalgic type of history painting is little more than a century old. After all, as Charles Eliot Norton lamented in 1889, the absence of venerable homes in the United States presented a serious cultural problem. "In our country," he wrote, "barren as it is of historic objects that appeal to the imagination and arouse the poetic associations that give depth and charm to life, such a home is even more precious than in lands where works abound that recall the past by transmitting its image to our eyes."[60]

Francis B. Mayer painted *Francis Street, Annapolis* (fig. 3-16) in 1876, the year he settled in the diminutive port town. He had a strong interest in local history, which residence in the quaint capital reinforced; in 1884 he helped to establish the Local Improvement Association of Annapolis.[61] Looking at *Francis Street* brings to mind Frederick Law Olmsted's wistful comment from the early 1870s that a walk through an older American village would show "the meeting-house closed, the church dilapidated; the famous old taverns, stores, shops, mills, and offices dropping to pieces and vacant."[62] Annapolis had not declined to quite such a dismal extent, but the notable point is this historic convergence of interest and concern by people like Olmsted and Mayer during the 1870s.

It had long been customary for artists to paint the homes in which they lived. We have anonymous examples from the early nineteenth century and one from William Sidney Mount a generation later.[63] During the mid-1880s, however, two important American painters did so; their techniques

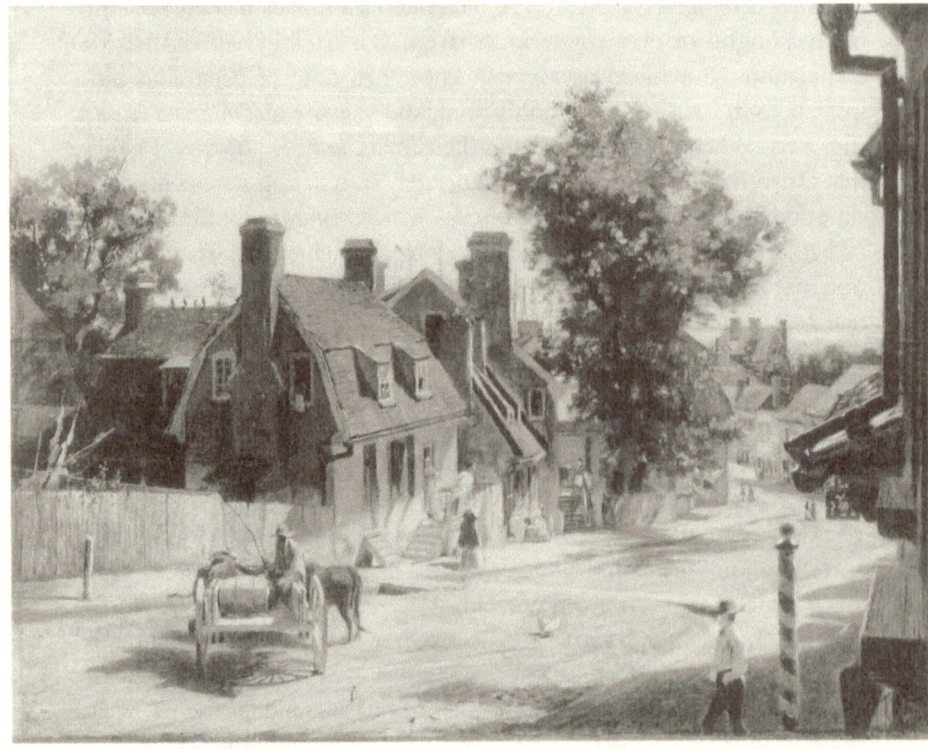

3-16. Francis B. Mayer, *Francis Street, Annapolis*, 1876. Oil on canvas, 15 3/4 × 20 1/2 in. The Metropolitan Museum of Art. Rogers Fund, 1939.

are indicative of distinct generations, yet each conveys a strong degree of sentiment. *The Old Homestead* by Jasper F. Cropsey (fig. 3-17) shows much of the house in poor condition—roof shingles missing and clapboards sagging—and two towering elms on the bluff above. John Twachtman's *My House* (c. 1886–1887) shows only the portico of a Greek Revival structure; the tree that dominates the northeast quadrant of the canvas appears to be an elm.[64]

Childe Hassam, a New Englander by birth, became part of the lively artists' summer colony at Old Lyme, Connecticut, early in this century.[65] We shall return in a later section to the importance of old elms there for his beloved compositions of colonial churches. In 1920, however, Hassam established a permanent summer home in East Hampton, Long Island, which had the same sort of early American charm as Old Lyme. He en-

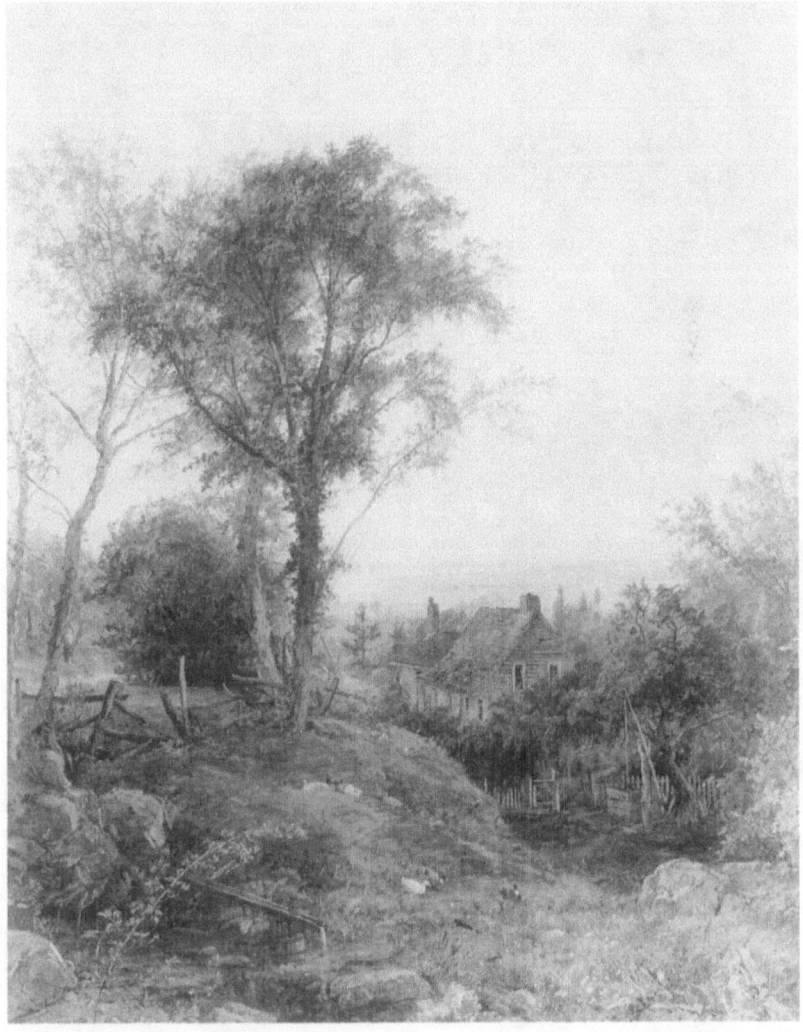

3-17. Jasper F. Cropsey, *The Old Homestead*, 1884. Oil on canvas, 60 × 48 in. Richard York Gallery, New York.

joyed etching the homes along Main Street because it was edged by venerable elms: hence *The Lion Gardiner House, East Hampton* (1920), *House on Main Street, East Hampton* (fig. 3-18), and *Village Elms, East Hampton—Aunt Phoebe's House* (1923).[66]

The reader will recall Braudel's observation—verging upon a stric-

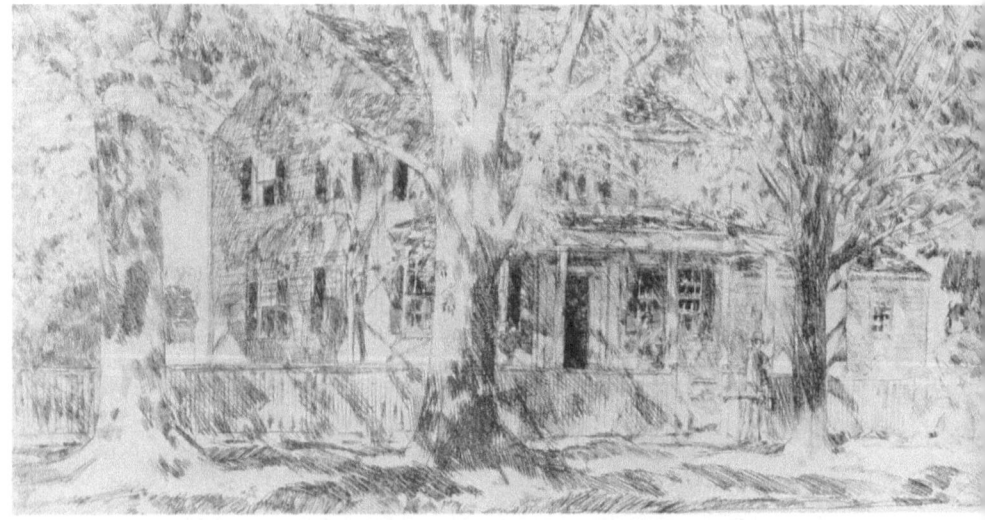

3-18. Childe Hassam, *House on Main Street, East Hampton,* 1922. Etching, 8 1/4 × 13 1/2 in. Courtesy Amon Carter Museum, Fort Worth, Texas.

ture—that "houses viewed from the outside are one thing, from within another." I doubt whether Hassam would have agreed. He is one of the few artists who seems to have painted interior scenes as well as exterior settings with equal pleasure. Perhaps because of his close association with the colonial revival, his interiors are very much what his exteriors might cause you to anticipate. His *Old Doorway, Nantucket* (pre-1900) is flanked by two huge trees which we see only partially, and *In the Old House* (1914) displays just what you would expect to find inside Aunt Phoebe's home in East Hampton![67]

Some members of the generation of artists following Hassam perpetuated his favored subjects, but with responses less tender and moods more austere. Edward Hopper's *Dead Tree and Lombard House* (1932) sends a chilling message, as does Walker Evans's familiar South Boston photograph, *Wooden Houses* (1936).[68] George C. Ault, a New York artist, was drawn repeatedly to the motif of a lifeless old home fronted by a tree that is dead and bare as a bone (fig. 3-19).[69]

Once again, however, it seems clear that such ambiguously unsentimental icons meant more to Charles Burchfield than to any other American artist. His *Lavender and Old Lace* (1939–1947) lacks people because the

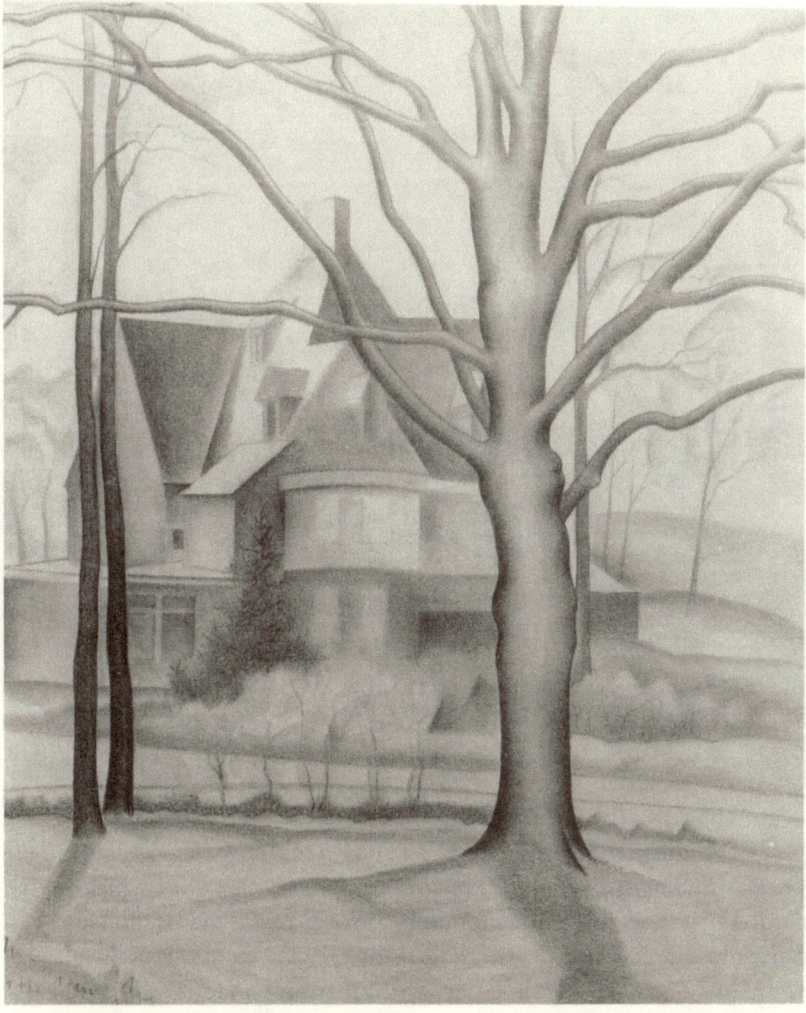

3-19. George C. Ault, *Victorian House and Tree,* 1927. Pencil on paper, 12 × 10 in. Collection of The Newark Museum. Gift of the artist, 1941.

Gothic cottage itself, covered with gingerbread, has reached the evening of its life. Burchfield explained in a journal entry dated May 31, 1947: "I am making it late twilight, I am adding elements . . . observed in other gothic houses; and added two huge elms back of the house, etc. In a word I have abandoned the idea of a specific house and locale, and [am] making it an expression of all I feel about gothic houses."[70]

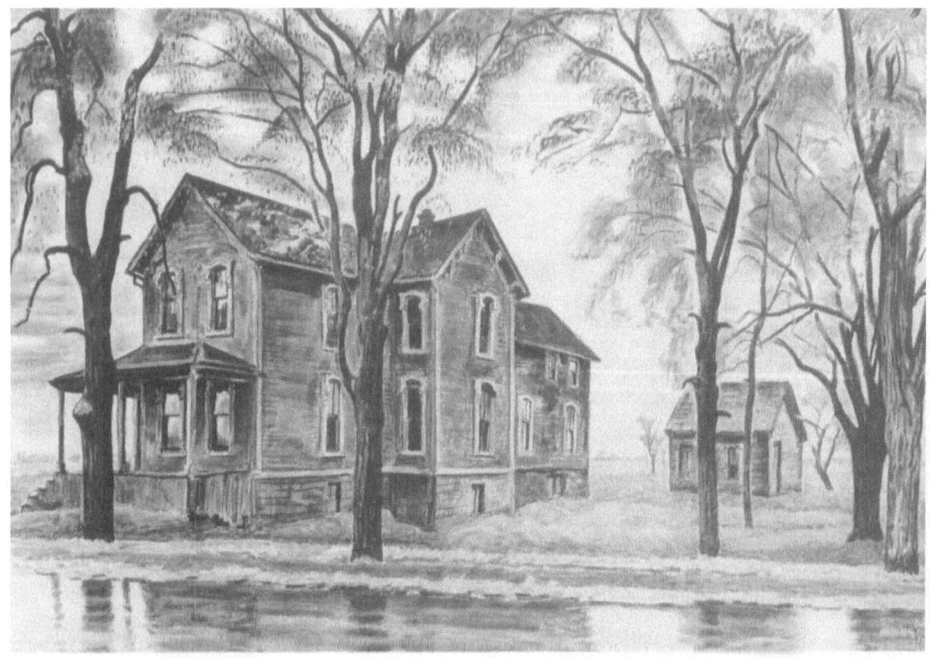

3-20. Charles E. Burchfield, *Old House and Elm Trees*, c. 1933–1940. Watercolor, 27 × 40 in. Virginia Museum of Fine Arts, Richmond. The John Barton Payne Fund.

Burchfield's other works along these lines are not only numerous but persistent throughout his career, such as *Trees and Houses* (1916), *Sulphurous Evening* (1929), and *The Great Elm* (1939–1941), of which he recorded that "memory and emotion play equal parts."[71] His ultimate (because most direct) assertion of these memories and emotions occurs in *Old House and Elm Trees* (fig. 3-20), in which there are no fewer than five elms and a large old home that could not be more barren, bleak, and lifeless.

Comparable British and Irish Symbols of the Past

These long-familiar associations linger on in diverse ways. Carl Carmer opened *Stars Fell on Alabama* with this description of the Van de Graaf place: "A lane of gaunt old elms, then a great blue-grey ghost of a house, dark and rambling." In E. B. White's *Stuart Little* (1945), white houses and elm trees in a New England town are emblematic of early American verities.[72] *The Wapshot Chronicle* by John Cheever takes place in a small coastal community in Massachusetts called St. Botolphs. It begins with an Independence Day parade, after which a horse and wagon plod past Mrs. Drinkwine's "charming white house" and "feathery elms." Cheever's is a chronicle of change and discontinuity, however, "for while the ladies admired the houses and the elms they knew that their sons would go away. Why did the young want to go away?" St. Botolphs was a community in decline.[73]

That social phenomenon, a significant circumstance in twentieth-century American history, provides us with a fundamental point of departure for comparisons with British and Irish culture. It is undeniable that old homes (and even associated elms) have figured prominently in the imaginative literature of Great Britain. John Ruskin wrote eloquently about the metaphorical meaning of old homes and the persistence of memory.[74]

In *Howards End* by E. M. Forster (1910) "houses are alive," and a particular one, which people compete to possess, is intimately tied to an "overhanging wych elm." Just as the house itself, called Howards End, is considered synonymous with England's past and future, so the elm is specified as an "English tree. . . . It was a comrade, bending over the house, strength and adventure in its roots." [76] (The selection of a wych elm hardly seems inevitable—a huge and ancient oak recurs throughout *The Forsyte Saga*, D. H. Lawrence chose an "old park of oak trees" for *Lady Chatterly's Lover,* and Joyce Cary preferred an immense lime tree for *To Be a Pilgrim*.[76]) As with American works, such as *The House of the Seven Gables,* some of Forster's characters care about the past and feel the "power of Home," while others do not. The sympathetic characters reveal the "instinctive wisdom the past alone can bestow." [77]

But what of the differences between such novels? Do they matter? More often than not, I find, the physical symbols may be similar but their meanings diverge. Forster himself, for instance, defined the essence of *Howards End* as "a hunt for a home." That certainly would *not* define the essence of *The House of the Seven Gables* or *Ethan Frome* or any of the many depictions of homes by Hopper and Burchfield. The English fascination with old country homes tends to be connected with concerns about the gentry, or about persons of new wealth and their relations with the aristocracy.[78] American usage is more likely to emphasize socially modest or even humble homes.

Above all, however, the British house is most often invoked as a symbol of order, community, or continuity. As Elizabeth Bowen says of Bowen's

Court: "I am ruled by a continuity that I cannot see." The country homes described by Henry James, E. M. Forster, and Ford Madox Ford are meant to elicit positive feelings for a living tradition or a cohesive connection to the natural landscape.[79]

The old home in American art and literature has more commonly stood for discontinuity, even for decay, and has more frequently been emblematic of social disintegration than communalism. In *Parade's End*, when Ford Madox Ford signals the demise of a social order with the cutting down of a great tree at Groby—and hence the truncation of an organic society—it is an American who cuts it down and severely damages the adjacent house in the process. Ford seems to imply that Americans are, or at least were then, indifferent to tradition.[80] Perhaps John Steinbeck cracked the kernel of a truth when he agreed with Thomas Wolfe, the self-destructive novelist: "You can't go home again because home has ceased to exist except in the mothballs of memory."[81]

In a vision that happens to be neither English nor American, and not so much Irish even as it is sui generis, William Butler Yeats begins his *Meditations in Time of Civil War* (1923) with a section rich in classical allusions called "Ancestral Houses," then moves to "My House" in lines that might have suited a Cropsey or a Gifford:

> An ancient bridge, and a more ancient tower,
> A farmhouse that is sheltered by its wall,
> An acre of stony ground,
> Where the symbolic rose can break in flower,
> Old ragged elms, old thorns innumerable,
> The sound of the rain or sound
> Of every wind that blows.[82]

Eight years later, in a poem called "Coole Park and Ballylee," honoring Lady Gregory, he specifies

> A spot whereon the founders lived and died
> Seemed once more dear than life; ancestral trees,
> Or gardens rich in memory glorified
> Marriages, alliances and families . . .[83]

Yeats concludes with stress upon discontinuity: "But all is changed," and with a "darkening flood" that has endured. How does an artist portray the permanence of change? Frequently by means of the four seasons motif, but equally often by using the motifs of decay and destruction.

Similarly Venerable Sites and Structures in American Culture

Although houses are very much at the core of my discussion, they do not convey the complete story. Other sorts of older structures have also served as symbols of tradition, especially when the so-called colonial revival flourished between the 1880s and roughly the third decade of the twentieth century.[84] (In a very real sense, the colonial revival has not yet expired. It gets reformulated in new molds.) Here, moreover, I must acknowledge the partially derivative nature of our phenomenon. The Victorian bishop and historian William Stubbs viewed an ancient church—he very likely had his own, at Navestock, in mind—as an epitome of English history. "Every old building," he noted, "church or not, has a history for every broken stone." John Ruskin wrote in much the same manner about Oxford Cathedral and added with scorn that swift, mindless, pattern-book building was indicative of a transient and improvised way of life.[85]

As far back as the mid-nineteenth century in the United States, as we have seen, James Fenimore Cooper warned that with swifter modes of travel "the half-hidden church, nestling among the leaves of its elms and pines, the neat and secluded hamlet, [and] the farm-house, with all its comforts and sober arrangements," would soon be lost from view.[86] During the early years of this century the old New England church, fronted by "aisles of elms," became a favorite subject for certain painters who cared about the past and wished to contrast it with the harsher lines and lesser quality of modern sites and structures. We find this expressed in Gifford Beal's *New England Street,* for instance, and to an even greater degree in such works by Willard Metcalf as *September Morning, Plainfield, New Hampshire* (1910) and *October Morning: Deerfield, Massachusetts* (1917).[87]

More than any other artist, however, Childe Hassam had the strongest urge to memorialize the venerable churches of New England, invariably fronted by elms, as testimony to the cultural continuity for which he yearned. On occasion he painted them with visual traces of the surrounding community. That is the case with *White Church, Provincetown* (1900) and *St. Marks in the Bowery* (1910).[88] Most often, however, he preferred to paint the church alone with its elms, and rarely with a complete steeple

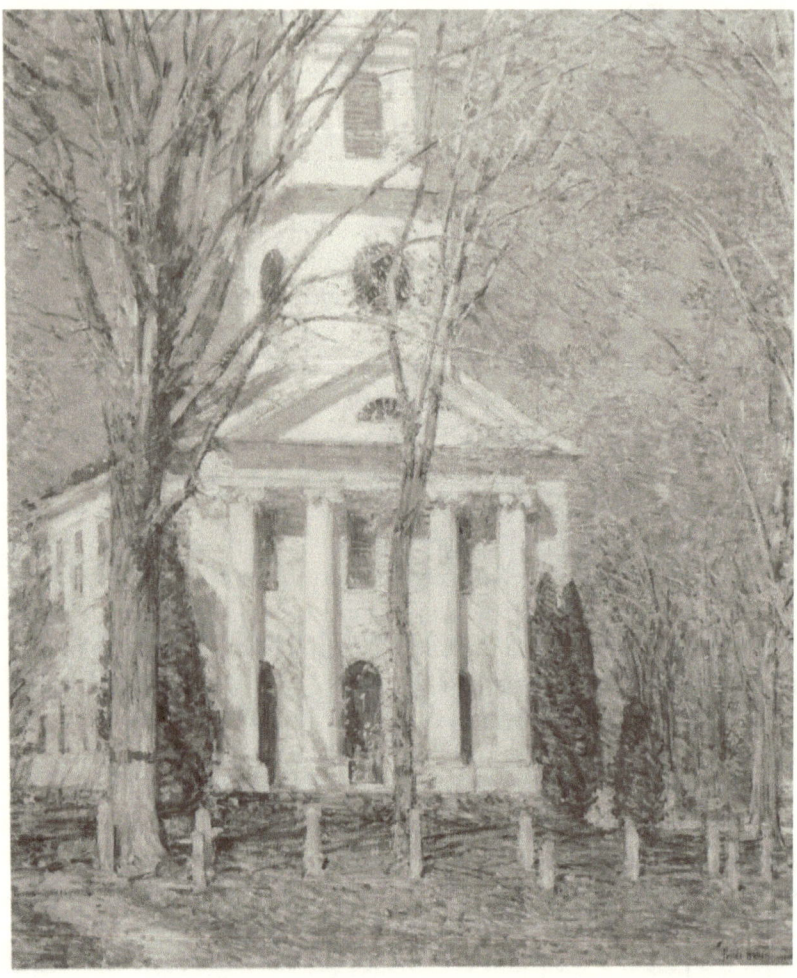

3-21. Childe Hassam, *Church at Old Lyme, Connecticut,* 1905. Oil on canvas, 36 1/4 × 32 1/4 in. Albright-Knox Art Gallery, Buffalo, New York. Albert H. Tracy Fund, 1909.

(fig. 3-21). His Palladian and Greek Revival churches are truncated. They do not, like Charles Demuth's, visibly point heavenward (fig. 3-22).[89]

Perhaps Hassam merely made an aesthetic decision to feature iconic elms in the foreground rather than steeples and indeterminate sky. I am persuaded, however, that this was only partially his rationale. Precisely because most Americans no longer lived in an age of faith, steeples aimed at Heaven, like so many pointers, seemed less meaningful. And precisely be-

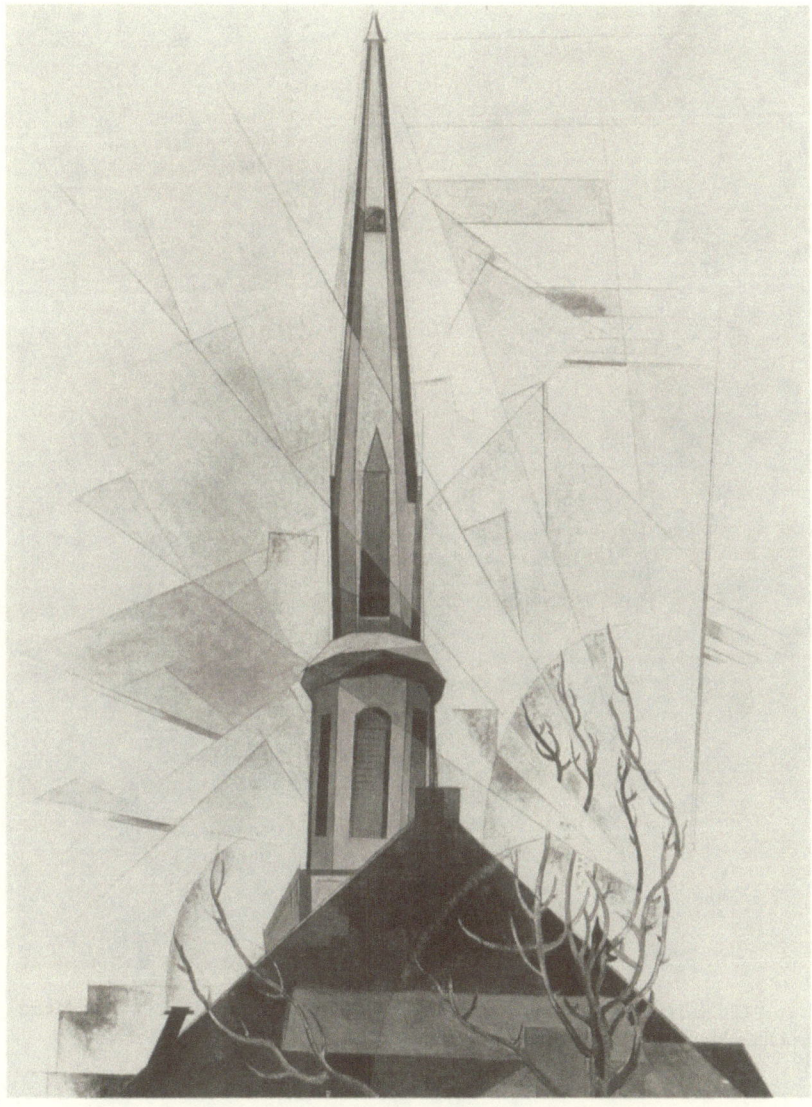

3-22. Charles Demuth, *In the Province,* 1920. Tempera, watercolor, and pencil on composition board, 19 1/2 × 15 1/2 in. Courtesy of the Amon Carter Museum, Fort Worth, Texas.

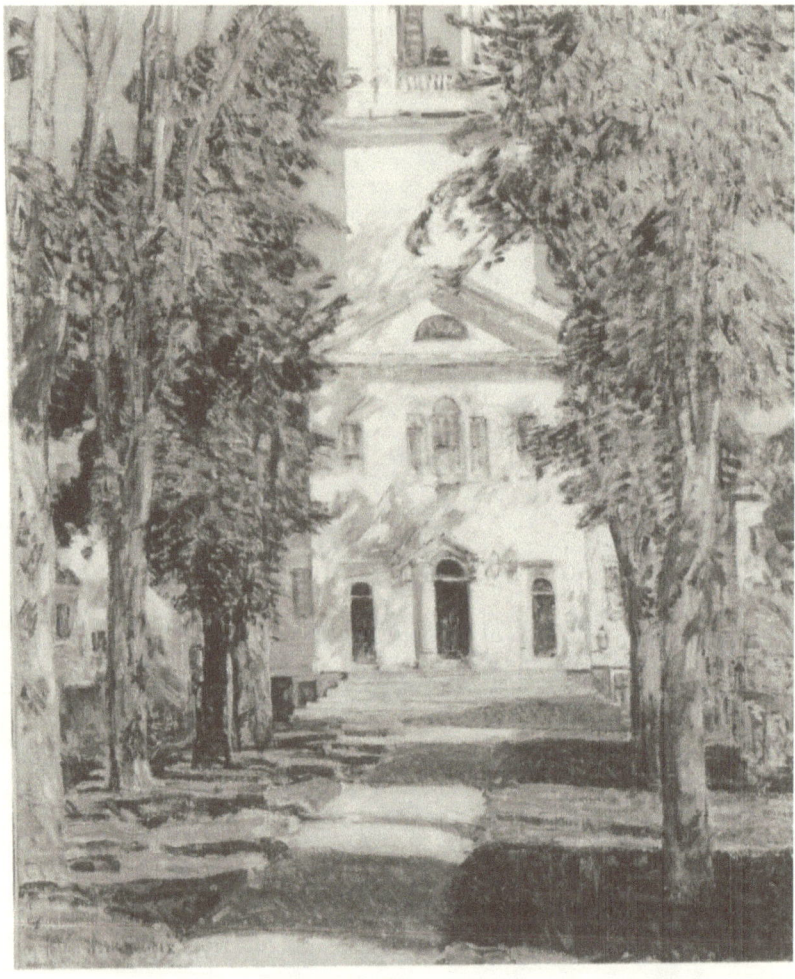

3-23. Childe Hassam, *The Church at Gloucester*, 1918. Oil on canvas, 30 × 25 in. The Metropolitan Museum of Art. Arthur H. Hearn Fund, 1925.

cause a foreground filled with venerable elms represented most explicitly the passage of generations preceding the present, Hassam wanted his elms in *Church at Old Lyme, Connecticut* as testimony to the historical process of *becoming* and as a palpable symbol of the quiddity of *being*.[90]

In *The Church at Gloucester* (fig. 3-23), Hassam's alley of elms leads our eye directly through the foreground, and they thereby serve as signposts of space as well as time. The elms throw marvelous shadows at each other and

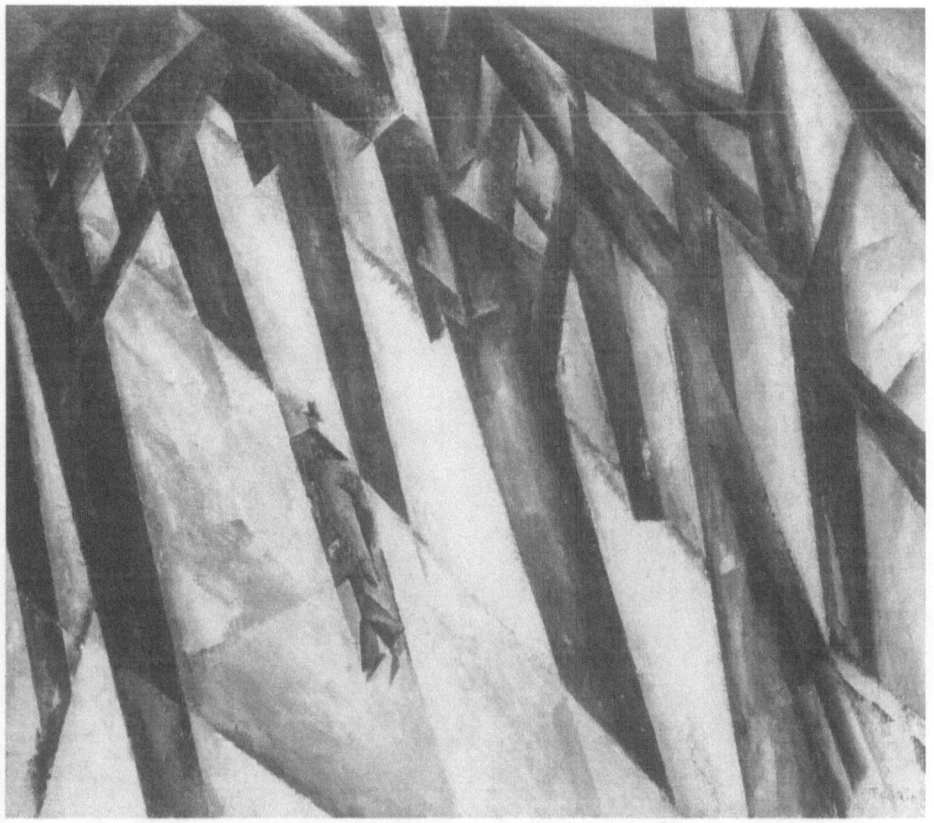

3-24. Lyonel Feininger, *Alley of Trees*, 1914. Oil on canvas, 31 3/4 × 39 3/4 in. The Metropolitan Museum of Art. Anonymous Loan (L.1980.63).

upon the church—more so than in his Old Lyme paintings. We have here Hassam's most wistful and haunting assertion of a past that is enduring even though no longer compelling for the secular society as a whole.[91] Notice, then, for purposes of comparison, that Lyonel Feininger eliminated the church entirely in his cubistic *Alley of Trees* (fig. 3-24). I am persuaded that Hassam would have said, "Here we see *Hamlet* without the prince."

The traditional New England church lingers on as a minor motif in American art, exemplified in a conventional representation by Robert Strong Woodward's *Enduring New England* (c. 1920–1930) and in the engagingly cubistic *New England* by Victor Candell (1952).[92]

We should acknowledge, however briefly, that other forms of vernacular

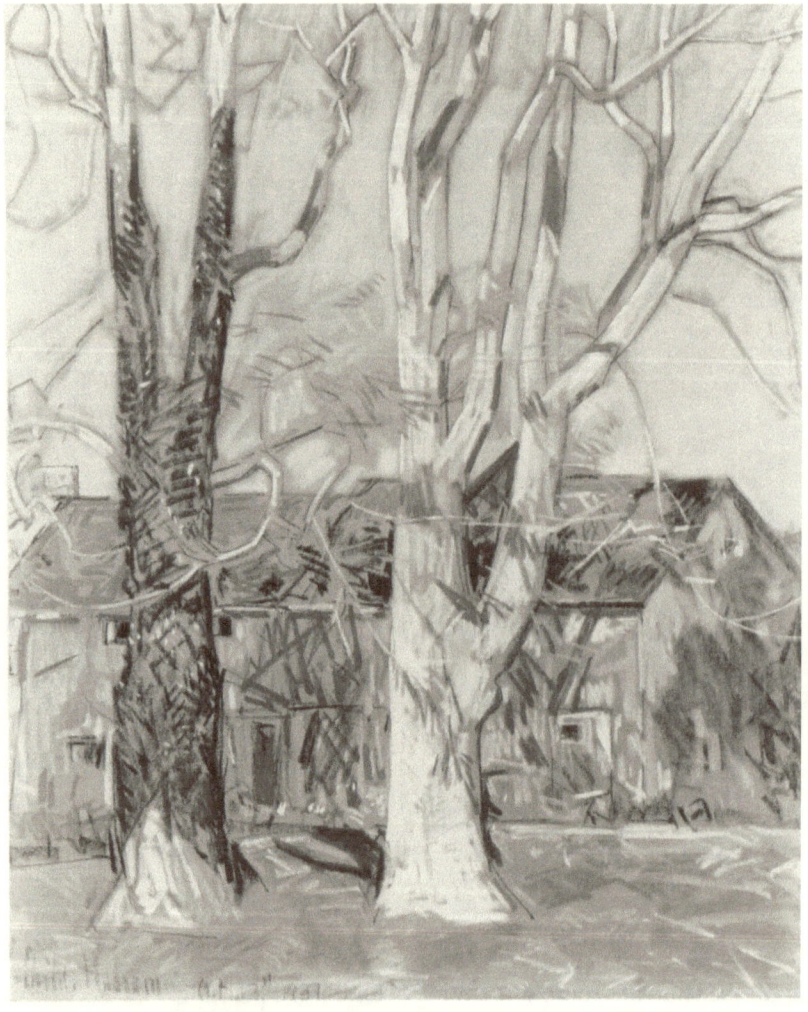

3-25. Childe Hassam, *Old Barn, East Hampton*, 1931. Pastel on paper, 24 × 20 in. Courtesy of Babcock Galleries, New York.

architecture have filled the role of *memor et fidelis*—mindful and faithful structures from the American past. One is the old barn, exemplified here in a pastel by Hassam (fig. 3-25). Another has been the old mill, illustrated by Charles Sheeler's *Old Slater Mill, Pawtucket, Rhode Island* (fig. 3-26).[93] The crisp contrasts in preciseness of technique, condition of the structures, and manner of presentation do not diminish, in my view, the romanticized message that these two works share in common.

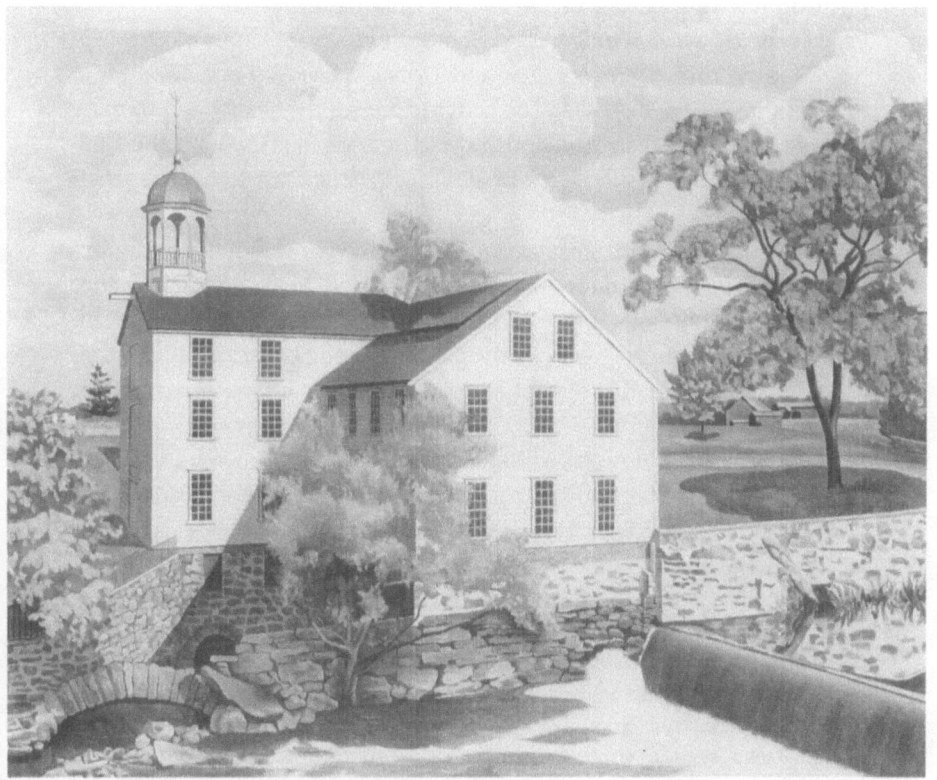

3-26. Charles Sheeler, *Old Slater Mill, Pawtucket, Rhode Island,* 1945. Oil on canvas, 29 ×
36 in. The Regis Collection, Minneapolis, Minnesota.

Still a third sort of structure that has been utilized is the old tavern, inn,
or village store. Charles Burchfield favored such buildings on occasion.[94]
When the African-American novelist and folklorist Zora Neale Hurston
wrote about Eatonville, Florida, the store porch became absolutely critical
as the center of community and embodiment of local black cultural traditions. It served as the focus for intergenerational connections and the
transmission of culture.[95]

Coda: Successions of Consciousness in American Culture

Americans as a people have responded in diverse ways to ancestral homes—
when they have responded at all. In the South, undeniably, the antebellum

mansion has long been a symbol of regional traditions. Thomas Nelson Page prepared an essay titled "The American Home—Source of Our Liberties" at the turn of the century, and Donald Davidson asserted in 1930 that "nothing more clearly . . . or better expresses the beauty and stability of an ordered life, than [the South's] old country homes, with their pillared porches, their simplicity of design, their sheltering groves, their walks. . . ."[96]

We encounter comparable sentiments in New England among figures so diverse as members of the Adams family, John P. Marquand, and Justice Oliver Wendell Holmes, an unsentimental man who wrote in 1925 to a Chinese friend: "One may . . . evoke the past by visiting houses built two centuries and a half ago. That is not long for China but it is long enough for romance."[97]

Hawthorne's self-designated romance, *The House of the Seven Gables,* begins by mocking mysterious genealogical pretensions and "an absurd delusion of family importance." At the end, however, a *via media* is achieved. Holgrave, the photographer who has been hostile to tradition throughout the story, gives a little homily to Phoebe Pyncheon, his bride-to-be:

> The happy man inevitably confines himself within ancient limits. I have a presentiment that, hereafter, it will be my lot to set out trees, to make fences,—perhaps, even, in due time, to build a house for another generation,—in a word, to conform myself to laws and the peaceful practice of society.[98]

He concludes by acknowledging that his temperament has an "oscillating tendency." That characteristic, in my view, is a significant aspect of his Americanness—especially his oscillations concerning past- versus present-mindedness.

A twentieth-century American artist made a bold observation fifty years ago and arranged it in strikingly visual terms for us (fig. 3-27). Philip Evergood explains the origins of *My Forebears Were Pioneers* in terms of an unusual scene that he witnessed in New England right after the catastrophic hurricane of 1938:

> We were driving from Cape Cod to New York, going through a little village with all the trees blown down, lying on the lawns, and there was a beautiful, austere old lady—beautiful because she was so ramrod straight—sitting in her

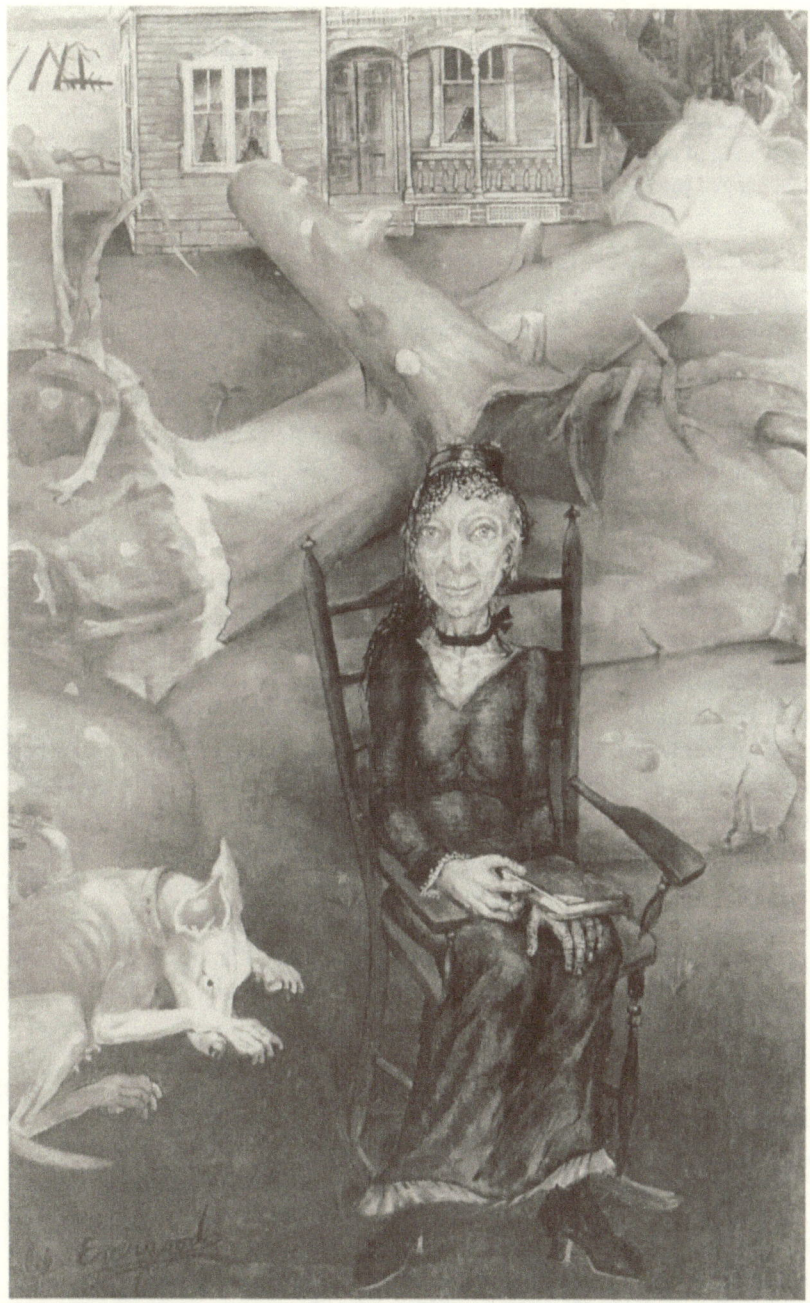

3-27. Philip Evergood, *My Forebears Were Pioneers,* 1939. Oil on canvas, 50 × 36 in. Georgia Museum of Art, The University of Georgia, University Purchase.

chair with an old dog at her feet and a Bible on her knee, calmly looking out at the cars going by, with the complete destruction of her house and trees lying all over the beautiful lawn. I was impressed by the way that old lady of pioneer stock was unperturbed by anything. Her grandfathers had fought Indians and come over on the Mayflower, and there she was with her Bible, not changed by all that turmoil of nature.[99]

It seems to me that this painting conveys several highly significant perceptions. First—a somewhat "revisionist" or at least neglected point—old houses and old trees do not *necessarily* make congenial companions. Building houses requires the destruction of trees, and nearby trees, in turn, may wreak havoc upon houses. Second, although it would appear that nature has overwhelmed culture (consistent with the temper of nineteenth-century American landscape art), those trees lying in the field *behind* the woman's house were presumably felled by the woman's pioneer forebears. And the house does not appear to be irreparably devastated. Far from it. But above all, the old woman is intact and her spirit is unbroken. A figurative family tree may have perished, but the clan's contemporary incarnation, represented by the house, the woman, and her dog, remain stalwart and self-assured. Although forces of discontinuity have done their utmost, they have not entirely prevailed.[100]

Evergood's painting concerns consciousness, and it brings us back once again to Henry James's intriguing concept of "successions of consciousness." That notion and this picture each convey an attitude toward and explication of cultural values. Historical art, like historical consciousness, can be concerned with ordinary—even anonymous—Americans. It also engages time and space. It has repeatedly memorialized old homes in powerfully metaphorical ways. And more often than not, a venerable French adage has been applicable: *la vieille maison a gardé son passé.*

Notes

1. See William H. Gerdts and Mark Thistlethwaite, *Grand Illusions: History Painting in America* (Fort Worth, 1988), p. 54. For a comparable issue in the study of American literature, see Susan L. Mizruchi, *The Power of Historical Knowledge: Narrating the Past in Hawthorne, James, and Dreiser* (Princeton, 1988), p. 4.

2. William Morris Hunt, *Talks about Art* (London, 1878), p. 80.

3. See the red-transfer printed earthenware plate made by Thomas Green of Staffordshire (c. 1847–1859), at the Henry Ford Museum, Dearborn, Michigan;

and the brown and white plate, also made by Green, at the Essex Institute, Salem, Massachusetts.

4. See the blue plate made by Mintons in 1905 at the Essex Institute, Salem, Massachusetts.

5. T. S. Eliot, "Little Gidding," from "Four Quartets," in *The Complete Poems and Plays, 1909–1950* (New York, 1952), p. 144.

6. Charles Coleman Sellers, "The Beginning: A Monument to Probity, Candor and Peace," in *Symbols of Peace: William Penn's Treaty with the Indians,* catalogue of Pennsylvania Academy of the Fine Arts exhibition, May–September 1976 (Philadelphia, 1976), n.p.

7. Ibid. See also Ann Uhry Abrams, "Benjamin West's Documentation of Colonial History: *William Penn's Treaty with the Indians,*" *Art Bulletin* 64 (Mar. 1982): 59–75. For the intense controversy in 1835–1836, when antiquarians discovered that Penn had not signed a treaty with the Indians, see Deborah D. Waters, "Philadelphia's Boswell: John Fanning Watson," *Pennsylvania Magazine of History and Biography* 98 (Jan. 1974): 28–29.

8. Helmut von Erffa and Allen Staley, *The Paintings of Benjamin West* (New Haven, 1986), pp. 68–69, 206–208. West's use of the date 1755 cannot be correct because he was born in 1734.

9. Located in the Chicago Historical Society and the Thomas Gilcrease Institute of American History and Art, Tulsa, Oklahoma.

10. See Alice Ford, *Edward Hicks: His Life and Art* (New York, 1985), p. 54; Susan Prendergast Schoelwer, "Curious Relics and Quaint Scenes: The Colonial Revival at Chicago's Great Fair," in *The Colonial Revival in America,* ed. Alan Axelrod (New York, 1985), p. 198.

11. Apparently this occurred because Hicks had only seen John Hall's 1775 engraving, for which his preparatory drawing was not reversed. West's original painting did not migrate from England to Philadelphia until 1852, three years after Hicks died.

12. See Ford, *Edward Hicks,* pp. 54–55, 60, 69–70. On May 23, 1775, Richard Henderson convened a House of Delegates for the projected colony of Transylvania (in central Kentucky) beneath a massive elm tree. The elm had great symbolic significance for Henderson. See Bernard Bailyn, *Voyagers to the West: A Passage in the Peopling of America on the Eve of the Revolution* (New York, 1986), pp. 538–539.

13. Martin P. Snyder, *City of Independence: Views of Philadelphia before 1800* (New York, 1975), pp. 141, 197; P. Lee Phillips, *A Descriptive List of Maps and Views of Philadelphia in the Library of Congress, 1683–1865* (Philadelphia, 1926), p. 74. For an unconventional rendition of *The Landing of William Penn* by Thomas Birch (c. 1850), see Matthew Baigell, *Nineteenth-Century Painters of the Delaware Valley* (Trenton, 1983), p. 27.

14. Actually Smith's painting was a close copy of John James Barralet's *Landscape View of Philadelphia from Kensington,* a 1796 watercolor in which there are two goats in the elm tree. See Snyder, *City of Independence,* p. 197.

15. *Edwin Austin Abbey (1852–1911): An Exhibition Organized by the Yale Univer-*

sity Art Gallery (New Haven, 1973), p. 2; *Symbols of Peace,* last page. Grooms's work is now in the Denver Art Museum.

16. See Henry T. Tuckerman, *Artist-Life: Or, Sketches of American Painters* (New York, 1847), p. 187; Jacob Abbot, *Marco Paul's Voyages & Travels in Vermont* (New York, 1852), p. 14; "A Tree Grows in Kansas: Tall, Old and Honored," *New York Times,* Sept. 7, 1980, p. 61.

17. See Roger G. Kennedy, *Architecture, Men, Women and Money in America, 1600–1860* (New York, 1985), p. 369; Maurice G. Baxter, *One and Inseparable: Daniel Webster and the Union* (Cambridge, Mass., 1984), p. 4.

18. Vincent J. Scully, Jr., *The Shingle Style and the Stick Style: Architectural Theory and Design from Downing to the Origins of Wright,* 2d ed. (New Haven, 1971), p. 145; Van Wyck Brooks, *Days of the Phoenix: The 1920s I Remember* (New York, 1951), pp. 2–3; David Levering Lewis, *When Harlem Was in Vogue* (New York, 1981), p. 210. During the 1920s Owen D. Young, chairman of General Electric, devised a major landscaping project for St. Lawrence University in Canton, New York: a quadruple avenue of elms nearly a mile in length. See Josephine Young Case and Everett Needham Case, *Owen D. Young and American Enterprise* (Boston, 1982), p. 387.

19. Baxter, *Webster and the Union,* p. 435; Karal Ann Marling, *George Washington Slept Here* (Cambridge, Mass., 1988), p. 67; *Washington Evening Star,* Dec. 7, 1937, p. A7. On Memorial Day in 1939 the Daughters of the Defenders of the Republic of the United States of America decorated elm trees (located behind Grant's Tomb) that are dedicated to twenty-two heroes of American wars. *New York Times,* May 30, 1939, p. 2.

20. David Tyack and Elizabeth Hansot, *Managers of Virtue: Public School Leadership in America, 1820–1980* (New York, 1982), p. 39. In 1881, when Walt Whitman visited Boston, he noted "especially the old elms along Tremont and Beacon streets." Whitman recalled with nostalgia that in 1860 he and Emerson had walked for two hours "between these same old elms" when Emerson "was the talker and I the listener." *Specimen Days* (1882), in *The Poetry and Prose of Walt Whitman,* ed. Louis Untermeyer (New York, 1949), p. 793.

21. Nathaniel Hawthorne, *The House of the Seven Gables: A Romance* (1851; Boston, 1900), pp. 96, 368, 381, 415, 422, 467. During the 1880s Herman Melville worked on a story about an aged mariner named Daniel Orme, which is the French word for elm. From the sketch that has survived, "Daniel Orme" was destined to be a reminiscence, at least in part, of Melville's own experiences almost half a century earlier on board the frigate *United States.* See F. Barron Freeman, "The Enigma of Melville's 'Daniel Orme'," *American Literature* 16 (Nov. 1944): 208–211.

22. Edith Wharton, *Ethan Frome* (1911; New York, 1950), pp. 162–169. See also Mary C. Crawford, *The Romance of Old New England Rooftrees* (Boston, 1902).

23. Ellen Glasgow, *The Sheltered Life* (Garden City, N.Y. 1932), pp. 6, 173. See also Walter Prichard Eaton, "Trees," *Century Magazine* 91 (Jan. 1916): 364–371. "The valley of the Housatonic, in the Berkshire Hills, is peculiarly rich in splendid

trees of many kinds, especially willows. Yet its elms stand out with a certain aristocratic aloofness, and demand, or, rather, compel, the chief attention. Over the well-kept village streets they spread magnificently, with the spring of a Gothic arch in their massive limbs, and oriole nests depending like tiny platinum ear-drops from the outer twigs. But along the river you see the whole tree; you are not aware of it as the under side of an arch, but rather as a complete and beautiful design, a mammoth vase rising on its graceful stem from the emerald meadows. There are five such elms in a row near my home" (p. 368).

24. *The Writings of James Russell Lowell* (Boston, 1897), 11:74. In 1900 some Harvard faculty disputed the tradition that Washington had stood beneath that stately elm when he accepted command. See "Attacks on Old Tradition: Prof. Channing Casts Doubt on the Washington Elm at Cambridge," *New York Times*, May 5, 1900, p. 1.

25. See Elizabeth Stillinger, *The Antiquers* (New York, 1980), pp. 21, 25. In 1936 the Bergen County Historical Society (New Jersey) sought to preserve an old elm tree in Ho-ho-kus under which George Washington is said to have spent a night during the American Revolution. See "Fund Sought to Save Historic Jersey Elm: Patriotic Groups to Be Asked to Preserve Tree That Once Sheltered Washington," *New York Times*, Nov. 30, 1936, p. 23.

26. Charles A. Fenton, *Stephen Vincent Benét: The Life and Times of an American Man of Letters, 1898–1943* (New Haven, 1958), p. 70.

27. Quoted in Herbert G. Gutman, *Work, Culture, and Society in Industrializing America: Essays in American Working-Class and Social History* (New York, 1976), p. 29.

28. In the Wadsworth Atheneum, Hartford, Connecticut. See John Samson, "Hawthorne's Oak Trees," *American Literature* 52 (Nov. 1980): 457–461, concerning the use of the Charter Oak in "Roger Malvin's Burial." For the "great Wayside Oak" near the inn at Sudbury, Massachusetts, see Marling, *George Washington Slept Here*, p. 174; and for the importance of the oak in German iconography, see Gerdts and Thistlethwaite, *Grand Illusions*, p. 146.

29. See "15,000 on the Mall Hail Constitution: Many Drenched by Rain," *New York Times*, Sept. 20, 1937, pp. 1, 9.

30. Frances Wright, *Views of Society and Manners in America*, ed. Paul R. Baker (Cambridge, Mass., 1963), pp. 104–105; Paul Russell Cutright and Michael J. Brodhead, *Elliot Coues: Naturalist and Frontier Historian* (Urbana, 1981), p. 22. Frank French wrote in "Trees," *Scribner's Magazine* 28 (July 1900): 29–38, "It is easy to recall many New England villages where ancient elms stand in double ranks along the main street . . . investing the very air with a sense of peace and serenity" (p. 32). See also Constance Cary Harrison, "American Rural Festivals," *Century Magazine* 50 (July 1895): 324, 326.

31. See Natalie Spassky et al., comps., *American Paintings in the Metropolitan Museum of Art* (Princeton, 1985), 2:250–254.

32. *The American Painting Collection of the Montclair Art Museum* (Montclair,

N.J. 1977), pp. 116, 219. See also Gifford Beal, *New England Elms*, in Christie's auction catalogue, *Important American Paintings, Drawings and Sculptures of the Nineteenth and Twentieth Centuries*, Dec. 5, 1986, p. 238.

33. See Fridolf Johnson, ed., *Rockwell Kent: An Anthology of His Works* (New York, 1982), p. 316.

34. John I. H. Baur, *The Inlander: Life and Work of Charles Burchfield, 1893–1967* (East Brunswick, N.J., 1982), p. 180.

35. Wright, *Views of Society and Manners in America*, p. 100; James Fenimore Cooper, "American and European Scenery Compared," in Motley F. Deakin, ed., *The Home Book of the Picturesque: Or American Scenery, Art, and Literature* (1852; Gainesville, Fla., 1967), p. 60.

36. For Thomas Cole it was a point of pride that the United States did not have ruined castles, cathedrals, etc. See his "Essay on American Scenery" (1835) in *American Art, 1700–1960: Sources and Documents*, ed. John W. McCoubrey (Englewood Cliffs, N.J., 1965), esp. pp. 101, 106, 108–109.

37. Jerome H. Buckley, *The Triumph of Time: A Study of the Victorian Concepts of Time, History, Progress, and Decadence* (Cambridge, Mass., 1966), p. 70.

38. Jean Starobinski, *The Invention of Liberty, 1700–1789* (Geneva, 1964), pp. 179–187; Victor Carlson, *Hubert Robert: Drawings & Watercolors* (Washington, D.C., 1978).

39. Rose Macaulay, *Pleasure of Ruins* (London, 1953); Stephen Bann, *The Clothing of Clio: A Study of the Representation of History in Nineteenth-Century Britain and France* (Cambridge, Eng., 1984), pp. 56–57.

40. See, e.g., Robert Goldwater and Marco Treves, *Artists on Art from the Fourteenth to the Twentieth Century* (New York, 1945), p. 281; Church, *Ruins at Baalbek* (1889), Yale University Art Gallery, New Haven, Connecticut; Theodore E. Stebbins, Jr., *Close Observation: Selected Oil Sketches by Frederic E. Church* (Washington, D.C., 1978), pp. 41, 43, 90, 93, 98–99; William S. Talbot, *Jasper F. Cropsey, 1823–1900* (Washington, D.C., 1970), pp. 21, 78–79, 87, 103–104.

41. See Brantz Mayer, "A June Jaunt: With Some Wanderings in the Footsteps of Washington, Braddock, and the Early Pioneers," *Harper's New Monthly Magazine* 14 (Apr. 1857): 598, 603–604. In mid-nineteenth-century American rhetoric, physical ruins of the European past, such as the Parthenon and the Colosseum, were compared to the prospective ruins of the Union if it should collapse. As Daniel Webster declared in 1837: "Fragments and shattered columns of the edifice may be found remaining; and melancholy and mournful ruins they will be." Quoted in Paul D. Erickson, *The Poetry of Events: Daniel Webster's Rhetoric of the Constitution and the Union* (New York, 1986), p. 116.

42. Thomas Nelson Page (1890), quoted in James M. Lindgren, "The Gospel of Preservation in Virginia and New England: Historic Preservation and the Regeneration of Traditionalism" (Ph.D. diss., College of William and Mary, 1984), p. 76. For *Ruins of Jamestown* (n.d.), painted by John G. Chapman, see Georgia

Stamm Chamberlain, *Studies on John Gadsby Chapman: American Artist, 1808–1889* (Annandale, Va., 1963), fig. 35.

43. Wayne Craven, "Asher B. Durand's Imaginary Landscapes," *The Magazine Antiques* 116 (Nov. 1979): 1121. See also Harry Levin, *The Power of Blackness: Hawthorne, Poe, Melville* (New York, 1958), Appendix, "Castles and Culture."

44. See Allen Guttmann, "Images of Value and the Sense of the Past," *New England Quarterly* 35 (Mar. 1962): 3–26. Jan Cohn, *The Palace or the Poorhouse: The American House as a Cultural Symbol* (East Lansing, Mich., 1979), emphasizes the home as an emblem of personal economic success and social stability based upon prosperity. For the historic "house essay," which helped to foster the idea of home as a shrine, see pp. 193–212.

45. See, e.g., Hermann Warner Williams, Jr., *Mirror to the American Past: A Survey of American Genre Painting, 1750–1900* (Greenwich, Conn., 1973).

46. Fernand Braudel, *Capitalism and Material Life, 1400–1800* (New York, 1973), p. 204. For an artistic affirmation of that statement by a remarkable American photographer, see Walker Evans, *Message from the Interior* (New York, 1966).

47. See Millicent Bell, *Hawthorne's View of the Artist* (New York, 1962). By using illuminated windows and open doorways, Edward Hopper succeeded in showing exterior structure and interior space in the same painting. See Gail Levin, *Edward Hopper: The Art and the Artist* (New York, 1980), plates 212, 290, 380, and 381.

48. Hawthorne, *House of the Seven Gables*, pp. 1, 19, 177. See also pp. 4, 6, 22, 64, 71, 118, 319.

49. Ibid., p. 178.

50. Ibid., pp. 380, 430. For a remarkable echo, see Hervey Allen, *Action at Aquila* (Philadelphia, 1938), p. 9.

51. See Richard Gill, *Happy Rural Seat: The English Country House and the Literary Imagination* (New Haven, 1972), chap. 1.

52. R. W. B. Lewis, *Edith Wharton: A Biography* (New York, 1975), pp. 104, 491. See also Joseph Hergesheimer, *From an Old House* (New York, 1926).

53. Walt Whitman, *Leaves of Grass*, ed. Emory Holloway (Garden City, N.Y., 1926), p. 488.

54. Quoted in William Barrett, *The Truants: Adventures among the Intellectuals* (Garden City, N.Y., 1982), p. 26.

55. See, e.g., *Cape Cod Afternoon* (1936) in *Survey of American Painting: Department of Fine Arts, Carnegie Institute* (Pittsburgh, 1940), pp. 252–253; and *House on the Cape* (1940) in Zane Probasco, *An American Collection: The Hunter Museum of Art* (Chattanooga, Tenn., 1978), no. 43.

56. The Museum of Fine Arts in Boston has a fine collection of Hopper watercolors of old houses, including *Houses of 'Squam Light, Gloucester* (1923), *House at the Fort, Gloucester* (1924), *Anderson's House, Gloucester* (1926), and *Hill and Houses, Cape Elizabeth, Maine* (1927).

57. In *The Mansard Roof* (1923) at the Brooklyn Museum, the billowing canvas

awnings offer respite from summer heat; see also *Pretty Penny* (1939), Smith College Museum of Art, Northampton, Massachusetts. For a sampler of Hopper's houses, see Levin, *Edward Hopper,* plates 208, 231, 264, 288, 290.

58. See Richard J. Koke, comp., *American Landscape and Genre Paintings in the New-York Historical Society* (Boston, 1982), 2 : 325–334.

59. Quoted in *American Art in the Newark Museum: Paintings, Drawings, and Sculpture* (Newark, N.J., 1981), p. 305. See also Charles Burchfield, *Garden of Memories* (1917), crayon and watercolor, Museum of Modern Art, New York. A very old woman in a reverie sits in front of her house, flowers on both sides of her. A larger old house looms in the upper left-hand corner. The colors are late autumnal—rust orange, faded green, and brown—and the woman looks ghostly. And see Allen Tate's poem "Reflections in an Old House" (1923), in *Collected Poems, 1919–1976* (New York, 1977), pp. 198–199.

60. Norton, "The Lack of Old Homes in America," *Scribner's Magazine* 5 (May 1889): 636–640. Cf. Charles Dudley Warner, "The Pilgrim, and the American of Today" (speech on Dec. 21, 1892), in *Fashions in Literature and Other Literary and Social Essays & Addresses* (New York, 1902), p. 136: "I know of a village of old-fashioned houses and broad elm-shaded streets in New England. . . ."

61. Some of his correspondence with John G. Hopkins (1886–1889), to whom he gave this painting, will be found in the Maryland Historical Society, Baltimore.

62. Quoted in Paul Boyer, *Urban Masses and Moral Order in America, 1820–1920* (Cambridge, Mass., 1978), p. 237.

63. See Nancy C. Muller, *Paintings and Drawings at the Shelburne Museum* (Shelburne, Vt., 1976), fig. 446 on p. 174; Alfred Frankenstein, *William Sidney Mount* (New York, 1975), fig. 102.

64. Talbot, *Jasper F. Cropsey,* p. 43; Theodore E. Stebbins, Jr., and Galina Gorokhoff, comps., *A Checklist of American Paintings at Yale University* (New Haven, 1982), pp. 156–157 and fig. 1632.

65. A contemporary of Hassam and another member of the group was Willard Metcalf, whose *Captain Lord House, Kennebunkport, Maine* (c. 1920), is a classic old New England house with elms flanking the front door. It is located in the Florence Griswold Museum, Old Lyme, Connecticut. See also Thomas D. Benrimo, "Old Lyme, Connecticut: Pencil Sketches with Notes by the Artist," *Scribner's Magazine* 64 (Aug. 1918): 165–172, in which five of the pictures feature elms. Old Lyme is described as "a quaint and charming example of the traditional New England village, with its broad, elm-shaded streets, winding lanes, and stately Colonial homes."

66. *The Magazine Antiques* 122 (July 1982): 90; and an exhibit at the Wunderlich Gallery, New York, 1985. See also Hassam, *Woodcutters (The Old Elm)* (1903) in Christie's [New York] auction catalogue for Dec. 2, 1988, pp. 190–191; and Lemuel M. Wiles, *Home Sweet Home* (1886), located at the Guild Hall Museum, East Hampton, New York, and reproduced in Ronald G. Pisano, *Long Island Landscape Painting, 1820–1920* (Boston, 1985), pp. 94–95.

67. See Probasco, *An American Collection,* plate 18; Alan Axelrod, ed., *The Colo-*

nial Revival in America (New York, 1985), pp. 267, 269. See also Willard Leroy Metcalf, *Old Homestead, Connecticut* (c. 1914), a late eighteenth-century house shown under bright moonlight. The painting is located in the St. Louis Art Museum, St. Louis, Missouri.

68. *Maestri americani della Collezione Thyssen-Bornemisza* (Lugano, 1983), p. 141; Evans's photograph will be found in the Fogg Art Museum, Harvard University, Cambridge, Massachusetts, and in Evans, *American Photographs* (Garden City, N.Y., 1938), pp. 164–165.

69. See Ault, *Old House, New Moon* (1943), in Stebbins and Gorokhoff, comps., *A Checklist of American Paintings at Yale University*, pp. 12–13, fig. 144. See, once again, Allen Tate's 1923 poem, "Reflections in an Old House," cited in n. 59 above, and Adrienne Rich, "From an Old House in America," in *Poems: Selected and New, 1950–1974* (New York, 1975), pp. 235–245.

70. Quoted in Baur, *Life and Work of Charles Burchfield*, pp. 200–201. The painting is located in the New Britain Museum of American Art, New Britain, Connecticut.

71. Found respectively in Christie's East auction catalogue, *Nineteenth and Twentieth Century American Paintings, Drawings, Watercolors and Sculpture,* sale no. 6377, June 24, 1987, fig. 139; the St. Louis Art Museum; Baur, *Life and Work of Charles Burchfield*, pp. 140–141, 180.

72. Carl Carmer, *Stars Fell on Alabama* (New York, 1934), p. 3; Scott Elledge, *E. B. White: A Biography* (New York, 1984), p. 256. See also Henry F. May, *Coming to Terms: A Study in Memory and History* (Berkeley, 1987), p. 79; and Theodore H. White, *In Search of History: A Personal Adventure* (New York, 1978), pp. 14–15.

73. John Cheever, *The Wapshot Chronicle* (New York, 1957), pp. 3, 17, 21. See also Elizabeth Shackleton, "Old American Houses," *Saturday Evening Post* 199 (Mar. 12, 1927): 30–31, 46 ("The place to see old houses is in the small, quiet village on its elm-shaded green. . . ."); Arthur Train, "Puritan's Progress," *Saturday Evening Post* 201 (May 25, 1929): 13, 197 ("the old-fashioned, white, wooden meetinghouse with narrow green blinds and tall thin spire, set in the grove of elms. . . ."). When Train enters his grandfather's old church in Framingham, Massachusetts, he finds it "empty save for the shadowy presences evoked by the traditions of the past."

74. See Gill, *The English Country House and the Literary Imagination*, pp. 18, 163; Martin J. Wiener, *English Culture and the Decline of the Industrial Spirit, 1850–1980* (Cambridge, Eng., 1981), pp. 70, 76.

75. E. M. Forster, *Howards End* (1910; reprint, New York, 1921), pp. 3, 22, 25, 206, 339.

76. Gill, *The English Country House and the Literary Imagination*, pp. 122–123, 148–149, 208. For the elm in French culture, see Henri Polge, "L'Orme au Village," *Annales du Midi* 88 (Jan. 1976): 75–91.

77. See Gill, *The English Country House and the Literary Imagination*, pp. 112–114, 203, 206, 222.

78. Ibid., pp. 112, 162–163.

79. Ibid., pp. 14–15, 83, 153, 172, 179, 183, 196–197, 220.

80. Ibid., pp. 100, 132. For direct support from a close analysis of *The House of the Seven Gables*, see Mizruchi, *The Power of Historical Knowledge*, pp. 89–92; and Harry Levin, *Grounds for Comparison* (Cambridge, Mass., 1972), pp. 337–338.

81. John Steinbeck, *Travels with Charley* (New York, 1962), p. 183.

82. *The Collected Poems of W. B. Yeats* (New York, 1956), pp. 198–199.

83. Ibid., pp. 239–240.

84. See Axelrod, *The Colonial Revival in America;* and for the special importance of elms, pp. 37, 47, 50, 103–105. See also Elizabeth Robins, "A Ramble in Old Philadelphia," *Century Magazine* 23 (Mar. 1882): 655–667; "The Tercentenary of Old Plymouth," *Scribner's Magazine* 67 (May 1920): 566–570. These five etchings by Sears Gallagher include "A Bit of Old Plymouth," "The Town Square" (showing a huge elm), "Old Commons House," "Old Curiosity Shop," and "Leyden Street."

85. Stubbs is quoted in John W. Burrow, *A Liberal Descent: Victorian Historians and the English Past* (Cambridge, Eng., 1982), p. 217. On Ruskin, see Roy Strong, *Recreating the Past: British History and the Victorian Painter* (London, 1978), chap. 2, "History Writing and History Painting."

86. Cooper, "American and European Scenery Compared," in Deakin, ed., *The Home Book of the Picturesque*, p. 66.

87. Respectively in Christie's East auction catalogue, *Nineteenth and Twentieth Century American Paintings, Drawings, Watercolors, and Sculpture*, June 24, 1987, fig. 125; *Selections of American Art: R. H. Love Galleries* (Chicago, 1986), fig. 55; Freer Gallery of Art, Smithsonian Institution, Washington, D.C.

88. *The Magazine Antiques* 127 (Mar. 1985): 537; Stebbins, *American Paintings at Yale University*, p. 65, fig. 642.

89. See also Demuth, *Church in Provincetown* (1919), in *Maestri americani*, p. 121.

90. In addition to fig. 3-21, Hassam also painted *Church at Old Lyme* (1903). See Richard J. Boyle, *American Impressionism* (1974: Boston, 1982), p. 146. In contrast to Hassam, Edward Hopper painted steeples as part of a roofline seen from close up, but not the rest of the church. See Levin, *Edward Hopper*, plates 203 and 221.

91. See generally Donelson F. Hoopes, *Childe Hassam* (New York, 1979).

92. Stebbins, *American Paintings at Yale University*, p. 172, fig. 1793; *American Painting Collection of the Montclair Art Museum*, p. 190, fig. 59.

93. See also Philip Evergood, *Through the Mill* (1940), in John I. H. Baur, *Philip Evergood* (New York, 1975), pp. 36–37. A few years ago the annual Thanksgiving card sent out by the Amica Mutual Insurance Company featured a watercolor by John Loughlin of Moffitt Mill in Lincoln, Rhode Island. "Once a utilitarian machine shop, dating from about 1812, it is now but a symbol of a less efficient, but simpler time." The card then declares: "Old buildings recall olden times—and old values."

94. See Baur, *Life and Work of Charles Burchfield*, plates 13, 14 and figs. 105,

106, 107, 120, 141, 143, and especially fig. 21, *Old Tavern at Hammondsville, Ohio* (1926–1928).

95. Robert E. Hemenway, *Zora Neale Hurston: A Literary Biography* (Urbana, 1977), p. 239.

96. Thomas Nelson Page Papers, box 9, folder A, Alderman Library, University of Virginia; Donald Davidson in Twelve Southerners, *I'll Take My Stand: The South and the Agrarian Tradition* (New York, 1930), p. 55. See also Carol Bleser, ed., *The Hammonds of Redcliffe* (New York, 1981).

97. See Malcolm Freiberg, "From Family to Nation: The Old House Becomes a National Historic Site," *Proceedings of the Massachusetts Historical Society* (Boston, 1987), 98 : 60–77; Millicent Bell, *Marquand: An American Life* (Boston, 1979); Holmes to John C. H. Wu, Sept. 6, 1925, quoted in Max Lerner, ed., *The Mind and Faith of Justice Holmes* (Boston, 1943), p. 429. See also Samuel Merwin, "Old Concord Seen Through Western Spectacles," *Century Magazine* 112 (May 1926): 32–40, which marvels at "a broad forest of elms" and locates the Alcott house "under immense old elms."

98. Hawthorne, *House of the Seven Gables*, pp. 22, 448. I must acknowledge that the marriage of Mrs. Gracedew and Captain Yule in Henry James's "Covering End" (1898) echoes the marriage of Phoebe and Holgrave in providing a union of all that is best in the modern and the traditional. The ultimate symbolism of that wych elm in *Howards End*, perhaps, is the reconciliation of progress and tradition.

99. Quoted in Baur, *Philip Evergood*, p. 47. Compare Walker Evans's 1935 photograph "Louisiana Plantation House," in which a huge uprooted tree lies on the lawn of a large house with pillars in front. Whereas Evans's focus is the tree, Evergood's is the old woman. See Evans, *American Photographs* (Garden City, N.Y., 1938), pp. 108–109.

100. For Evergood this was neither an isolated nor a parochial episode. As he noted: "Julian Levi, the painter, gave the picture its title. He and Bruce Mitchell came into my studio while I was struggling with it, and one of them said, 'It's funny, Phil, how you seem to deal with topical subjects. I don't see things that way.' And I said, 'Well, it is topical now because we've had a hurricane and I saw the old lady sitting there on her lawn, but I don't like to feel that it will always be topical. I don't paint to put over topical ideas. I feel very conscious when I develop a theme that it must have universal connotations before I want to put it down in paint.'" Baur, *Philip Evergood*, p. 50.

Index

www.ingramcontent.com/pod-product-compliance
Lightning Source LLC
Chambersburg PA
CBHW030925180526
45163CB00002B/465